"Thoroughly researched and beautifully written, *Intended for Evil* blazes with vivid detail. Sillars had me at 'hello.'"

Lynn Vincent, *New York Times* bestselling author of
Same Kind of Different as Me and *Heaven Is for Real*

"*Single death: tragedy. Million deaths: statistic.* Sometimes attributed to Joseph Stalin, sometimes to others, that formula certainly holds true for writing about the Khmer Rouge's murder of 1.7 million Cambodians. So Les Sillars was wise to tell the story of one man, Radha Manickam, and his journey through Communist hell during the 1970s. It's also a tale of coming to Christ and surviving through God's grace. If you want to understand that era, *Intended for Evil* is a great book to read."

Marvin Olasky, editor-in-chief of *World*

"The Khmer Rouge's murderous regime in Cambodia was one of the worst events in human history and perhaps the purest Communist revolution the world has ever seen. And yet we know very little about it. *Intended for Evil* is the remarkable and intimate story of a man who miraculously survived the Khmer Rouge and later returned to Cambodia as a missionary. His story of faith in the midst of suffering, torture, and the now infamous 'killing fields' will leave you stunned."

William J. Bennett, former secretary of education,
bestselling author, and host of *The Bill Bennett Podcast*

"*Intended for Evil* is one of the most compelling stories I have read of life under the tyrannical despotism of Cambodia's Communist rulers, the Khmer Rouge. From 1975 until 1979, when the Vietnamese invasion brought the downfall of the regime, Radha Manickam experienced the brutal public murder of commune members who displeased the Communist cadres, cynical political deception, constant surveillance—often literally by children—and a complete suppression of normal human relations.

Most extraordinarily, Radha experienced a compulsory marriage to another prisoner who might have caused his death had she reported his Christian faith to the authorities. In an astonishing example of God's miraculous providence, his bride turned out to be a Christian, and the two of them endured a harrowing few years surviving first the Khmer Rouge and then the brutal uncertainties of Vietnamese rule over Cambodia.

In *Intended for Evil*, Les Sillars has drawn an astute and vivid portrait of a young man encountering one of the most wicked political regimes of all time. It is an exceptional book."

David Aikman, former *Time* correspondent
and author of *One Nation without God?*

"*Intended for Evil* reads like a gripping novel—a thriller, a totalitarian dystopia, a horror story. But it's history, not fiction. Les Sillars's book is also an inspiring account of the resiliency of the Christian faith against the most extreme opposition."

—**Gene Edward Veith**, provost emeritus, Patrick Henry College

INTENDED
FOR EVIL

INTENDED FOR EVIL

A SURVIVOR'S STORY OF LOVE, FAITH, AND COURAGE
IN THE CAMBODIAN KILLING FIELDS

LES SILLARS

BakerBooks
a division of Baker Publishing Group
Grand Rapids, Michigan

© 2016 by Les Sillars

Published by Baker Books
a division of Baker Publishing Group
P.O. Box 6287, Grand Rapids, MI 49516-6287
www.bakerbooks.com

Printed in the United States of America

Library of Congress Cataloging-in-Publication Data is on file at the Library of Congress, Washington, DC.

ISBN 978-0-8010-0909-9

16 17 18 19 20 21 22   7 6 5 4 3 2 1

To Radha and Samen

Contents

Author's Note

Y ou should call this guy," David Aikman told me in the fall of 2013. We were in a hallway at Patrick Henry College, where we both taught. David, a senior *Time* correspondent for many years, had heard from mutual friends an incredible tale about a Cambodian Christian who had survived the Khmer Rouge in the late 1970s. According to David, this person wanted someone to write down his stories. He passed along the email address of one Radha Manickam of Seattle.

As my knowledge of Pol Pot and the Khmer Rouge at the time consisted of a hazy recollection of a movie, *The Killing Fields*, I had no idea where this might lead. But I sent Radha a note, and we set up a phone call. Radha mentioned his forced marriage, the loss of almost all his family, and seeing people murdered. I promised to do some reading and call him back.

I soon realized that the Khmer Rouge regime was one of modern history's greatest catastrophes—and one largely forgotten in recent years. I found the Khmer Rouge both horrifying and fascinating. No other government in modern history has killed a greater percentage of its own citizens? The most totalitarian government ever attempted? Torture, starvation, and mass executions? Civil war and bloody revolution? Because of the Vietnam War, the American military was involved in Cambodia and even, said critics, partly responsible? And Radha, then a new Christian and the slightly spoiled son of a wealthy merchant, had lived through it all? Wow.

So in January 2014, I started interviewing Radha; we had long conversations at least weekly for a year. Every time we spoke, he told me something else that made my jaw drop: people sliced open before his eyes, treks through the jungles, unbelievable deprivation, and a faith that survived many doubts and much anger. The story he told was stunning. I hope I've done it justice.

The human memory is often less than completely accurate, but Radha's story was remarkably consistent with what I was learning in my investigations about life under the Khmer Rouge. For example, when Radha described how the leaders of his village were purged in the summer of 1978 or communal dining areas were instituted in the fall of 1976, I later read in various historical and scholarly studies that, yes, the Central Committee in Phnom Penh had instituted just such a policy around that time.

Radha's story also matched the many memoirs of Khmer Rouge victims; what he described for me corresponded to the experience of many, many other people. He seemed rather reluctant to dwell on the more sensational details, which made him all the more credible to me.

Quotation marks indicate my best attempt to represent accurately the substance and tone of Radha's conversations as he recalled them, but of course the dialogue is not verbatim; obviously, it's difficult for anyone to recall exactly what they said thirty-five years ago. Where possible, I confirmed dialogue with Samen or others.

A note on spelling "Angka": it's also commonly spelled "Angkar" (pronounced with a silent "r"), but many of the scholars writing closest to the time of the Khmer Rouge tended to prefer the shorter version, so I went with that.

I owe a great debt to the many scholars and writers who have written about Cambodia and the Khmer Rouge. For background, I relied on respected books of history, social science, or journalism by David Chandler, Ben Kiernan, William Shawcross, François Ponchaud, Karl D. Jackson, Donald Cormack, and Elizabeth Becker. These writers and others are cited where appropriate in endnotes, but I'd like to express my admiration for their careful and diligent scholarship. Where my summaries or interpretations of Cambodian history, personalities, and events fall short, the fault is entirely mine.

Prologue

But God will redeem me from the realm of the dead; he will surely take me to himself.

—Psalm 49:15

The second time Radha Manickam tried to commit suicide, it was by singing "This World Is Not My Home." It seemed appropriate. He was lying atop a termite hill next to a small, sputtering fire in a northwestern Cambodian rice paddy in January 1978. He was twenty-five years old, and after three years under the brutal regime of the Communist Khmer Rouge, he weighed around ninety pounds. It was raining.

He and the rest of his plowing crew were spending the night out in the rice fields with the water buffalo. The wet, gritty surface of the termite hill rose a few feet out of the soggy rice paddy. His only covering was a thin blanket one yard square. In the darkness around him, his fellow workers were trying to sleep. *Chhlops* (child spies) were likely sneaking among the dikes, ferreting out imaginary treason, and Khmer Rouge soldiers were patrolling the area. A Bible verse came to Radha's mind: "Come to me, all who are weary and heavy-laden, and I will give you rest."

Radha was so very weary. He didn't think he could keep going, driven by the soldiers to do more and more work on less and less food with a few scant hours of sleep per night. The regime was not equally harsh everywhere, but everywhere it was harsh and nowhere was it free.

Cambodia had become the realm of the dead. Khmer Rouge propaganda declared, "Everywhere in the country, in the countryside, in the factories and in the units of the Revolutionary Army, joy, enthusiasm, and emulation prevail."[1] But the countryside contained far more unmarked mass graves than revolutionary enthusiasm. In its doomed attempt to create an agrarian utopia, Pol Pot's regime would through policy decisions, cynical deception, and stupefying violence murder more than 1.7 million people.[2] Mao's and Stalin's Communist regimes killed far more people, but no other government in modern history has destroyed nearly a quarter of its own citizens. If Communist Vietnam had not ousted the Khmer Rouge in 1979, that figure surely would have been even higher.

Some victims died relatively quickly—shot or clubbed or tortured to death. Others lingered for months or years until they died of starvation or some wretched disease.

Millions of Cambodians weren't in the grave just yet, but they were dying on the inside. Pol Pot once boasted that the Khmer revolution was the purest, most Communist revolution the world had ever seen. He was probably right; no other government has ever tried to exert such totalitarian control over its citizens.[3]

Pol Pot and other Khmer leaders tried to reshape the identities of an entire nation in their determination to create the "new socialist man." The regime commanded how and where people would live, work, eat, sleep, and marry. Leisure time did not exist.

Much Khmer Rouge ideology resembled, ironically, key elements of Christianity turned inside out and upside down. This was not deliberate, for the Khmer Rouge knew little of the Bible. Pol Pot insisted that everything about the revolution was Khmer in origin.

16

Yet everywhere in Cambodia under the Khmer Rouge were shadows of biblical truth and practice—love, worship, community, confession, transformation, unity, judgment, virtue, purity, equality—all hideously distorted. It's as if some alien intelligence, attempting to create the most un-Christian society possible, distilled decades of totalitarianism from around the world into one ghastly system and then unleashed it on a small, unsuspecting country.

Many Khmers resisted, to the degree they were able, by shutting down. Do your job; don't complain; keep your head down; and most important, trust no one. Over time, people's souls shriveled. In one sense, even the Khmer Rouge themselves were dying on their feet. They were soldiers of socialism for whom murder was not a crime but the prelude to a new society.[4]

Surrounding Radha as he lay on the termite hill were endless stretches of shallow water broken up by dikes and stands of trees. He saw no way out. *Lord*, he prayed, *I really want my rest. Take me home*. He waited, and the rain kept falling. *If you aren't going to take me home, I'm going to help you.*

So he began to sing in English. With water dripping off the bushes around him, he lifted up his voice and sang, perhaps not as loudly as he could but quite clearly, about how this world was not his home. "I'm just a-passing through / My treasures are laid up somewhere beyond the blue." It's a bouncy, country gospel tune called "This World Is Not My Home" that he had learned at Maranatha Church in Phnom Penh. He learned it soon after he became a Christian in 1973. He hummed it to himself in the fields while plodding behind the water buffalo, along with "Call for the Reapers" and "Bringing in the Sheaves." "Power in the Blood" was one of his favorites.

His voice drifted out over the rice paddies. Had he stopped to listen, he probably could have heard voices and people rustling, but he didn't. He gradually became aware of a voice. It said, "I have a plan for your life."

Radha kept singing, but inside he also spoke to God. *If you really have a plan for my life*, he thought, *you should help me now.*

Just then a group of soldiers stepped out of the darkness. They had been hanging around the communal kitchen under the tin roof and out of the rain, as was their custom, but had gone for a walk, picking their way across the tops of the dikes. They heard the strange music and headed over to investigate. Their leader, a skinny fourteen-year-old named Sal, carried an AK-47.

"Comrade," he demanded, "what language are you singing in?"

Radha had expected this. He was tired, and this was the easiest way out of the rice field. It was probably the only way.

He just had to say "English" and, ideally, Sal would just shoot him on the spot, although there was an excellent chance he would be clubbed to death and his body dumped into a shallow grave. It didn't seem like such a bad way to go—suicide by praise song.

But as Sal was speaking, Radha heard the voice again. "I have a plan for your life," it repeated.

Radha didn't really know what he was doing because he couldn't think clearly, but he changed his mind. "It's not really a language," he lied. "It's just some sounds I put together."

Sal bought it. "Go to sleep," instructed the teen, laughing. "You have to go work in the morning."

Radha rolled over and went to sleep.

1

Civil War

There is no faithfulness, no love, no acknowledgment of God in the land. There is only cursing, lying and murder, stealing and adultery; they break all bounds, and bloodshed follows bloodshed.

—Hosea 4:1–2

In early August 1973, "Live and Let Die" by Paul McCartney was on its way to the top of the charts, *American Graffiti* was set to dominate that summer's box office, and President Richard Nixon was reeling from recent revelations that he'd tried to cover up the Watergate break-in.

Nixon was also facing some awkward questions about secret carpet-bombings in Cambodia. For the previous three years, the US Air Force had executed an intense bombing campaign designed to aid Cambodia's pro-American government, the Khmer Republic, in a brutal civil war against the Khmer Rouge, Communist guerrillas backed by North Vietnam.

Those questions got much sharper on August 7. At 4:30 that morning, an American B-52 navigator forgot to flip a switch, and so the plane homed in on a radar beacon placed in a ferry town on the Mekong River instead of its intended military target. Thirty tons of bombs came shrieking out of the dark sky and flattened the middle of Neak Luong, a city of about ten thousand people east of Phnom Penh. Shocked residents found the city's main street reduced to a line of craters filled with flames, concrete, twisted steel, and some scattered human remains. The bombs killed 137 and wounded 268, most of them soldiers of the Khmer Republic and their families.

American officials initially described it as "no great disaster," but it was soon recognized as one of the worst bombing errors of the Vietnam War. "Yesterday afternoon a soldier could be seen sobbing uncontrollably on the riverbank," read one *New York Times* report. "'All my family is dead!' he cried, beating his hand on the wooden bench where he had collapsed. 'All my family is dead! Take my picture! Take my picture! Let the Americans see me!'"[1]

In a comfortable, second-story apartment on the western side of Phnom Penh, a young man named Manickam Radha (in Cambodia, family names come first followed by given names) saw the TV news reports about Neak Luong. He was deeply angered that the American ambassador came out to the town and offered victims' families about one hundred dollars each in compensation. Radha was generally pro-Khmer Republic and pro-American, but this felt like a slap in the face of every Cambodian.

Radha was not by birth an ethnic Khmer, but he had been born in the country and identified very strongly with the Khmer people. He was twenty, quite slim, and on the tall side for an Asian at five feet six inches. Playing soccer kept his body in shape, and he had handsome, classically Indian features inherited from his father, Manickam Chetia, who had emigrated from that country in the 1940s. A passport photo from the 1930s shows *Appa* (the affectionate Tamil word for "father") as a sharp-looking young man with short hair parted to the side, a broad forehead, and strikingly intense dark eyes. He was a warm father in the Asian sense. That is, he was seldom openly affectionate and didn't smile much, but he was generous and often took in relatives in need of help. His kids thought of him as a bit of a perfectionist. He was also thrifty and hated to waste food; he would rinse off yesterday's rice and munch it down, while the kids preferred it cooked fresh.

The elder Manickam had developed a severe case of arthritis, which was worsened by the fact that he was a very big man by Asian standards, standing about five feet eight inches and weighing well over two hundred pounds, with a paunch befitting a prosperous Cambodian businessman. He could still walk in 1973 but needed two canes to get around.

Radha was his eldest child, born in 1953 to Ve Meenachi. She too was fairly tall, about even with Radha, and quiet in the manner of properly respectful Cambodian wives. *Amma* (Tamil for "mom") was a kind and giving soul who loved to cook. She often made extra food for her family just to have something to share with the neighbors. Her mother was Vietnamese, her father Indian. A line of children followed Radha in the next two decades: Indira (sister), Ravy (brother), Dhanam (sister), Selvem (brother), and Annapoorani (sister). Lakshmi (sister) had just been born earlier in 1973. The last sibling, Murugan (brother), would be born in June 1975.

Radha was for the most part a good son, at least as far as his parents knew. He had skipped his high school classes sometimes but never enough to get into serious trouble. Manickam was serious about his Hindu faith, while Radha was outwardly respectful but couldn't get into it. It seemed to him that Hinduism had too many gods. And the Theravada Buddhism of the Khmer people held no pull for him.

Radha thought of himself as "normal" even though as an ethnic Indian he was part of a tiny minority inside the Khmer nation, and his family was moderately wealthy in a country marked by poverty. His father often traveled to India and Hong Kong on business, bringing back perfume and jewelry for the girls and the latest toys for the

21

boys. Ravy was briefly the envy of his friends when in the mid-1960s he got the first battery-powered metal toy car in the neighborhood.

Radha's grandfather on his dad's side immigrated to Cambodia in the early 1940s to seek his fortune. He started an arts and crafts shop in the "Old Market" at Siem Reap, once the Angkorean capital, about two hundred miles north of Phnom Penh. Radha's father followed a few years later.

Grandfather and Manickam were devout Hindus and Brahmins, members of the highest-ranking caste in India. Grandfather never trimmed the fingernails on the pinkie and ring fingers of his left hand. He was the only Indian in town, so the nails of "Grandpa Indian," which were so long they curled, were quite the curiosity to local children.

Grandfather easily made connections in Cambodia, then a French protectorate. The Manickam family's long-standing ties to Cambodia's royal family began with a gunfight. Once in the early 1950s, he accompanied a French general on a car trip from Siem Reap to Phnom Penh. On the way they were attacked by a group of Khmer Issarak, nationalists fighting for independence from France. Grandfather's "long gun" helped protect the party when the general's bodyguards ran out of ammunition. Both the French authorities and the king of Cambodia himself, Norodom Sihanouk, awarded Grandfather medals. Grandfather's long gun was stolen some years later, and Sihanouk made sure the weapon was returned. It isn't clear exactly how the gun was returned, but family lore said it involved some sort of appeal over the radio, possibly combined with threats in low places. Anyway, Grandfather got his long gun back. Every time Sihanouk visited Siem Reap, Grandfather would drop by with an offering of food or a gift. Sihanouk loved Indian curry, and Grandfather, who loved to cook, never needed an appointment.

Manickam, over time, leveraged the family association with Sihanouk into several businesses in the capital. The family had some rough patches financially, even going bankrupt in 1967. It didn't help

22

that in the mid-1960s the economy was tanking, in part because during one of Sihanouk's occasional shifts to the political left he nationalized the import/export business. The family's finances got so dire that Manickam sent Radha southwest to Sihanoukville, a coastline city, for eighteen months to live with some friends. Fourteen-year-old Radha had to take a bus to school, carry water for the household, and sell watermelon seeds in his spare time to send a bit of money back home. He hated it—every second.

But Radha came home to Phnom Penh in 1968 when business started picking up, and by 1970, Manickam had recovered nicely. He became the only authorized distributor of Sanyo appliances and Suzuki motorcycles in the country. He gave Sihanouk four white 350cc bikes for his motorcade, ordered special from Japan.

The Cambodian civil war began in 1970 with a coup that was initially quite profitable for Manickam and many other Cambodian businesses. But the coup was really a cliff at the end of a tragic decline.

In the 1960s, Phnom Penh had been a beautiful, vibrant city of perhaps six hundred thousand, built at the junction of the famous Mekong River and the Tonle Sap, a river flowing southeast from Cambodia's largest lake. Under King Sihanouk, the "Pearl of the East" had orderly, tree-lined avenues, shaded promenades and squares, sparse traffic, sleepy cafés, and a light, open feel. Many buildings featured elements of Buddhist temples, such as multitiered roofs, golden spires, and gables, all ornamented with figures from Buddhist mythology. To visiting writers, the Kingdom of Cambodia looked like a peaceful place, despite the war in Vietnam raging just across the border to the east. Some referred to Cambodia's "provincial charm"—the country had been a French protectorate until 1953. True, the countryside was full of poor farmers who eked out a living from rice paddies and fish traps and banana groves, and unrest ruled in certain areas, but overall it was better off than some of its neighboring countries.

Sihanouk was beloved among the Buddhist peasants, in part because he had stage-managed the 1953 "crisis" that led to the country's independence from France.[2] The farmers viewed him as something less than one of the god-kings of Cambodian legend, perhaps, but certainly more than an ordinary man. He was Samdech Euv, "Papa King."

The business and elite classes, however, thought him a populist trickster, a violent and patronizing figure whose self-serving tactics and corruption had mired the country in poverty. They were especially angry that Sihanouk had been allowing the Communist North Vietnamese, at war with the Republic of South Vietnam and its US ally, to run troops and supplies up and down the Ho Chi Minh Trail through Cambodia's eastern jungles since the mid-1960s. Many Khmers regarded it as a failure to stand up to the Vietnamese.

Sihanouk had hoped the deal with North Vietnam would keep Cambodia out of the conflict; it didn't work. Sihanouk's decision to allow North Vietnam access to the trail was a huge military advantage to the North Vietnamese and prompted the United States to begin secretly bombing the Cambodian border regions in 1969.

That deal was one of many factors that prompted General Lon Nol to lead a 1970 coup that deposed Sihanouk, abolished the monarchy, formed the Khmer Republic, and set off a wave of anti-Vietnamese violence within Cambodia.[3] In one instance, Khmer Republic troops shot some eight hundred Vietnamese living in the country and dumped their bodies into the Tonle Bassac (a river that roughly parallels the Mekong) to float down toward Vietnam.[4] The Vietnamese Communists, who rightly saw Lon Nol and the new Khmer Republic as an American ally, promptly invaded Cambodia. They supposedly did so to help Cambodian Communist guerrillas—a small and largely ineffective group that Sihanouk had driven into the forests in the 1960s, dismissing them in a jocular comment as "Khmer Rouge."

In response to the Vietnamese invasion, the United States poured arms and aid into the Khmer Republic. Nixon also authorized a massive expansion of the incredibly destructive B-52 campaigns—hundreds of planes flying tens of thousands of sorties—in an attempt to blow the Vietnamese and Khmer Communists out of the Cambodian jungles and prevent them from attacking US forces in Vietnam. Tons of bombs flowed out of each plane's belly like strings of eggs from a gigantic flying fish, plunging to earth at nearly the speed of sound. The explosions ripped apart buildings, shredded stands of large trees into toothpicks, threw dirt and rocks hundreds of feet into the air, and left behind huge smoking craters.

From his high school desk, Radha heard the B-52s rumble overhead and felt the building shake from the blasts. While out walking, Radha and his friends would talk politics and wonder about the conflict raging just out of sight. They'd see the bombers or fighters go by, and then a helicopter or twin-engine plane from the Cambodian air force would roar past and drop leaflets urging support for the Lon Nol government.

When the leaflets first started falling, Radha and his teenaged friends would rush over to pick them up and pore over the messages, searching for some clue as to what was going on. But they soon stopped. The messages were always the same: the Khmer Republic is the best government for Cambodians and will stamp out corruption, Sihanouk is a traitor, and so on. After a few months, the traffic pushed the unread pamphlets into gutters, and the wind blew them into piles on boulevards and in people's yards.

Radha slowly began to notice the American influence seeping into Phnom Penh. In place of traditional sarongs and elaborately patterned shirts, people wore bell-bottom pants (known as elephant ear pants), short skirts, and big collars. The uniform for girls at Radha's school was a modest blue skirt and long-sleeved white shirt, but their clothing after school was different. Radha would often notice a girl on the streets wearing a miniskirt, sporting bobbed hair and bangs, and was surprised to realize she was a classmate.

The changes went beyond clothing. Cambodian traditionalists listened with alarm to the beats of American-style rock music thumping from boom boxes mounted on the shoulders of teens loitering near Independence Monument. They heard of strange new dances in the clubs. They noted with disapproval youngsters lining up to see the latest box-office attractions. And they scowled at the disrespect when long-haired young Cambodians roared through the streets on motorbikes and scooters, forcing their elders to jump out of the way. Some viewed all this as mounting chaos in the midst of civil war, while others saw it as the much-needed liberalization of a society that had suffered too long under the burdens of monarchy and tradition.

Radha was no radical, but he thought some change was in order. He graduated from high school in 1972 and started working for his dad as a bookkeeper. Appa's Khmer wasn't great, so Radha often handled negotiations with Khmer clients and customers. He had longish hair and usually wore elephant ear pants and a shirt tailor-made from some of the fine fabric his father imported and distributed. His shirts tended to be silk and designed with bright colors—royal blue, yellow, sometimes cream, but never orange. If you wore orange, people called you a monk.

Radha's crew of friends was well off and maybe a little arrogant but, like him, seldom openly rebellious. Above all, they respected family. Some were Khmer, Cambodia's majority ethnic group, but others were from Cambodia's minority populations of Chinese and Vietnamese. Minorities in Cambodia tended to be merchants and professionals and were better off than the average Khmer in Phnom Penh and way better off than the legions of Cambodian farmers. Radha and his friends just thought of themselves as Cambodian.

Radha never went out to bars, and his relations with girls stayed at the level of casual flirting. The closest he came to dishonoring his parents was when he and some buddies in the Republican Army thought a restaurant was charging too much for their dinner. They stuffed some of the dishes into their pockets so the waiter couldn't find the plates and charge for the dish. They got away with it. Another time he went up to a fruit stall and began to argue loudly with the owner. "This fruit is rotten!" he declared just for the fun of watching the owner get angry as customers stared curiously.

It was an odd way to have fun amid a war, but Radha, like many residents of Phnom Penh, was trying to ignore the possibility that the Khmer Rouge might win. They had limited faith in Republican troops but were convinced that the United States, having spilled American blood for about a decade battling Communism in Vietnam, would never allow the Communists to take over the country right next door. The Americans had been propping up the Lon Nol regime for years; surely they wouldn't just throw all that away. Moreover, all the aid that ended up in private pockets meant some people had money to spend—lots of it. For much of the civil war, right up until mid-1973, clubs were filled, restaurants were booked, and luxury car lots were dealing. For the Manickams, business continued as much as reasonably possible; Appa kept the Suzukis and the Sanyos coming into the country.

Denial, as they say, is not just a river in Egypt.

By the time Neak Luong was destroyed in August 1973, Phnom Penh was in desperate straits. The civil war had become a brutal and bloody stalemate. The notoriously incompetent and corrupt Republican forces barely held the major cities despite a massive influx of American arms and aid, while fanatical Khmer Rouge troops controlled most of the bombed-out countryside. They had gradually gained enough strength to take over the war in Cambodia from the Vietnamese. What had been essentially a Vietnamese invasion had morphed into a civil war: Khmer vs. Khmer.[5]

The stalemate couldn't continue. Phnom Penh's population had more than tripled to two million as refugees streamed in, some fleeing the American bombs and others the Khmer Rouge's expanding reign of terror. Refugees found a city on the verge of starvation, bombarded by Communist rockets, and crowded with the sick and wounded. Slapdash ghettos of tarp-roofed shelters and palm-branch huts filled and spread. The destitute newcomers flooded into the markets and loitered on the streets, mixing with the thousands of Republican Army veterans who had been wounded and discharged and then left to fend for themselves. Many who had lost limbs or were otherwise disabled hung out at the markets begging for food or a few riels to buy some potent rice wine. But the shopkeepers and citizens became less generous as they felt more overwhelmed. Returning veterans, some drunk and on crutches, were known to threaten shopkeepers with grenades if they didn't offer a suitable handout.

Food had to come through an American airlift into Phnom Penh's airport or via ship up the mine-infested Mekong River, and there wasn't nearly enough. Khmer Rouge rockets pounded the city, and Khmer Rouge saboteurs slipped through Republican lines to lob grenades into crowded theaters and markets. The task of caring for the refugees fell to private charities, mostly American, that were well intentioned but couldn't keep up. For those with money, life continued but always with smoke and the echo of explosions in the background.

The United States had withdrawn its forces from Vietnam following the Paris Peace Accords in January 1973, and that freed up American airplanes for sorties into Cambodia. By August 1973, historians later discovered, the United States had dropped 2.7 million tons of bombs on Cambodia, making it the most heavily bombed country in history (the Allies dropped two million tons of bombs in all of World War II).[6] While the carpet-bombing rattled the Communists, it certainly didn't stop them.

When the B-52 campaign into Cambodia became public in America, incensed anti-war activists charged that Nixon had been telling the public he was trying to end the war in Vietnam even as he extended it into a neutral country. Even today, nobody knows how many Cambodian civilians died in the attacks, although it was likely in the tens of thousands despite the efforts of American airmen to avoid Cambodian settlements.[7]

Critics later charged that the American bombing itself destabilized the countryside and drove furious, grief-stricken peasants who had lost family members in the attacks into the arms of the Khmer Rouge.[8] In later interviews, Khmer Rouge officers described what they saw when they would visit the farmers after bombings. "Their minds just froze up and they would wander around mute for three or four days. Terrified and half-crazy, the people were ready to believe what they were told. It was because of their dissatisfaction with the bombing that they kept on co-operating with the Khmer Rouge, joining up with the Khmer Rouge, sending their children off to go with them. . . . Sometimes the bombs fell and hit little children, and their fathers would be all for the Khmer Rouge."[9]

In short, critics said, American policy made possible the rise of the Khmer Rouge.[10]

However, American officials have pointed out that the United States needed to protect its troops in Vietnam.[11] The North Vietnamese, not the Americans, extended the Vietnam War into Cambodia by using the Ho Chi Minh Trail and then handled the heavy fighting for the first year of the war in Cambodia. Without support from Vietnam (itself a Soviet client state), the Khmer Republic might well have been able to keep the Khmer Rouge a jungle-bound and mostly impotent guerrilla movement.

Moreover, at the urging of the Chinese, soon after an enraged Sihanouk was ousted in 1970, he agreed to become the public face of the National United Front of Kampuchea. It really was just a front for the Khmer Rouge; Sihanouk legitimized the same Communist guerrillas he had chased into the forests a few years earlier. Thousands of farmers joined the Khmer Rouge at Sihanouk's urging when he spoke to them over the radio from Peking. Had Sihanouk retired quietly to France after the coup, the Khmer Rouge may never have gotten off the ground. The Chinese, for their part, supported the Cambodian Communists not only during the civil war but also during the Khmer Rouge regime. There was lots of blame to go around.

And then came Neak Luong.

Under pressure to keep his campaign promises, Nixon had reluctantly announced an August end to the Cambodian bombing. As late as July 1973, Nixon was still warning of dire consequences in the region if the B-52 attacks ended. On August 15, Congress took the decision out of his hands, declining to reauthorize more funds for the bombing, although US aid to the Cambodian government continued. Without American air support, however, the future of the Khmer Republic looked very, very dim. The Khmer Rouge prepared for a final assault on the capital.

It was about to get ugly.

2

Talking Theology

For the message of the cross is foolishness to those who are perishing, but to us who are being saved it is the power of God.

—1 Corinthians 1:18

After the American bombs stopped, the Manickam family continued with daily life. What else could they do? They had some hope—American aid was still flowing, and the American embassy still operated. In the fall of 1973, Radha was going after work to daily English classes at a private school. Tuition was steep, so most of the students were teenagers or young adults from well-off families. Radha's first teacher was a Cambodian who had been educated in Australia; his accent struck Radha as odd. An American who was picky about diction taught the second section of the course, and those lessons—that desire for precision in language—stuck with Radha.

At the English school, Radha met Huoth, who spent his days working for his family's prosperous brick and tile factory near Phnom Penh. Huoth was on the quiet side but cheerful and accommodating. He dressed a bit sloppily compared to the other kids from wealthy

31

families, wearing fewer silk shirts and more denim pants. Around four in the afternoon, he would pick up Radha on his small Honda motorbike and give him a lift to class, which ran from about 5:00 to 7:00 p.m. After class, they would drive down to the Mekong River to hang out with friends and perhaps buy some snacks at a street vendor—watermelon seeds, roasted peanuts, or fried bananas, and maybe a Coke. Later, Houth's dad gave him a Vespa scooter, which they thought of as an old person's ride. They were both glad when Huoth got a Jeep on his eighteenth birthday. Radha was twenty.

In late September, several weeks after the carpet-bombing ended, Huoth invited Radha to a different English class. The "Mata School" was, Huoth pointed out, free. Free sounded good to Radha.

On that first day, Radha didn't notice that the school had a sign out front that read "Maranatha Church." School was held in the corner apartment on the second floor of a building on a busy intersection just west of central Phnom Penh. Inside the small room, a few dozen Cambodian students crowded onto wooden benches and the floor. The plaster walls stood bare except for a blackboard. Bars covered the windows, and a ceiling fan barely cooled the room on the stickier days. Up front was an athletic-looking American in his twenties with a dark brown mustache and long hair. Radha and Huoth found a couple of seats, and the students passed around copies of an English book. Radha also soon noticed the most beautiful American woman he had ever seen. She was tall, with light brown hair, a gracious smile, and easy manners.

The teacher's name was Todd Burke. He instructed the students to open their books to "Matthew." He read a short passage in a clear, confident manner, and then the students—most of whom knew at least a little English—repeated it back to him. After reading several passages, Burke would, with an interpreter's help, explain the more difficult words and stories and answer students' questions. Radha thought Burke seemed bossy and overbearing, but he liked the American's accent and crystal-clear voice. The thought of another glimpse of the American woman also drew him in until he discovered that her name was DeAnn Burke—Todd's wife.

The Burkes had come to Phnom Penh in September 1973 as independent missionaries with very little support.[1] Todd, then twenty-three, was an adventurous risk-taker and a strong charismatic who had just graduated from Oral Roberts University. He and DeAnn had been inspired by the missionary biographies of Adoniram Judson and Hudson Taylor, and they came to Cambodia loaded with enthusiasm and naiveté. They knew the US bombing had just stopped and the Communists could well take over soon. Within two weeks of arriving, Todd had arranged an evangelistic crusade attended by several thousand people and started teaching English and Bible classes.

The Burkes found Cambodians to be friendly and generous. The couple learned how to do the *sampeah*, the palms-together gesture of respect and greeting accompanied by a slight bow. According to the Burkes' memoir, *Anointed for Burial*, over the next eighteen months their ministry involved many healing services, much speaking in tongues, and regular exorcisms. They also started caring for orphans.

The Burkes ran three English classes each day. The evening session, which Radha attended, soon mushroomed into an informal church. Radha found the stories in this English book, the Bible, interesting, even compelling. After a few weeks, the class began reading from Luke. Gradually he realized he had heard most of these stories before, just not in English. Years earlier, an uncle had given him a Khmer translation of the Gospel of Luke. His uncle wasn't a believer; he just knew Radha liked to read. Radha found the healing miracles especially appealing. Soon the class switched to the Gospel of John, and as he continued to attend the class, the stories began to make sense. Huoth, he soon realized, was already a Christian.

Maranatha Church also had several Cambodian pastors and lay leaders, including Nou Thay, who worked with the church's young people. He was gentle and sincere but forthright, a man with a very soft voice whose mother, known as Grandmother Rose, had been one of the first and most prominent Christians in Cambodia. He had worked with the Christian and Missionary Alliance churches in Phnom Penh but left the denomination when he embraced charismatic teachings and soon joined the Burkes' ministry.

Radha met with Thay one evening instead of attending the English class. "Can you explain to me a little more about this Jesus?" Radha asked. Thay took out a Khmer Bible and, beginning at Genesis, began to explain some basic doctrine. "Little brother," he said in his soft voice, "Jesus was God, and He is God. He's the Creator of all things." Radha wondered how one person could save everyone in the whole world from their sins.

Thay told him that God was like a parent who can cover up for that child's mistakes. Jesus, the Son of God who had become a man, had never committed any sin, so He could pay the penalty for the sins of the whole world. "All who sin must die," Thay told Radha. "But He took our place. Jesus is the perfect sacrificial lamb who can save the world."

Radha objected, asking why if Jesus was God, how could He come into the world as a man? "He's so powerful everyone would die!"

Thay told him that to save us, Jesus became like one of us. "He wants to be in tune with humans," he said. "He has to live with their suffering, and then He can die for us."

Radha never thought much about the suffering part of the conversation until much, much later.

That evening Radha believed that Jesus was the Savior of the world. He went home and told his parents, "I just became a Christian."

"What do you mean, you just became a Christian?" his father barked. Manickam wasn't exactly talkative, and he believed that when he spoke it should be the final word. His father sat and glared, and in the glance Radha could see three hundred years of anticolonial resentment.

About eighty Indian families lived in Cambodia in the early 1970s. Every October 2 they rented a Phnom Penh theater and got together to celebrate Gandhi Jayanti, the birthday of Mahatma Gandhi. It's a national holiday in India, marked by prayer meetings and Hindu ceremonies all over the country. The Indian Cambodian families, most of them headed by successful businessmen, would watch an Indian documentary about Gandhi and Indian independence. They feasted on red curry (with meat), green curry (without), and all kinds of delicacies. They congratulated themselves that Gandhi had been the greatest of all world leaders because of his teachings on nonviolence and because he taught that one should love everybody from all religions. The whole event celebrated Indian liberation from British oppression and, along with that, their liberation from British religion, which meant Protestant Christianity. Many Cambodians—Khmer, as well as minorities—also nursed strong anti-Catholic sentiments that grew out of their experience under French colonialism.

Priests, artists, and teachers belonged to Manickam's Brahmim caste. He diligently fulfilled his duties as a caste member: he worshiped and burned incense to his chosen deities every evening; he studied the Vedas, Hinduism's oldest scriptures; and he practiced *dharma*. That is, he tried to live in a morally upright way to build up virtue in this and successive lives.

Manickam knew his oldest son was hanging around some Christians, but he didn't know it had come to this. Radha wasn't surprised to see his father's dark face start to turn pink. "Don't you understand anything from our fellowship with Indian people?" Manickam demanded. "How the British treated Indian people?"

Radha did, but he still believed in Christ. He wasn't trying to provoke his parents, exactly, but he also knew he had never resonated with his father's religion. And while some things about Christianity were hard to understand, other parts made a lot of sense. Manickam was unhappy with the whole thing but relented and allowed Radha to keep attending Maranatha Church.

By becoming a Christian in Cambodia in 1973, Radha was joining a tiny minority that was experiencing a modest revival in the crucible of the civil war.

The vast majority of Cambodia's population was (and is) ethnic Khmer. By far, the dominant religion is Theravada Buddhism, but it's mixed with spiritism and animism from Cambodia's ancient past, as well as the Hinduism that dominated the region until the thirteenth century.

The Mekong Delta, which since the 1800s has been part of Vietnam, was home to some of the area's first evangelical Christian Khmers back in the early 1920s. A population of Khmers called Khmers Krom lived on the Vietnamese side of the border, where evangelical missionaries had been ministering. Cambodia also had a long-standing but small Catholic presence because of the French influence throughout Indochina but no Protestant Christians. Until 1923, Catholic French and Cambodian leaders banned protestant missionaries in Cambodia, and evangelical Christians were nonexistent.

Two couples—David and Muriel Ellison and Arthur and Esther Hammond—with the Christian and Missionary Alliance were the first evangelical missionaries in the country in 1923. The Ellisons came to the city of Battambang to plant churches (and in 1925 opened the Bible School there), while the Hammonds moved to Phnom Penh to begin work on a Khmer translation of the Bible. Within ten years, as Don Cormack describes in *Killing Fields, Living Fields*, evangelical Cambodians were ministering in eleven of fourteen provinces.[2]

But the work was hard and converts were scarce. In 1932, King Monivong issued a royal edict forbidding proselytizing. Although it was unevenly enforced, traveling Cambodian evangelists were arrested, beaten, and sometimes killed. Local pastors and church members suffered harassment and worse from neighbors and officials.

Christians faced another wave of persecution beginning in 1941 under the four-year Japanese occupation of Cambodia. In the late 1940s through the early 1950s, Christians suffered yet more persecution during the uprisings of nationalist guerrillas called the Khmer Issarak, but the Lord protected the believers. Cormack writes, "They were preserved in times of bloody ambush by day, and raids on their villages at night, in trains derailed by mines and in remote areas where they were surrounded by hostility and contempt."[3]

In 1949, the Bible School moved to a site on the banks of the Bassac River in Phnom Penh. The Hammonds finished their Khmer translation of the Scriptures in 1954 and presented a copy to King Sihanouk, who declared freedom of religion throughout the country. That began a decade of relative peace and security for Cambodian evangelicals. Churches grew as a small core of key leaders trained at the Bible School in Phnom Penh. Most didn't survive the Khmer Rouge in the 1970s.

The peaceful period ended in 1965 when Sihanouk, leaning away from the United States and hoping to curry favor with Communists in China and Vietnam, expelled all foreign missionaries; it worked. Evangelical leaders estimated that in 1965 there were seven hundred baptized believers and maybe another two thousand adherents. After five years of persecution, only a handful of churches remained in Phnom Penh and Battambang, and a few house churches were scattered in rural areas. By 1969, perhaps three hundred Cambodians in total called themselves evangelical Christians.[4]

After the 1970 coup, the pro-US Lon Nol government reopened Cambodia to missionaries, and the Khmer Christians no longer faced official persecution. The Christian and Missionary Alliance resumed its work alongside the Khmer Christians, while other agencies such as Overseas Missionary Fellowship rushed in.

These groups found many people receptive to the gospel. As civil war raged around them, Cambodians desperately sought a source of hope. Amid the refugee camps, brothels, fear, and hot, crowded streets, under screaming rockets and jagged shrapnel, as Cormack described it, young Cambodian Christians began praying and evangelizing with passion. By late 1973, the three hundred believers had become 1,200, and by 1975, the three main evangelical churches in Phnom Penh had become thirty, along with many other house churches and Bible studies. One church began in a grounded houseboat along the banks of the Mekong River. The Bible School reopened, Khmer pastors held evangelistic crusades that attracted thousands, and on Christmas in 1974, the churches gathered in the stadium for a huge Christmas pageant.

Several thousand believers lived in Phnom Penh alone. Churches in Battambang, Siem Reap, and other cities also grew significantly. "Gone now were the platitudes, the social niceties, the easy banter of earlier days," Cormack writes. "Talk of eternal things was straightforward and undiluted. People living in the shadow of suffering and death have a unique capacity for isolating and focusing on the truly vital and essential issues of life."[5]

Despite the war, the months after Radha's conversion were for the most part happy. His father gave him permission to attend Sunday services only, but he was in church every time the doors opened. He went to Sunday worship and many of the weeknight Bible studies. Sometimes his brother Ravy, who was fifteen, even came with him. Appa wasn't happy about that either.

Radha soon developed a small group of close friends in Maranatha Church. Along with Huoth, there was Van, who worked for the Phnom Penh police, another young man named Van who was a student at a university, a Vietnamese medical student named Thy, and a few others. One friend, Hach, worked in the Pacific Restaurant near the Central Market. He lived in the church because he was afraid of being conscripted into the military. Bands of Republican troops used to roam through the city corralling young men and hauling them off in trucks for some perfunctory training before sending them to the front where they became targets for Khmer Rouge mortars.

The friends would ride around in Houth's Jeep and listen to Khmer artists like Ros Sereysothea, a chanteuse known as "The Golden Voice," and crooner Sinn Sisamouth, the "King of Khmer Music," on the radio. Phnom Penh had a thriving music scene, and one could hear echoes of the Beatles and the Rolling Stones in the Khmer bands that made their way from the provinces to play in the city's swinging clubs.

The group often spent late evenings on the church roof. Instead of talking politics, as Radha had done with his high school friends, they'd open their Bibles and talk about theology, pray, and sing. Sometimes they spoke in tongues, but Radha refrained. He read 1 Corinthians in more detail, and it seemed to teach that God does not give the same gifts to everyone.

Radha began to have serious doubts about charismatic teaching, but he was excited about the gospel, as was his circle of vivacious and passionate friends. Five or six of them, usually including Radha and Thy and one of the Vans, piled into Houth's Jeep several times a week and headed down to the Mekong riverfront to evangelize. To DeAnn it seemed that they really were ready to lay down their lives for the gospel. One day she was struck with Radha's exuberance as he stood in the back of the Jeep loading up guitars and helping his friends climb aboard. As the truck pulled out, he turned and gave her a wide, cheery smile as he waved good-bye.

The group often stood on the retaining wall down by the river and preached, where another street evangelist, an older Chinese-Cambodian man, would set up a table on a corner with a hand-cranked record player. He'd play recordings of the gospel and Radha would stand nearby and try to talk to passersby. Most ignored their Cambodian Bible Society tracts and attempts to engage them in conversation. Some would shout "Traitor!" at them or accuse them of abandoning the *only* Khmer religion—Buddhism.

A few people tried to win the conversation. If Jesus is God, one person asked Radha once, then why is Buddha older than Jesus is? Jesus, Radha replied, was there at creation. Radha told someone else that Buddha was a vegetarian because he knew he didn't own the animals. Jesus, who created the animals, had the authority to let men eat them. For a good Buddhist, this was an obnoxious line of reasoning, but Radha enjoyed getting a reaction.

Always in the background was the rumble of war or the clatter of helicopters overhead. Radha seldom ventured into the refugee camps in Phnom Penh, but one day a rocket landed in one near Maranatha Church. A square mile of ramshackle huts and old wooden buildings was soon ablaze. Hundreds rushed to the scene to help, including Todd and DeAnn. They saw residents bleeding from vicious shrapnel wounds and reeled at the stench of burnt flesh and homes. The sun was red from the roiling smoke. DeAnn felt like she was on the edge of hell.

They helped load wounded and burned people onto three-wheeled bikes and into taxis to get them to hospitals, and soon had blood on their clothes and hands. Todd picked up a man to put him into the back of a taxi and the bottom part of his leg, which had been slashed through the bone just below the knee, fell off. Todd wrapped it in a cloth and put it on the seat beside the victim, then dashed off to help somebody else.

Radha and several of the other youths jumped into a car to come help. They spent hours trying to pull victims out of collapsed, smoking buildings. By the end, they were dragging out bodies.

All that day Radha could feel his anger rising against the Khmer Rouge and against Sihanouk, who he felt bore much of the responsibility. Throughout the war Sihanouk had appealed on the radio for Cambodians—particularly those with some education, who he said would be necessary for rebuilding the country—to join the Communists. Many did, which both mystified and frustrated Radha. Here were the results: innocent people buried in burning rubble.

During this time, Radha frequently joined an armed night patrol in his parents' neighborhood. He prowled around the streets and alleys carrying a rifle but never flipped off the safety catch. Radha hated guns and didn't think he could have shot anyone. As head of the household, the elder Manickam was supposed to be on patrol but because of his arthritis was in no condition to go out. So Radha went to a training session during which an officer showed the group how to shove a clip into an automatic rifle and pull the trigger. That was it—no instruction in military tactics, no other weapons training, nothing. People referred to the watch duty as the "commando" patrol, but Radha didn't feel much like a commando. He prayed constantly that he wouldn't encounter any Khmer Rouge, and he didn't. Not then.

3

Two Worlds

Then I said, "For how long, Lord?" And he answered: "Until the cities lie ruined and without inhabitant, until the houses are left deserted and the fields ruined and ravaged, until the LORD has sent everyone far away and the land is utterly forsaken.

—Isaiah 6:11–12

One Sunday in early 1974, Radha noticed a bunch of believers heading to the rooftop of Maranatha Church. Pastor Thay explained that they were all going to be baptized. "Do you believe that Jesus saved you from your sins?" he asked Radha. He did, and so he went up to the roof where there was a large, tiled water reservoir. When it was his turn, he climbed into the tank, and Todd Burke lowered him under the water onto his back and said, "I baptize you in the name of the Father, and of the Son, and of the Holy Ghost." Radha didn't have any dry clothes to change into afterward, so he walked home dripping wet with the waters of baptism.

"What happened to you?" asked his father when he came in the door. "Fall into the river?"

Radha steadied himself. "No," he replied. "I'm really a Christian today. I was baptized. This is the next step."

"Wrong," growled Appa. For the elder Manickam, to have the son of a Brahmin convert to Christianity was bad enough. Baptism crossed a line that he couldn't overlook. But Radha refused to back down. They argued, as fiercely as an Asian son would dare against his father, and that night Radha moved out of the house. He soon found a job as an accountant for a fish seller in the city's main marketplace. He slept in one of the company trucks in a spot down by the river.

Radha, then twenty-one, was a new man in Christ, spiritually speaking, but that wasn't always reflected in his life. While working in the fish shop that spring, he and another worker carried in from one truck a big basket of fish that weighed about four hundred pounds. It wasn't his job; he was the bookkeeper. He was just kind of showing off his twenty-one-year-old muscles, but one of the laborers objected; carrying baskets was his job, and he expected to be paid for it. They argued in the street until finally Radha lost his temper and cracked the guy on the forehead with a bamboo carrying pole. He felt bad about it later.

Radha's job at the shop required him to take a driver and one of the trucks to a fish farm about twelve miles north of Phnom Penh for nighttime pickups. The Republic still controlled the major cities as well as narrow bands of land along some of the major roads. Once, on the way back, a couple of motorcycle police stopped them. Per usual, the officers expected a little something, perhaps a few bills slipped across in a handshake. *The cops are exceptionally polite*, Radha thought, *always wanting to shake hands.*

So Radha climbed out and walked back, leaving the driver in the cab with the engine running. He offered the cops a small catfish or mudfish each, but one of them kept pushing for something bigger. Radha kept resisting politely. While the cops were grumbling in the glare of their motorcycle headlights, Radha eased quietly back up to the door of his truck, then suddenly jumped in the cab. "Go!" he yelled at the startled driver, who shoved it into gear and jolted out onto Highway 5.

The cops hopped on their motorcycles and gave chase. Radha, peering out the window, saw one of them pull up next to the truck. "Push him off the road!" snapped Radha. The driver yanked the wheel over. The cop and his motorcycle swerved off the road and bounced into the ditch. The second officer stopped to check on the first; Radha and the driver kept going.

Radha was glad to get away with it but later felt a pang of regret. Nobody had enough money, and the cops were paid so poorly that they couldn't survive apart from a handshake-delivered "bonjour." It occurred to him that Jesus fed five thousand people with a few fishes; he'd had a truckload of fish and run off the road a guy who probably needed it to feed his family. The bribes weren't right but neither was what he'd done.

Appa eventually softened, perhaps from seeing some positive changes in his son, and Radha moved back home. Radha's parents, meanwhile, had been planning to upgrade their living quarters from their apartment in west Phnom Penh. Appa bought a row house on a cul-de-sac a few blocks southeast of the Central Market. Soon they were settled in the upper stories, with a display area on the street level for the motorcycles. The elder Manickam also rented the ground-floor units of the buildings across the street to store the Sanyos and company vehicles, a half-dozen small cars and trucks, Isuzus and Daihatsus.

Still, Radha had a streak that made him willing to risk his father's anger. For example, he used to sneak one of the display Suzukis out the door for joyrides when Appa was out of the house. It was risky, of course, because Appa would have been furious, but Radha always got home in time to wash the bike thoroughly and gas it up.

For Radha, 1974 was like living in two different worlds. One was war and rockets, chaos and blood and fear; the other was fellowship and peace, worship and prayer and song.

One Sunday that spring, Radha was walking home from church about 11:00 a.m. The morning was nice and sunny as he strolled down Nehru Boulevard. He was wearing his good Sunday clothes with his black shoes. He watched people shopping, gossiping, and sitting at patio tables outside restaurants. When he reached the corner of Kampuchea Krom, something whizzed overhead, and he ducked. Then he heard a massive boom behind him on Nehru. He spun around, saw the smoke, and then dashed back a half block to where the rocket had hit—the place he had passed less than a minute earlier.

A crowd had already gathered. Radha could see a couple of mangled motorbikes, and then gradually he recognized body parts scattered around the street—a hand, a leg. He saw blood oozing along the ground, flowing away from the point of impact. He turned and walked home.

Radha didn't want to see that anymore, didn't want to be reminded of how quickly his life could end. He felt peace at the thought of going to heaven, but his family was another matter. What would they do without him? He was his dad's voice when dealing with Khmer businessmen, and his brothers were not yet ready to step into that role.

On another day, Todd, DeAnn, Pastor Thay, Huoth, Radha, and about fifteen other church members piled into three vehicles and headed west on National Road 4 to the village of Kampong Speu. At the market square, they brought out guitars and a group of eight launched into some gospel songs in four-part harmony. Radha sang bass. A small crowd soon gathered, and when the songs were finished, they wandered among the people, witnessing and handing out tracts. Radha and a few friends hiked over to a nearby military base called Chbar Mon to witness for an hour or two and then returned to the market.

Radha stood in the square and watched the Burkes, Pastor Thay, and his friends smiling as they approached people to share the gospel and felt an intense kind of joy. Just before noon, they gathered at the tiny river that was next to the town. Some jumped in for a cooling swim with much laughing and splashing, and then they had a picnic lunch.

He would always remember that day a little wistfully. This seemed to him what the Christian life was supposed to look like. Here were his church leaders fulfilling the Great Commission, and next to them his brothers and sisters in Christ were living lives of ministry in sweet fellowship.

Late that afternoon they drove back to Phnom Penh, and on the way they could hear the war thundering in the distance. It continued all that evening and all night long.

The room was dark and completely packed. When everyone had settled, DeAnn began to play softly on her guitar "O Holy Night." When she began to sing, the hair on the back of Radha's neck stood up. They lit the candles, beginning with one and spreading from person to person, and Radha felt almost overcome with love for Jesus.

It was Maranatha Church's candlelight Christmas Eve service in 1974. He couldn't have explained how the service symbolized living in the dark of sin and coming into the light of the gospel through the witness of friends, but he felt it—strongly. Jesus brought everything into the light, and nothing needed to be in the dark anymore.

That January Radha turned twenty-two, and days later the Khmer Rouge were surrounding Phnom Penh. To its residents, the darkness seemed closer than ever. Radha could see how crowded the city was; refugee camps were everywhere. Many children came in from the countryside with distended bellies, swollen hands and feet, and lightened skin, the symptoms of malnutrition and impending starvation. But there was little enough food in the city. Rockets were landing day and night. The airport was closed frequently, while Khmer Rouge ambushes and underwater mines made it increasingly difficult to get supplies up the Mekong River.

The power was often out, and Republican officials, trying to anticipate attacks, called curfews at any hour of the day or night to get the population undercover. People walked down alleys, trying to avoid main streets, as they seemed more likely to be hit by rockets. Inflation wiped out the local economy. More and more, people traded in gold or American dollars, one of which might be worth thousands of riels.

The Manickams bought a fifty-pound bag of white rice that came in on an American airlift. The first pot they cooked for a meal tasted kind of sweet, almost like a dessert. It was depressing, not because it tasted bad, but because it was a reminder that Cambodians had been reduced to eating imported rice when their own country was covered in rice fields devastated by civil war.

They often ate by candlelight in those weeks, so candles and kerosene lamps sat all over the house. One evening, Grandma, Amma's mother, came into Radha's room to ask him to refill her lamp. She was a spry, energetic woman named Sami Heng. She had a head for business and kept her long graying hair tied up in a bun in traditional Vietnamese style. Radha spilled some of the kerosene on his hand and jerked it away, right over the candle on his desk. Suddenly flames were flickering on his hand and forearm. In a panic, he tried to wipe it off on his chest, but the kerosene kept burning, so now his shirt and then his chest hair were on fire.

Grandma, after screaming for a second, scurried from the room and returned a few seconds later with a wet scarf. She flung it over his body, and together they put out the fire. Radha ended up with minor burns on his hand, but a large section of skin on his chest was seared, and soon a massive blister appeared.

He did not go to the hospital. Everybody had heard the stories about how the hospitals were stacked full of wounded Republican

Army veterans, and the conditions were terrible. Only the most desperately ill went there for treatment—and only if they had no other choice. Instead, the next day Grandma pulled out some dark Vietnamese fish sauce and dabbed it on the blister. The salty sauce was supposed to prevent infection. It stung horribly, and Radha could hardly keep from yelling.

Despite the burns, he continued to work at the fish market. He handed over whatever he earned to his mother, and she gave him a small allowance back. It was almost the family's only income during this period. The Manickam family businesses had slowed down drastically, and their electronics and appliances were stacking up in the warehouse across the street from the family home.

The Republican Army had showed surprising grit and endurance after the American bombing ended in August 1973, fending off the Khmer Rouge through the dry-season campaign that ran from November until the rains came again in mid-June 1974. But the Khmer Rouge resumed the attack in the fall, and by January 1975, the end was near.

American aid was continuing to arrive but not nearly enough to support the Khmer Republic much longer. With the South Vietnamese losing ground steadily, the United States' long and discouraging attempt to stave off Communism in the region was about to end in failure. On August 9, 1974, Nixon resigned in the aftermath of Watergate. By early 1975, President Gerald Ford, who would shortly approve the complete withdrawal of US personnel from South Vietnam, was unable to convince Congress to prop up the Cambodian government and its leader, Lon Nol, whom Western observers widely dismissed as corrupt and incompetent. Many of his senior officers infamously grew wealthy by padding the number of troops under their command and pocketing the salaries of the "phantom soldiers." Many Cambodians, however, regarded Lon Nol as a true patriot.

Around Phnom Penh and the major Cambodian cities, the Khmer Rouge pressed ever closer. By January, the Communists had closed off the Mekong. One after another, towns outside Phnom Penh's perimeter fell to the Khmer Rouge. The more victories they gained, the more captured artillery they brought to bear on the capital. The United States authorized a massive airlift that spring, but there was no hope that enough food for two million people could arrive through one airport under frequent rocket attack.

In the spring of 1975, most of the people wealthy enough to buy plane tickets out of the country left, along with almost all the foreigners. Todd and DeAnn Burke flew out on March 29, taking with them five orphans who would be adopted by families in the West. Even then, the Burkes hoped one day to return to Cambodia. Lon Nol left the country on April 1 with half a million dollars at the request of US and Cambodian officials who hoped his departure would help negotiations with the Khmer Rouge or persuade the US Congress to authorize more aid. Radha saw Lon Nol on TV getting on the airplane; he was weeping as he climbed the steps.

On April 12, the Americans evacuated their embassy in Phnom Penh.

Radha and his friends continued meeting at the church for as long as they could. Pastor Thay set up a twenty-four-hour prayer vigil, which Radha attended almost daily. Cormack describes packed churches across Phnom Penh on April 13, Easter Sunday. "Though a thousand of us die," said Pastor Thay in what would be his final sermon at Maranatha Church, "ten thousand will be raised up!"[1]

A day or two later, Pastor Thay walked into the church, where about twenty of Radha's friends were praying earnestly for their country. He looked at them all sadly for a moment. "The Lord has not answered our prayers," he said. "Go home. You can't come back here now. It's not safe."

Radha choked up, and some of the others burst into tears.

4

Streets of Fear

We, too, clung to shreds of hope and believed to the last moment that it would not be so bad.

—Nazi survivor Viktor Frankl in *Man's Search for Meaning*

Radha was up by 7:00 a.m. on Thursday, April 17, with the rest of his family, pacing, watching, wondering. It had been an extremely long week. Radha peered out the second-story windows of the Manickams' row house. The neighborhood was eerily quiet.

Radha and his father went out onto the balcony, coffee cups in hand, and watched the street below. It was mostly empty. Then they noticed their neighbors in nearby apartments dropping bundles over the sides of their balconies and then ducking back inside. Radha and Appa peered at the bundles—they were green and looked like clothing—and realized that soldiers and officers of the Republican Army were getting rid of their uniforms.

In the middle of the morning, they saw people running and shouting and waving white flags. "Something's not right," Appa said. "Let's go inside." Radha was confused. A week after the American

50

delegation had been evacuated on helicopters, he still couldn't believe the Americans would let Phnom Penh fall to a bunch of Communist guerrillas. So why were those people waving white flags?

Radha and his father went into the apartment and closed the curtains. Later that morning they saw them—squads of Khmer Rouge soldiers walking in single file down their street. They wore loose black cotton pants that came down to mid-calf and shirts with buttons and breast pockets (often called "pajamas"), a black Chinese cap, and a red and white check-patterned krama (a sturdy traditional Cambodian garment used as a bandana or child carrier or other useful purposes) either around their waists or necks. Most had "Ho Chi Minh sandals" cut from old tires on their feet. They looked very young, younger than Radha's twenty-two years, and also thinner and much, much tougher. They were mostly filthy, reflecting months or years of warfare in the jungle. They didn't smile, and they didn't act like victors. Ravy, who was seventeen by then, thought the Khmer Rouge were much more frightening than the Republican troops. The Communists looked grim, menacing, and unpredictable. Many carried rocket launchers or AK-47s slung from shoulder straps.

The young soldiers moved down the street, pulling on the metal roll-up doors. They shot the locks off the Manickams' warehouses and went inside. A few minutes later they emerged and tied a bit of red string on the door handle that signified *this is now ours.*

They also went into the garage where the Manickams parked their three cars and two trucks and tied white flags onto those they claimed. Then they came out, and Radha and his dad eyed them from behind the curtains as the soldiers approached the family's front door. They glanced at the door and moved on, much to the family's relief.

When Appa was out of the living room, Radha pulled back a curtain a little and peeked out. His father happened to come in just then and yanked him away from the window. Appa warned Radha to stay back because they could shoot him through the window.

Radha thought back to the last "revolution" he had experienced in March 1970 when the national legislature, led by Marshal Lon Nol and Prince Sirik Matak, deposed Prince Norodom Sihanouk and founded the Khmer Republic. At the time, the city felt wild and crazy. People rioted and ran around shouting and waving clubs, but it ended without much bloodshed. This was different. There were no riots, no screaming—just many grim peasant youths carrying big guns. It looked much, much more dangerous.

Around noon, Amma made some lunch. They sat on woven mats on the floor, as was their custom, and picked at their rice and fish. None of Radha's six siblings seemed hungry, from the oldest sister, Indira, at nineteen, down through the baby sister, Lakshmi, who was two. Amma was about seven months pregnant.

They had a Phnom Penh radio station on the dial, hoping for some news, but it was silent until the middle of the day when a couple of different voices spoke in turn. One was Hem Keth Dara, leader of a group called the Monatio, or National Movement, which included the Supreme Patriarchs of the two main Buddhist sects and a senior Republican general. Another was General Mey Sichan, one of Lon Nol's top staff.

They appealed for everyone to remain calm and said that all military personnel of the Khmer Republic should put down their arms. A speaker was saying that officials of the Khmer Republic would begin negotiations with the revolutionary groups, when suddenly they were cut off, and confused sounds, voices, and scuffling were heard. A new voice—harsh and cold—then came on, saying the United Front had taken control of Cambodia and was entering the capitol through force of arms. There would be no negotiations with the Khmer Republic. Then the radio went dead.[1]

Later that day the power went off. The Manickams ate a hurried meal and then sat through the evening, watching the candles and waiting, but for what they did not know. The war was over, obviously, and Radha hoped that the bloodshed was too. But what would happen to their business, to their family? Who was in charge? Radha prayed heartfelt prayers that God would protect them all. Eventually they all went to bed, and after a long while, they fell asleep.

The Manickams didn't realize that while they had been watching and waiting on April 17, ten thousand Khmer Rouge troops had drifted into the city like scattered clouds of poisonous gas. Most, like the soldiers outside the Manickams' window, traveled on foot in single file. Some of the Khmer Rouge troops came in military vehicles; others, upon entering the city, soon commandeered Mercedes, Jeeps, trucks, bicycles, pedicabs, mopeds, and scooters.

Many residents of Phnom Penh—even those who hated Communism—were initially giddy that the war was over. They were sick of the ostentatious corruption of the Lon Nol regime, sick of the war, sick of the rockets, sick of the food shortages. They'd had enough of refugees from the countryside flooding the city, of nighttime terror, of death—they were just sick of it all. And maybe those young Khmer Rouge soldiers who had been bombed out of their minds in the jungles deserved to win this one. Communist or capitalist—what did it matter? What could be worse than the civil war? Were they not all Buddhists? Buddhism is a moderate and reasonable faith, and Cambodian people bend like young bamboo in the breeze of fate. Surely the time for Khmers killing Khmers was over. Perhaps life could return to what it was before all this began.

So when they saw the black-clad soldiers moving down the streets, they reveled in relief. In the morning sunshine, they waved white flags from windows and sheets from doorways. They hung white shawls from trees and wrapped white handkerchiefs around their arms. Khmer Rouge and Republican Army soldiers, in a few isolated instances, met in the street, joked, embraced, and slapped one another on the back. Citizens lined the streets clapping and cheering and shouting, "Victory!" and "Congratulations, comrade!" and "Peace, peace!" Throughout Cambodia, citizens broke into celebrations on city streets. They took pictures of residents and Republic soldiers standing in happy groups behind piles of surrendered rifles. For a while, it looked like Sihanouk's prediction would come true—that a national "fête" would break out if foreign troops left Cambodia.[2] People sang Khmer folk songs, danced Khmer dances, chanted Communist slogans, and for a few short hours believed all would be okay.

Then hope vanished like the illusion it was. By mid-morning troops started looting shops in Phnom Penh. The Khmer Rouge threatened over loudspeakers and the radio to shoot or hang offenders on the spot, while their own troops rampaged through the commercial district. Soldiers shot locks off doors and ripped shop doors off hinges with ropes tied to Jeeps and then stuffed their pockets with everything from watches to liquor to ballpoint pens.

Soon the Khmer Rouge had control of every major intersection in the city and were stopping traffic in the name of the Khmer Rouge's revolutionary organization. "Angka requests the use of your car," they would politely inform the driver. Angka, however, often didn't know how to drive. The young guerrillas would jump in, take off, and promptly crash into some other comrade's newly liberated truck. Despite the confusion, however, the Communists solidified their hold on the city. They seized weapons and tanks, took over buildings, and forced government troops to remove their uniforms.

Scattered outbreaks of revenge also surfaced when Communist soldiers encountered unarmed Khmer Republic troops, and individual Khmer Rouge soldiers brutalized and shot civilians for no good reason.

The deliberate, systemic violence began around 9:00 a.m. on April 17 when the Khmer Rouge started evacuating the city at gunpoint. The Communists emptied businesses, markets, houses, apartments, orphanages, clinics, pagodas (Buddhist temples)—anywhere people lived or worked. They wouldn't get around to the Manickams' neighborhood until the next morning, April 18, and were still clearing cities and villages across the country for two more weeks.

On that first day the Khmer Rouge concentrated initially on hospitals, into which thousands of casualties of the civil war had been packed—sometimes in appalling conditions, stacked in stinking hallways smeared with blood.

Troops stormed into Phnom Penh's largest hospital, Preach Ket Melea, shouting, "Out! Everybody out! Get out!" The Communists forced at gunpoint the doctors and nurses who had not yet fled and every last patient—hundreds of them, regardless of condition or consciousness—into the street, where the temperature was more than one hundred degrees Fahrenheit. Relatives or friends pushed the beds of patients unable to walk, holding up bottles dripping plasma or serum. "One man carried his son, whose legs had been amputated. The bandages on both stumps were red with blood, and the son, who appeared to be about twenty-two, was screaming, 'You can't leave me like this! Kill me! Please kill me!'"[3]

A couple of Khmer Rouge guerrillas burst into the operating room of surgeon Haing Ngor that morning as he was sewing up a Republican soldier whose abdomen had been punctured by shrapnel from a grenade. One Khmer Rouge put his rifle barrel to Haing's head, but he told them the doctor had just left and the guerrillas ran out the back door in pursuit. He and his medical team fled the clinic, knowing the patient would die anyway. "There was something excessive about their anger," Haing writes. "Something had happened to these people in their years in the forests. They had been transformed. They were not like the Cambodians I had known."[4]

When Haing got to the streets, he saw a female Khmer Rouge who was just as dusty and angry as any of her male comrades. She shoved a terrified prisoner in front of her and waved her pistol around. "Everybody is equal now," she shouted. "The revolution has arrived!" People, she said, had to choose: "No more masters and no more servants! The wheel of history is turning! You must follow Angka's rules!"[5]

Father François Ponchaud, a Catholic missionary, witnessed from his mission the "hallucinatory spectacle" of patients dragging themselves along. "I shall never forget one cripple who had neither hands nor feet, writhing along the ground like a severed worm, or a weeping father carrying his ten-year-old daughter wrapped in a sheet tied round his neck like a sling," he writes in *Cambodia: Year Zero*. One man's foot was dangling, attached to his leg by nothing but skin; Ponchaud denied him permission to stay at the mission. "Refusing shelter to the sick and injured makes one feel that one has lost one's last shred of human dignity. That is how the first evacuees left, about twenty thousand of them."[6]

The guerrillas also began to "cleanse" the city of books, magazines, and printed material of all kinds. They stormed into government ministries, the Royal Palace, businesses, temples, and the libraries of the universities and private residences. They flung books and binders of records and sheaves of paper onto the streets and carted more off to the city dump. They burned down whole libraries, including those of Phnom Penh University and Buddhist University. They collected paper riels from all over the city, including from the vaults of the country's central bank, the Banque Khmer de Commerce, stuffed them into sacks and burned them in the streets.

Refugees later reported seeing Communist soldiers invade homes for invalids and then hearing shots as they murdered patients in their beds and chairs. Then they moved into residential neighborhoods, banging on doors and ordering people out. Sometimes they were polite—"Angka requests that you leave the city immediately"—and sometimes they screamed, but they always got their way because they shot or bayoneted anybody who resisted.

The euphoria was gone by midmorning, and by sunset fear covered the streets like rainwater on a rice field. Democratic Kampuchea had arrived.

On April 18, Radha woke up around 6:00 a.m. to the sound of loudspeakers blaring on the street below. He looked out the front window. A couple of Khmer Rouge soldiers were pushing a bicycle down the street with a portable PA system balanced on the seat.

They said Angka Loeu required everyone to leave the city for three days. Leave immediately. The Americans would be bombing all the cities in Democratic Kampuchea very soon. People were told to take only the possessions they would need for three days, no more. They could return in three days, but they had to leave the city now.

Who or what is this "Angka Loeu"? Radha wondered. *And do we really have to?* Angka translates roughly to "organization," and *loeu* means either "upper" or "on high." Then they began hearing scattered gunshots in the neighborhood. The Manickams looked outside again and saw people on their street and on neighboring streets slowly come out their doors, carrying sacks and suitcases, and begin trudging north. Farther down the way, soldiers were going house to house, banging on doors. "Out!" they barked. "Everyone must go!" Dark shapes sprawled out on a few of the doorsteps in the soldiers' wake.

Appa told the family to get some food together. "We're going," he said.

So the Manickams, including Grandma, hurriedly packed up some rice, vegetables, a bit of meat, some cooking utensils, and some clothes. Radha threw into a sack the gold watch his father had given him, a beautiful piece, and also his Khmer Bible. It was about five inches wide by eight inches tall and four inches thick, with fine white paper and red gilding. On the front, it said "Bible" in French in gold letters. It was heavy, but he wasn't going to leave without it.

Then he looked around for something to carry their goods with and saw one of the Suzuki motorbikes, a display model. He grabbed the handlebars and was about to roll it out the door when his father stopped him. "Don't take it, son," he said. "You won't get far."

"What do you mean?" Radha asked.

"You can't own anything anymore," he replied sadly.

So they rolled one of the kids' bicycles to the front door, hauled out three suitcases, and piled them atop the handlebars and seat. They gave each of the older children a bag. Appa took his canes and one of his Sanyo radios and made sure that two of his most important family idols had been carefully wrapped and stored in one of the suitcases. Amma had Lakshmi by the hand. As Appa was standing at the front doors locking up, a Khmer Rouge soldier came up. "Leave it," he said. "Angka will take care of it."

Appa looked at him but said nothing and then slowly turned to his family. They set off down the street, joining a group of other glum-looking city dwellers who trickled into a tributary that joined larger and larger rivers of people, hundreds of thousands of them, flowing slowly through the streets of Phnom Penh.

When Radha and his family joined the crowds, the soldiers were pushing people out of the city, but no one could hurry. Appa's canes and Amma's pregnancy made them slow, but it didn't matter much because the crowds could only shuffle along. They headed north with the rest of the crowd, and then Appa decided they should try for the French embassy, which was on the far side of the Central Market, to the northwest. When they hit Neayok Souk, they turned left and began to work their way around the south side of the market.

They didn't get far. The Khmer Rouge relentlessly funneled the crowds, inching along, onto the main arteries. When the Manickams tried to leave the main road, a soldier shoved Appa in the chest with his rifle. "You're going to see Angka Loeu," the soldiers said, not letting anyone leave the main roads. They found themselves on Route 182 heading west. The young children carried their bags of clothes and some supplies, while the older children and adults carried packs or pushed the bicycle with the suitcases. Somewhere along the way, they picked up a two-wheeled cart in which they put all their food.

Radha looked at the side streets as they slowly passed. Most were empty. The whole city had been stuffed into Phnom Penh's thoroughfares. Most people had food and clothing, but others also carried TVs on their shoulders or furniture in their carts. Some carried live ducks and chickens in cages and pulled behind them pigs on leashes. Those in the middle of the street could see only the heads and shoulders of the people packed in around them.

That's how the day wore on. It was brutally hot, it was crowded, and it stunk. Children wailed, women and the elderly cried, and the sick, wounded, and injured moaned, but there was no chatter or even conversation. "Don't say anything to anyone," Appa instructed. "Keep moving. Don't look at people." Drawing attention to yourself appeared to be the quickest way to get shot. Nobody wanted to be recognized, especially those who were trying to hide the fact that they had been wealthy or educated in the old Phnom Penh or had served in the Republican Army. The Communists' intentions weren't exactly clear, but it was hard to miss the hostility in those hard-eyed young soldiers.

Some people were pushing their belongings in small cars, mostly Peugeots and Renaults, that rolled easily. To save gasoline hardly anybody started their vehicles. The line was moving so slowly it would have been pointless. Radha watched as a couple of soldiers, country boys fresh out of the jungle, approached one of the cars. They waved the owners away with the muzzles of their rifles, started the car, and lurched off down the street, scattering those around them. They crashed into the side of a house, extracted the car from that mess, and then bashed into a tree. The soldiers got out and left the wreck for the owners to come collect their belongings.

On another occasion, Radha heard an engine revving behind him and turned to see a Jeep weaving through the crowd with Khmer Rouge soldiers hanging off the sides and sending bursts of bullets into the air. People had to hustle out of the way or be run over. Radha watched the Jeep disappear down the road. It covered more distance in a couple of minutes than his family had traveled that whole day.

By about 8:00 p.m., the Manickam family had made it to the home of Radha's Aunt Thy. She lived on a street right near Route 182 on the western side of Phnom Penh in a neighborhood that had yet to be evacuated. Aunt Thy was not a blood relative; Grandma had adopted her years before. At this point Thy, her husband, her father-in-law, and a couple of young cousins named Saravanan, seven, and Chandara, five, joined the Manickams. There were fifteen in their party. Amma, Appa, and Grandma tried to hide the pain, but they had struggled all day just to pick up their feet. Radha and some of his siblings went out to find some food, but all the nearby stores had been looted. As they returned, they saw all around them in the alleys and yards thousands of people settling in for the night, laying out blankets on the ground and searching for empty buildings. Small fires twinkled up and down the street. Inside Aunt Thy's house, the Manickams cooked some of their rice and had a small meal.

When the soldiers first pushed them out of the house, nobody had much time to wonder whether the Americans really were going to bomb Phnom Penh. It had seemed plausible at first. Radha, like many in the city, wanted to believe that the victors had peaceful intentions. He couldn't imagine any other reason the Khmer Rouge wanted everybody out of their homes.

But as the day wore on, Radha began to wonder. That night he lay on a mat and pondered the possibilities. *If it was just a trick, what was the point?*

5

The Khmer Rouge

Secret work is the essence of all that we are undertaking.

—Nuon Chea, Brother Number Two, *Pol Pot's
Little Red Book: The Sayings of Angkar*

The evacuation of Phnom Penh was, in fact, a trick—an especially malevolent one. Many besides Radha were confused about the Khmer Rouge's intentions because the Communist leadership, particularly Pol Pot and his chief political officer Nuon Chea, were obsessive about secrecy. Few outside their inner circle knew exactly what they had in mind; few outside the inner circles of the Central Committee even knew who the leaders were. Pol Pot didn't reveal himself as the leader of the Khmer Rouge or even acknowledge, officially, that the Khmer Rouge was a Communist organization until the Chinese insisted he do so in a 1977 speech.

But the Khmer Rouge had a plan—and it wasn't a good plan. It owed much to Mao's Great Leap Forward and his Cultural Revolution, both of which had killed millions of people. It was a naive, simplistic, and unrealistic plan. And Pol Pot and his inner circle chased it relentlessly.

61

During their years in the jungle, the Khmer Rouge built a few thousand poorly equipped troops into an organization that was crafty, deceptive, and just powerful enough to win a civil war, but Pol Pot knew that in 1975 he probably could not control the entire country purely through force of arms. He simply didn't have enough troops to put down a populist revolt.[1]

However, he did have just enough soldiers and popular support to intimidate the rest of the population into compliance, especially in a Buddhist culture that placed a high value on order and respect for authority. By emptying the cities, Pol Pot disconnected any potential networks of "counterrevolutionary" forces, especially ex-Khmer Republic military personnel, leaving potential rebels isolated, unarmed, on the move, and powerless.

The evacuations were far more than a mere strategy for gaining and maintaining power. Khmer Rouge leaders would later claim they emptied the cities because they had no way to feed all those people, but hints about the Communists' intentions had surfaced as far back as 1972. In the middle of the civil war, the Khmer Rouge began setting up prototype "cooperatives" in the "liberated" rural regions they controlled. The first detailed account of these areas came from Ith Sarin, a left-leaning former bureaucrat. He spent nine months in the *maquis* (a French word that referred to the Cambodian jungles) preparing for Khmer Rouge membership, only to return to Phnom Penh as a dedicated anti-Communist. His book *Regrets for the Khmer Soul* describes a shadowy organization called "Angka" that bore all the signs of a fledgling totalitarian Communist state.[2] Children and youth went through rigorous political indoctrination designed to instill a "collective spirit" and class-consciousness, not to mention a mortal hatred for the Republican government. Cadres, officials responsible for implementing Angka's directives, forbade liquor, gambling, and illicit sex.

Some of the farmers at first welcomed the Khmer Rouge, who cracked down on theft and corruption among former local Republic officials and even provided food and medicine to needy families. Only later did the farmers sense they had made a deal with the devil. Ith also cited what was to become a defining aphorism for the Khmer Rouge: "One must trust completely in Angka, because Angka has as many eyes as a pineapple and cannot make mistakes."[3]

Prior to that point, however, the history of Cambodia's socialist militants provided few obvious clues of what was coming. For most of the 1960s, the Cambodian Communists were an irritant to Sihanouk but were no serious threat to his power or a significant force in the war in Vietnam. When the Americans began dropping bombs on Cambodia's border regions to disrupt the Communist Vietnamese, US intelligence officers presumed the Cambodian Communists were working closely with the North Vietnamese, the South Vietnamese insurgents called Viet Cong, the Chinese, and any other Communists in the area.

That wasn't accurate. Operating over the years under a variety of organizations, Cambodia's Communists had long and with good reason suspected that the North Vietnamese were hoping to absorb fellow Communists all over Indochina into a coalition controlled, of course, by the North Vietnamese. The Communist regime in Hanoi also held a condescending attitude toward their Cambodian brethren, and there was some vicious racial tension, especially in Cambodia's rural areas, between Khmer and Vietnamese that went back centuries.

Vietnamese soldiers in the 1800s supposedly gouged out Khmer prisoners' eyes and salted their wounds. Every Cambodian knew about the nineteenth-century Vietnamese ruler who, according to the story, ordered three captured Khmer soldiers buried up to their necks. His soldiers then lit a fire between them, balanced a brazier on top of their heads, and set a teapot on it. "Don't spill the master's tea," taunted the Vietnamese as the Khmers died in agony. The Vietnamese perspective, of course, was that the Khmers were treacherous savages who had committed their own share of atrocities over the centuries. After the Khmers revolted against Vietnam's rule in 1840, the emperor at the time ranted, "I am so angry that my hair stands upright. Hundreds of knives should be used against them to chop them up, to dismember them."[4]

More recently, for a century (until Cambodian independence in 1953) French officials had imported into Cambodia and then educated tens of thousands of Vietnamese bureaucrats and soldiers to administer the protectorate. The French viewed the Vietnamese people as industrious and reliable and the Khmers as lazy and indolent, overly inclined to lounge in hammocks while watching their rice grow. This favoritism produced a minority class of educated and relatively wealthy Vietnamese whose descendants—national estimates ranged from three hundred thousand to seven hundred thousand—controlled much of the trade and retained their ethnic language and dress.[5] Individual Khmers and Vietnamese could be friends, but the favoritism produced a resentment that persisted through Sihanouk's reign and, unsurprisingly, generated much hostility, especially among poor Khmers, that on occasion manifested in racial massacres.[6] The Cambodian Communists were prepared to accept a certain amount of aid and direction from Vietnam, but they were deeply suspicious.

Cambodian Communists felt strong enough to begin armed attacks on Sihanouk's forces by 1967, beginning with the Samlaut Rebellion and continuing with small-scale attacks. The North Vietnamese government had discouraged armed resistance to Sihanouk, instructing the Cambodian Communists to agitate politically instead. The Cambodian Communists were furious when they later discovered that the North Vietnamese actually preferred Sihanouk in power because his deal with them made it easier to keep the Ho Chi Minh Trail open. In the eyes of the Cambodian Communists, the Vietnamese had sold out any chance of a Cambodian Communist revolution to protect their own interests.

By the end of the 1960s, the Khmer Rouge had a few thousand troops, trained and supplied mostly by the Chinese and North

Vietnamese, and several thousand guerrillas drawn from the rural areas. Some Cambodians were attracted to the Communists' egalitarian rhetoric, others were sick of the perennial corruption in Phnom Penh, and others had suffered at the hands of Sihanouk's forces throughout the years.

Their leader was Saloth Sar, who in 1977 revealed himself to the world as "Brother Number One," or Pol Pot. He became general secretary of the party's Central Committee in 1963. Pol Pot was in many ways the opposite of Sihanouk. They shared a thirst for power, but where Sihanouk was flamboyant, impulsive, and self-seeking, Pol Pot was disciplined, secretive, and zealous. Rather than turn the party into a cult of personality, he kept himself hidden and made Angka the ultimate authority.[7] Sihanouk believed, said, and did what was politically expedient; what was good for him was good for Cambodia. Pol Pot burned inside for a Communist Khmer society.

Pol Pot was born in 1925, the youngest of seven children, to a prosperous rice farmer living in the northwest near Tonle Sap, the country's largest freshwater lake. According to his brothers, Pol Pot never worked in the fields, and a neighbor later described him in that period as "very serious, and he would not gamble or allow children such as myself to play near his home."[8] At nine years old, Pol Pot was sent to Phnom Penh to live with his cousin and older sister; his cousin had borne a son to one of the royal princes and his sister was a minor consort of King Sisowath Monovong.

From 1936 to 1942 Pol Pot attended a Catholic prep school in Phnom Penh where he became literate in French and Catholic doctrine and received the rudiments of a classical education. He was a serious but average student throughout high school. Still, he earned a scholarship to take a technicians' course at the Ecole Française de Radioélectricité in Paris, one of the first one hundred young men and women to earn such government support.

In 1951 in Paris, he joined a Marxist circle of fellow Cambodian students. It was a heady time to be a Communist in France, which had the strongest, most aggressive Communist Party west of Eastern Europe. As historian David Chandler has noted, with Stalinism nearing its peak, the victory of Communism in China, and a decisive confrontation happening in Korea, Communism must have seemed like "the wave of the future" to the young Cambodians in Paris.[9]

Friends later described Pol Pot in his young adult days as gentle and shy—and yet still a charming and strangely persuasive young man who "would not have killed a chicken."[10] He was bright enough but less interested in electronics than in reading and Marxist discussions. Friends said he was pining for his girlfriend back in Phnom Penh, a beautiful young woman from a wealthy family. He also met several others, such as Ieng Sary, who would become comrades on the Central Committee back in Cambodia. He would have most of them executed in the purges he set raging through the party starting in 1976.[11]

Pol Pot lost his scholarship to the technical school in mid-1952 and returned to Phnom Penh the following January. A short time later, he joined the Vietnamese-run Indochina Communist Party, and his girlfriend dumped him to become the junior wife of a rising star in Sihanouk's government. In 1956, he instead married an elegant, austere young woman named Khieu Ponnary whom he had met in Paris. She was from an elite Phnom Penh family and eight years his senior. They both found work as teachers in Phnom Penh.

Pol Pot was by all accounts a skilled teacher—eloquent, unpretentious, and fond of his students. One acquaintance said he "could explain things in such a way that you came to love justice and honesty and hate corruption."[12] He spent the 1950s and early 1960s working with both the aboveground political efforts of Cambodian leftists and Communists and the underground groups that Sihanouk's forces had pushed into the forests. He also lived for a time with the North Vietnamese Communists. In 1963, he became general secretary of Pracheachon, which renamed itself the Communist Party of Kampuchea in 1966. Even then he was self-effacing, one who deliberately melted into the background while planning to take control.

Pol Pot learned the basics of Communism in Paris, but it is likely that he and the others who formed the backbone of the Khmer Rouge leadership in the 1960s adopted the more radical elements of their ideology after returning to Cambodia. He would later claim that the Khmer Rouge were "building socialism without a model."[13]

That was ridiculous. Leftist scholars used to split hairs about the degree to which Khmer Rouge ideology reflects classic Marxist concepts, but the outlines are clear.[14] It was the philosophy of Mao executed with the speed and violence of Stalin, all shot through with ultranationalism and xenophobia. Pol Pot visited China in the mid-1960s and from Mao adopted concepts such as autonomous revolution, voluntarism, and continuous class struggle, which he thought would give Khmers a model by which to become independent of the Vietnamese.[15]

Pol Pot's goal was to create a new society that was purely socialist and purely Khmer. First, the regime had to crush the old society and everything connected to it: religion, free markets, private property, schools, political and economic institutions, as well as traditional ideas of morality, sexuality, and family.

He turned socialism into Cambodia's national religion, enforced by Angka with the legalism of Pharisees and pretensions to the omniscience of Big Brother. Following Mao (with object lessons from the French Revolution), Pol Pot elevated farmers and agriculture—everything rural. In Paris, he had read Jean-Jacques Rousseau and seemed to see humans as "noble savages" who had been corrupted by the institutions of a predatory urban society.[16] By emptying the cities, he eliminated private property, thereby abolishing capitalism and instituting socialism in one brilliant stroke.

The Khmer Rouge also wiped out almost all scientists and technicians, thinking that the experience of farmers must be superior to the book learning of academics. As one Khmer Rouge saying put it,

"The rice paddy is the university," and another, "The spade is your pen; the rice field is your paper."[17]

Pol Pot saw himself as taking exceptional measures to save the Khmer nation.[18] He believed life was pure class warfare—one that required and justified violence. Murder was not a crime but "the necessary prelude to the birth of a new society." [19] To execute the revolution, you had to crush what existed; after the revolution, you had to crush the counterrevolutionaries who survived; and then to maintain the revolution, you had to crush all revisionists and traitors who might attempt to undermine it.

This new society required the creation of the "new socialist man" dedicated to only the collective.[20] The Khmer Rouge had what one theorist calls a "high modernist orientation"—that is, the overweening confidence in "science" that prompts totalitarians to try mind-bogglingly tyrannical social engineering projects.[21] They believed humans are blank slates who could, with enough force, be molded into any shape they chose; thus, they planned to "restructure" the individual completely and force society into new, collectivist patterns. Home life would be defined not by the family but by the cooperative. Work would be done not for personal gain but in the context of a "battalion" for the good of the collective. People would be "tempered" through abolishing "privateness." Khmer Rouge president Khieu Samphan, for example, said that even thoughts were unacceptably private: "To become a true revolutionary, you must . . . wash your mind clean."[22]

Khmer Rouge ideology also had some distinctively Khmer elements based in the legend of the Angkorean Empire. For the five hundred years or more prior, Cambodia had been kicked around by its more powerful neighbors, Siam (Thailand) and Vietnam, which both regarded the Khmer nation as a buffer state between their aggressive cultures. Cambodia also had suffered foreign colonization by China in centuries past and more recently by France. To survive, Cambodian rulers had a long history of playing one regional power against the other in futile attempts to preserve its territory and dignity. The description fit Sihanouk pretty well.

But Cambodia hadn't always been weak, according to the romanticized version of Khmer history to which the Khmer Rouge (and most Khmer rulers after 1900) appealed. From the ninth through the fifteenth centuries a series of brutal Khmer god-kings, notably Jayavarman VII, built an empire with the wealth generated by slave labor and a vast system of irrigation dams, reservoirs, and canals for growing rice. They dominated the entire region, exacting tribute and fear from kingdoms in Thailand and Vietnam. They also built the famous temple complex, Angkor Wat, still the world's largest religious site ever discovered and the symbol of Khmer identity.[23] Although it is falling into ruins today, it features tall, beautiful towers, massive stone sculptures, and intricate Hindu and Buddhist carvings in which snakes play a prominent role. Armies of slaves toiled for years under the lash of whips and the broiling sun to build it.

The historical reality of the Angkorean Empire was perhaps not quite as glorious as Pol Pot had imagined, but it had been impressive. The Khmer Rouge intended to restore the lost glory of the Angkorean era by similar means: grow and sell enough rice to buy the equipment to build a modern, industrial state.[24] Only instead of being a feudal nation founded on patronage and slave labor, the new Democratic Kampuchea would consist of only comrades wholly devoted to the cause—the "new socialist man." Khmers had to do everything and only the Khmer way, with no outside help or direction. This was the principle of *aekâreach mâchaskar*, roughly translated "independence-mastery." Using Khmer Rouge propaganda, officials would later repeat this phrase endlessly, innocent of the irony that the concept itself had been lifted from Mao's Cultural Revolution.

Members of the Khmer Rouge, like all good Communists, despised religion in general. "Every citizen of Kampuchea has the right to worship according to any religion and the right not to worship

69

according to any religion. Reactionary religions which are detrimental to Democratic Kampuchea and Kampuchean people are absolutely forbidden," declared the Khmer Rouge constitution in a gorgeous bit of Orwellian doublethink.[25] The Buddhist doctrine of karma—that people suffer misery or prosper now according to their actions in past lives—clashes with an ideology of class warfare. The regime immediately executed almost all bonzes (Buddhist priests) as "bloodsuckers" on the people.[26]

But the Khmer Rouge co-opted elements of Buddhism that fit their purposes.[27] For example, like Buddhist doctrine, Khmer Rouge ideology rejected the quest for material wealth and embraced (in theory) disciplined personal transformation. As the awareness of self is an illusion for a good Buddhist, so the Khmer Rouge demanded that all Cambodians submerge their identities into the collective. Individuals were to free themselves of all emotional ties or obligations to other people and submit wholly to the state, for the "wheel of revolution which never stops" (perhaps a nod to the Buddhist *samsara*, the eternal cycle of reincarnation) will inevitably "crush all who place themselves in its path."[28]

Just as Buddhist converts take new names to symbolize their new identity, so the Khmer Rouge gave all under their power new, shorter names. Saloth Sar himself became Pol Pot. Film shot by official Chinese propagandists in 1977 shows him flashing a bright smile in a smooth, unlined face under a brush cut. He plays perfectly the humble yet confident leader as he applauds back at the cheering and saluting crowds.

Pol Pot spent the majority of the civil war lurking in the *maquis*. He had retreated in the 1960s to the camps the Vietnamese had helped construct in the country's northeast jungles. In the words of one historian, the *maquis* was where "with a group of like-minded colleagues, he lost touch with everyday Cambodian life, polished his Utopian ideas, nourished his hatreds, and thought about seizing power."[29]

And that's why, as soon as he seized power, Pol Pot emptied the cities.

———————

The next day, April 19, the soldiers were back with the sun, waving their machine guns and barking at the groggy people to "get up! Now! Angka says you must keep moving!" Only this morning, instead of forcing the crowds west, the soldiers pushed them back east a few blocks to Mao Tse Toung Boulevard. Then they went north until they hit Kampuchea Krom Boulevard, one of the city's main arteries, and headed west again out toward the airport.

Wrecked cars and trucks littered the streets, along with human bodies already bloated after a day or two in the blazing heat. Some had been murdered outright by the Communists. Many others, elderly or ill when forced out of their homes, had been abandoned by weeping family members and left to die, sometimes in agony.

That day the bodies began piling up even faster; thousands of Cambodians perished in those initial days of the "liberation." With the power grid down, the water system stopped working. Under the blazing sunshine, those who had failed to bring water soon began drinking whatever they could find in open barrels, gutters, and rapidly drying puddles brown with muck and worse. Dysentery took hold, and the constant diarrhea dehydrated its victims even further. That disease (along with typhoid fever, cholera, malaria, and many others) would plague countless Cambodians for the next four years. Keeping clean was next to impossible, and so the illnesses spread.

No bathrooms were available, of course, and no one could leave the road or escape the crowds. People had to relieve themselves on the side of the street, sometimes as a family member held up a blanket for a shred of privacy. Soon the stench of excrement was mixed with the odor of human corpses. The smell was so rank and pervasive that sometimes people would lie down to sleep next to a

71

mess of drying diarrhea, unaware that the source of the stench was right next to them.

Because of the stress, the heat, the disease, and the lack of water and food, pregnant women frequently miscarried, and without medical care, some lost so much blood that they died. Across the city, groups of tearful family members would gather around a shrieking woman on her back beside the road or in the backseat of a car. Radha glanced at his mother, toiling along behind her belly, and prayed.

By late afternoon, the crowd had more or less stopped. Radha, Indira, and Aunt Thy searched for food. Radha found a sow and a piglet in a pen that, somehow, was unattended. He tied them up with some rope he found nearby, and they carried them back to the camp. A fellow evacuee agreed to butcher them in exchange for the heads. That night Grandma cooked up a good meal, and they ate by firelight.

On April 20, the soldiers were back again by 6:00 a.m., and again they reversed direction and pushed the crowds east, back toward the downtown. Radha wondered again who, exactly, was in charge. Angka didn't seem to know what it was doing. Around midmorning, the Khmer Rouge began herding the crowds onto Yothapol Khemarak Phoumin Boulevard, which led south past the downtown and then curved east toward the Bassac and Mekong Rivers. They flowed south along the eastern edge of Phnom Penh's downtown.

Around midday, Radha noticed more Khmer Rouge shaking down passing travelers. He watched as a pair approached a group and demanded something. The evacuees shook their heads, so the soldiers grabbed their hands, checked their wrists, and then searched their packs.

When the Manickams came up, the soldiers said that Angka required the use of their wristwatches. Radha spoke up quickly; he had hidden his watch in his pack. "I'm very sorry," he told them, "but we already gave ours to some of your comrades." The soldiers glanced at his wrists and then waved them on. The Manickams plodded by, Appa leaning on Radha and Ravy while the rest of the family trailed behind.

A few hours later they approached the Bassac River and turned south onto National Road No. 2. Not long after that the Manickams suddenly noticed that Amma and the two youngest sisters, Lakshmi, who was two, and Annapoorani, five, were missing, along with Aunt Thy and her relatives.

They called out and searched the crowd. The rest of the family moved over to the side of the road and stopped, trying to avoid the notice of the soldiers. Radha, his stomach tightening, could see the fear in his father's eyes. Who saw what happened? Hadn't they been in the front? How could they have gone ahead so quickly? They couldn't be far behind because the soldiers were pushing everybody along. And then they realized that at the time Amma had been pulling the cart carrying all their food, including their rice.

They wanted to go back to look for her, but clumps of Khmer Rouge soldiers, smoking cigarettes and drinking bottles of Pepsi, loitered along the street as far as they could see in both directions. The soldiers shouted at those who stopped to rest and kicked at those who refused initially to move. The Manickams tried once or twice to head back against the flow, but the soldiers screamed and pointed their weapons at them.

Going back looked hopeless, so they continued on. Maybe she had somehow gotten ahead of them, or maybe she would be able to catch up. They didn't know whether to hurry up or slow down. They kept glancing around, backward and forward, hoping, but Amma and the girls were gone.

6

Into the Countryside

Kum is a Cambodian word for a particularly Cambodian mental-
ity of revenge—to be precise, a long-standing grudge leading to
revenge much more damaging than the original injury. If I hit
you with my fist and you wait five years and then shoot me in
the back one dark night, that is *kum*. . . . Cambodians know all
about *kum*. It is the infection that grows on our national soul.

—Haing Ngor, *A Cambodian Odyssey*

Many families were missing members at this point. The
crowds were overwhelming, and the Khmer Rouge were
relentless in keeping people moving. The Manickams
kept heading south down Highway 2, which ran out of Phnom Penh
and roughly parallel to the Bassac River. When they stopped to eat,
Indira found some cucumbers and jicama (a kind of white tuber)
down by the river, and Radha and Ravy found some coconuts. They
ate some, saved the rest for evening, and then got up and kept going.
They watched constantly for Amma and the girls.

As the Manickam party approached a concrete bridge over a
stream at the village of Krong Ta Khmau, just a couple of miles

south of Phnom Penh, they saw that a couple of Khmer Rouge had set up an informal checkpoint. Two boys, perhaps sixteen years old, came up to the family and began to interrogate Manickam: Where did he come from? What was his business? Was he in the military?

However, Manickam's Khmer wasn't great even when he was alert, and now he was exhausted and in pain. He leaned on his canes and tried to answer, but the youths kept yammering at him. And the less he understood, the more aggressive the soldiers became. They kept insisting that Manickam had been in the military. "You must not lie to Angka! Tell us! You were in the military!" they said.

These two peasant boys harassing his father—an arthritic, vegetarian Hindu who could barely speak Khmer—was just too much for Radha. His mother and sisters were missing, and now they had to contend with a couple of ignorant, idiotic teens in black pajamas. Somewhere in the back of his mind he knew it was dangerous, but he didn't care. He stormed up from the back of their group. "What's wrong with you?" he yelled at the soldiers. "Can't you see he's sick and old? He can barely walk! He needs two canes! He was *not* in the army!"

The soldiers looked startled and then uncertain. Radha paused, trembling. He had seen more corpses in the last two days than in his entire life. Boys just like these had killed many of them. Some would have shot Radha on the spot and then possibly machine-gunned his entire family. Instead, they mumbled something and let the Manickams pass.

When they got over the bridge, they noticed that Indira, his oldest sister, was also missing. She was outgoing and, although a little chubby by Cambodian standards and taller than even Radha, quite pretty. Radha found her a few minutes later and started yelling at her—she had crossed the bridge before the rest of the family—but the scare was nearly more than Appa could take, and he teared up. It was the first time Radha had ever seen his father cry.

That evening they found another pig and someone to butcher it. They also met a Chinese family and traded some of their vegetables for some "broken rice" (the leftovers after the good white rice grains have been milled and separated out) and soy sauce. Grandma cooked up a decent meal, and they were glad to get it, although Appa found some nails and small pebbles in his rice. That night Radha lay awake under the stars, surrounded by the crowds of other city folk sighing and shifting. He heard occasional cries of small children. He wondered where Amma and the girls were and if they were safe. Then he fell asleep.

The Khmer Rouge put them on the road again early the next morning, and the next few days were distressingly similar. The crowd would plod along the road all day, getting hotter, thirstier, and ever more footsore, until noon. Then they would take a break and eat a bit of lunch, in some shade if they could find it, until the soldiers came by and yelled, "Up! Keep moving!" at which time they would heave themselves wearily to their feet again.

On the fifth or sixth day after Amma disappeared, his father cried out, "Meenachi!" Radha snapped his head up and saw his father was struggling ahead on his canes. There was Amma, shuffling down the pavement toward them as fast as a woman who was seven months pregnant could, arms out, sarong flapping around her legs. "*Anner!*" she sobbed. "*Anner!*" (*Anner* is the Tamil marital equivalent of "honey.") They met in the street, and their fellow evacuees barely spared a glance; they had their own problems.

Lakshmi and Annapoorani were with some farmers a bit farther up the road at a village called Prek Long. Amma explained that on the day she got lost she had been straggling at the back of the family caravan when a wheel came off the cart. Thy and her family tried to help fix it, and when Amma looked up just a few minutes later, everybody else was out of sight in the crowds; the family hadn't seen her stop. Amma and Thy grabbed the girls and tried to catch up, but it was too late.

They stopped in the middle of the road, desperately scanning the crowd. She was scared and disoriented, and she doubted that she would ever see her husband or the rest of her children again. But Amma and Thy hurried the girls back to the cart, selected some of the supplies and, leaving the cart behind, started down the road with the herd of city dwellers, a child hanging onto either hand. At least she had Thy with her, but then Thy and her husband decided to try to find a place off the main road to settle; by this time the soldiers were letting people stop if they could find a rural family to take them in. Amma insisted on continuing down the road, hoping to find her family. After some discussion, they separated. Now it was just Amma and the young girls.

Not long after they separated, she heard a truck lurch up behind her as people shuffled out of the way. It paused near her, and she called out to the driver. She explained that she had lost her family and asked if she could ride in the truck for a short time. The driver looked at her swollen belly and the two exhausted children. Then he nodded, and Amma hurried around to the back and awkwardly hoisted the children and herself aboard. The truck continued, and Amma clutched the children to her sides and stared hard at the faces of the people they passed, ready to jump off if she saw Appa or anyone else she recognized.

But she didn't, not that day. The truck rumbled slowly down National Road No. 2, which followed the curve of the Bassac as it turned east for a few miles and then hooked right to wander, roughly parallel to the Mekong, southward into the Mekong Delta. After a while, the truck entered the village of Prek Long and stopped.

Amma figured she must have passed the family by that time and slipped out of the truck with the children. She was near the main square of a village, with a marketplace and stores and huts on stilts nearby. A stream of city folk was still passing, but she was more than five miles out of Phnom Penh by this point and the crowd had thinned somewhat. Khmer Rouge loitered in the street, but not as many as near the city. She sat down by the roadside and pulled out a bit of food for herself and the girls. She was exhausted and desperate.

A family of banana farmers who lived by the road happened along just then. They looked curiously at this very pregnant woman with two small children. She had obviously come from the city and looked like she was in trouble, so they offered their help.

In the end, the family agreed to look after her girls during the day while Amma hunted for the rest of her family. For the next four days, Amma got up, cooked a pot of rice and put it on her head to eat later, then trekked carefully up and down the road, avoiding the soldiers as much as possible. She stopped now and then only to eat, until finally she found her family.

The Manickams were together again and grateful to be in a place that seemed, under the circumstances, remarkably hospitable. They also discovered that Prek Long was far enough. That is, the Khmer Rouge were allowing the villagers who lived there to stay in their homes, and Phnom Penh residents could stay too, for a while, if they found a village family to put them up.

The family that agreed to look after the girls took in all the Manickams. Besides the bananas, they grew rice, vegetables, and tobacco and managed well enough for their own three children. Feeding another twelve mouths was a daunting prospect, but they treated the Manickams kindly. They offered a place to sleep under their hut, corn to mix with their rice, and bamboo beds for the adults and some of the children. Radha thought it was a huge break.

For a day or so it was, but within a couple of days the Khmer Rouge–appointed village leader stopped by to see who among the "New People" might be able to join the work crews. He picked Radha and Indira to head out to the rice fields the next morning.

Radha had heard the phrase "New People" before. It carried a lot of baggage in Democratic Kampuchea. New People or "April 17 people" were those who had been evacuated from the cities. In the eyes of the revolutionaries, they were enemies, corrupt urbanites, elites, business owners, and army officers who had resisted the revolution. Farmers and landlords had grown rich exploiting the peasants. Intellectuals, doctors, lawyers, monks, and teachers thought—and their thinking was tainted by Western ideas. As one memoir put it, the list went on and on: "The rebellious, the kind-hearted, the brave, the clever, the individualists, the people who wore glasses, the literate, the popular, the complainers, the lazy, those with talent, those with trouble getting along with others, and those with soft hands. These people were corrupted and lived off the blood and sweat of the farmers and the poor."[1]

The farmers and the poor were the virtuous country folk, "Old People" or "Base People." Old People were those in the early "liberated zones" who had supported the Khmer Rouge in the war with the Khmer Republic. Initially, Old People could keep a few of their possessions or animals or a small garden. They could (depending on their personal history and past enthusiastic support for Angka) join the Khmer Rouge and so enjoy even more freedom, more status, and more food.

New People who survived the initial takeover were at the bottom of the social heap. The existence of a social hierarchy was a heavy irony in a regime that was in theory attempting to create a classless, egalitarian society, but Khmer Rouge ideology had no room for "forgiveness." Instead, Cambodian society has a word for a grudge that leads to disproportionate revenge—revenge far worse than the original offense and so brutal that it destroys an enemy so they never can rise again: *kum*. The Khmer Rouge ideology encouraged *kum* in the peasants who formed the backbone of the Communists. Proper "revolutionary consciousness" was, at its heart, burning rage against class enemies.[2]

So the Khmer Rouge regarded New People as unredeemable, forever tainted by their capitalist background and, therefore, less than human. They were simply slave labor, and once they were unable to work, they became "parasitic plants" as one saying put it.[3] New

People got the worst jobs and the least food and could not become official party members. Cadres enjoyed taunting New People with a saying, roughly translated: "Keeping you is no gain, losing you is no loss."[4] The Khmer Rouge planned to squeeze every bit of labor from them, and then if they died, they died.

Of course, none of this was obvious in the first months of the regime. So when the village leader came by to recruit Radha and Indira for New People work teams, they showed up at sunrise with all the other youths from Prek Long, were assigned to crews, and headed over to nearby fields. There they followed a tractor pulling a plow, yanking up the grass by hand and piling it up for burning. Radha had never before worked in a field. He found it hot, tiring, and extremely frustrating. Why did they need all these people to pull grass by hand? Hadn't they heard of harrows? Could they at least get some rakes if they had to do it by hand?

He and Indira came home that night to some grim news: Lakshmi was very sick. After being lost with Amma, she had seemed OK but soon became listless and then developed a terrible fever. The normally cheerful, sunny little girl lay on a bed under their host family's hut, her tiny body burning. Amma and Grandma hovered over her but could do little except watch. It could have been anything from sunstroke to typhoid fever. No doctors were in the village, and their host had only some traditional remedies, including a dark liquid of uncertain origin. Radha thought the stuff made her worse.

On the evening of the third day of her fever, Radha came home from the fields and knelt by her bed. As he watched, she broke into convulsions. He tried to hold her down with a hand on her chest. She clasped his hand in both of hers, brought it up to her mouth, and with her eyes rolling back into her head, bit down on one finger as hard as she could. Radha gasped and yanked it away. After some minutes that seemed to last for days, she calmed down and closed her eyes. She seemed to fade and sink and settle. Her breathing slowed. That night she died.

Amma, Grandma, and the older daughters dissolved into tears and wailing, while Appa and Radha sobbed. *Lakshmi didn't deserve this*, Radha thought. None of them did. Of all his brothers and sisters, Lakshmi had been Radha's favorite. Back in Phnom Penh, when he came home she would run to him and clamp onto his calf like a barnacle, giggling while he walked around and pretended to try to shake her off. Sometimes she would crawl onto his lap and fall asleep on his chest. *How could God allow this?* he thought.

Appa finally got up and went to sit in front of the hut, his canes beside him. Over the next several hours, Radha watched his father's grief calm, but it didn't go away. It stayed and settled over him, heavy and dark as the night. His head drooped, the temperature dropped, and dew formed on the grass. Radha came outside, shivering a little, as the sky lightened in the east. "Appa," he said. "Appa, please." No response.

That morning their hosts agreed, with their sympathies, to let the Manickams bury Lakshmi in their rice field. Amma wanted to go out to the burial, but Grandma wouldn't hear of a pregnant woman going to a graveside. You never knew what being around a body could do to the baby. "You stay behind," she insisted. "You don't come."

Amma and Grandma wrapped Lakshmi in some fine cloth they had brought, and Radha and Indira carried her gently out to a corner of the rice field, accompanied by the farmer and his wife, and buried her. Appa stayed where he was in front of the hut. Radha lingered at the grave after the others returned to the hut. He was angry, but he didn't know at whom. Mostly, he felt empty. He prayed, asking God to give him and his family strength and comfort.

Appa was still sitting in front of the hut when Radha returned from the rice field. By late morning, he still hadn't spoken and had hardly moved.

Finally, Appa struggled to his feet and limped into their sleeping area under their hosts' hut. He opened a suitcase, dug through the

81

clothes and supplies, took out his two Hindu gods and put them into a bag. Amma watched him with anxious eyes. He left the shelter and started down the path through the trees and tall grass to the Bassac River. Amma whispered to Radha, "Go with him!"

As Appa hobbled along with his canes, Radha followed quietly some yards behind. Appa found an open spot in the grass on the bank of the river and climbed down into the brown water. Appa's jaw was clenched, and Radha could see a vein in his temple. Then Appa set aside his canes and took the idols out of the bag. They were about eight inches high, intricately carved from ivory and delicately painted. One was Genashe, a son of Shiva with the head of an elephant. He was the god of wisdom, the one who removes obstacles, a patron of the arts and sciences. The other was Lakshmi, the wife of Vishnu and the one after whom Appa had named his daughter. She was the embodiment of beauty, the goddess of wealth, love, prosperity, and good luck. She protected her worshipers from financial difficulties and misery.

Appa stood in the water, looking at the gods in his hands. Then he threw them as far as he could and one after the other they dropped into the river.

Radha was stunned. Appa turned around and saw his son, the Christian, but neither said anything. Radha reached down and helped his father clamber onto the bank, and then Appa took his canes and labored back to the house.

7

Water Buffalo Island

Do not mortals have hard service on earth? Are not their days like those of hired laborers? Like a slave longing for the evening shadows, or a hired laborer waiting to be paid, so I have been allotted months of futility, and nights of misery have been assigned to me.

—Job 7:1–3

The Khmer Rouge took great pride in the fact that they took Phnom Penh almost two full weeks before their North Vietnamese brethren took Saigon on April 30, 1975. They didn't see it as merely a victory against a weak and corrupt regime whose primary ally and patron abandoned it in its hour of greatest need. Rather, it was a resounding defeat of the massive resources and military might of the United States and everything it stood for.[1] The Americans had tried to impose their will on Kampuchea and had been defeated by the strength, resolve, and revolutionary consciousness of the Khmer people. Pol Pot instituted a new calendar for a new era; 1975 became "Year Zero."

So in the summer of 1975, the Khmer Rouge began serious construction on their agrarian utopia. In early May, about a week after Lakshmi died, the leader of Prek Long came by the hut. He said Angka required everybody to register and took the names of everybody in the family. A few days later, the Manickams were given a tiny piece of land in the middle of a rice field about a half mile from Prek Long. Theirs was one of about fifty plots for the families Angka had deemed suitable for a new settlement, at least for now. The Manickams dug in some posts and built a makeshift hut with a tarp. It provided some shade, but with no trees anywhere nearby, it offered little protection from either the daytime heat or the nighttime chill.

Appa still had his radio. The Khmer Rouge broadcasts made for dreary listening, but a few weeks later, the family heard something worth hearing: Angka required foreigners to register, and those who did would be allowed to leave the country. Foreign nationals should proceed to Wat Champa (*wat* is the Khmer word for a Buddhist temple) on National Road No. 1.

The Manickams talked it over, and staying in Cambodia seemed unlikely to lead to a bright future. The next morning they got up early, well before dawn, and slipped out of their shelter. The eleven in their party—Grandma, Appa, Amma, Radha, and the other five remaining children, as well as the two cousins, slipped out of their settlement and headed back north along National Highway No. 2. The crowds from the original evacuation were gone, and they made much better time. They found someone to ferry them across the Bassac in a small boat and began making their way north and east along backcountry roads toward the No. 1, about four miles away.

Soon the road took them through a small village. The local leaders noticed them and approached. "Where are you from, comrades?" they asked. "Come, stay here with us. We have a fine village, and you should not move any farther because it is almost time to start planting rice."

"That is very kind, comrades," Radha said. He made some small talk and then excused himself to join his family. The Manickams found an empty plot in an out-of-the-way area of the village and sat down to rest. It was nearing noon, so they prepared and ate some rice and a few vegetables. Then, when nobody was looking, they quietly packed up their belongings and slipped out of the village to resume their journey.

This happened a few more times over the next two days, which was how long it took to get to the No. 1 and then cover the roughly two miles west back toward the city and Wat Champa. Appa was leaning heavily on his canes, and Amma was getting—and looking—ever closer to her due date. The No. 1 still had people heading east away from the city, but a few, like the Manickams, were going back toward Phnom Penh. The Khmer Rouge soldiers just stood and watched them pass. A few bodies still littered the roadside.

The Manickams got to the temple at night and bedded down on the grounds. Many New People, as well as foreign families, were living on the grounds, hoping to leave the country. The *wat* housed no monks.

The next morning some Khmer Rouge set up a table under a big tree at the temple gate and a line formed. When Radha and his father got to the front, they explained that they were Indian citizens and wanted to return to India. The officers listened politely. The Manickams were clearly not Khmer, plus they had their passports. The officers questioned them in detail concerning their background and history. Once an officer asked a question in English; it was a trap. Selvem started to speak, but the family hushed him up, and that seemed to end the interview. They registered each member of the family. "Tomorrow," the officers said, "we'll take you back to Phnom Penh. From there you can leave the country. Sleep here tonight on the grounds. We'll keep your passports."

Radha and his father paused. This was unsettling, but they had no choice. They slowly turned and went back to their camp.

The next morning the Manickams climbed into the back of a GMC truck along with some other New People. It was only a couple of miles, but pushing through the travelers reduced the truck to a crawl. Radha watched them go by, and his stomach churned. They had just lost possession of the most important documents they owned—proof of their Indian citizenship. How could they enter any other country without passports? *God*, he prayed, *please protect us.*

Soon the truck crossed the bridge over the Mekong and rolled into Phnom Penh's downtown area. The streets were almost empty. A couple of right turns took them past the US Embassy and then onto Samdech Sothearos Boulevard. They went through the gate of what had been the villa of the US ambassador until the delegation was evacuated a few days before the fall of Phnom Penh.

The grounds were grim. The once carefully tended trees had been reduced to piles of ash under blackened cooking pots. The villa's furniture had been hauled into the yard and hacked into pieces—also for firewood. People had been sleeping in the yard, stretched out on the beds that had yet to be burned. The villa itself looked empty.

Radha helped his family down from the truck and glanced around at the several dozen people standing or sitting around the grounds. A Khmer Rouge soldier took them into the villa and motioned them into an empty, carpeted room. They sank down, grateful for a break inside a real building with a real floor.

Radha began to survey the villa. A few doors down the hallway he came to a bathroom with a toilet and a bidet. Idly, he pushed the bidet's button and watched the water shoot a few feet into the air as a young Khmer Rouge soldier passed by the doorway. He glanced in. "I didn't know the Americans had well water in here," he said and came into the room. He pushed the button himself and gazed curiously at the stream. Then he bent down and took a slurp.

Radha froze. *Should I tell him?* he wondered. The boy had a machine gun, and Radha saw no way the conversation could end well. He said nothing and walked out.

Radha kept exploring and soon found the villa's kitchen. The cupboards were bare except for a couple of jars of grape jelly and mango jam. Radha rummaged a bit more and found a dry, stale baguette someone had overlooked. He took it all back to the room. He broke off pieces of bread and spread some jam on them for the family to eat.

A couple of soldiers passed the door. "Hey," they said, "why are you putting axle grease on your bread?" The Manickams turned to the door, the children still chewing. Apparently the soldiers couldn't read the labels on the jars and had passed up the jelly earlier. "It's not grease," Radha explained carefully. "It's fruit."

"Fruit?" they said. They came in and sniffed the jars, then they confiscated the lot and left. Radha was angry with himself for not hiding his discovery, but that evening the soldiers butchered a pig they found in the street. The whole compound had pork in their rice stew.

The next morning the Khmer Rouge assembled the would-be emigrants in the courtyard. "The train tracks have been damaged," a soldier said. "We can't get you to the border, so you'll go to one of the new settlements for now. These trucks will take you." Radha looked at his father, and they knew they wouldn't be leaving Cambodia—not yet, anyway. The Khmer Rouge still had their passports. The Manickams climbed again into one of the trucks.

It took them over to Highway No. 2, the same one they had taken out of Phnom Penh some weeks earlier and then headed south. The bodies along the roadways were still there, Radha noticed.

The truck dropped them off in a rice field settlement west of the Bassac called Koh Krabai—or Water Buffalo Island. Craters from the B-52 bombings dotted the countryside so that stands of trees had sudden gaps and the rice fields had basins and small ponds in unlikely places. It was still May. They found themselves back under a makeshift shelter, with Radha and Indira preparing rice fields or clearing brush most days. Sometimes the older children were assigned minor tasks around the village. Grandma, Appa, and Amma hung around the shelter and waited. Their food from home soon ran out, but the Khmer Rouge began providing some rice and vegetables and sometimes a bit of meat that the family cooked in their shelter. It kept them alive, but they were all losing weight. Amma, who should have been comfortably round, looked gaunt.

Then Radha came down with malaria. One day he woke up chilled and shaking, asking for blankets. He fell into convulsions and Appa had to hold him down to keep him on his mat. After an hour or so of chills, a fever set in. The thought of eating turned his stomach; he could barely drink water.

This continued for a couple of weeks. He tried but usually failed to keep down the little he ate and grew weaker by the day. His father went to the village leaders for some medicine but returned with only some black pills, a traditional remedy. Radha tried one; it tasted like burnt rice mixed with a bit of honey.

In early June, Khmer Rouge leaders came by and instructed everybody to register (again) with the village leaders and report their family history, past employment, and so on. They were looking for former employees from the Lon Nol regime. They announced that Sihanouk was returning to reestablish the monarchy, and to help prepare for the return of the king they needed knowledgeable people with experience to help restore and rebuild the country. They hoped to find government workers of all kinds—especially teachers, professors, and students.

The New People huddled in their shelters and huts that evening to talk it over in private. They still wanted to believe that Sihanouk could set things right. But could they trust these Khmer Rouge? They had killed many people, yes, but it had been during war, right? Surely this madness couldn't continue. A couple of days later, a few dozen families from the Water Buffalo Island settlement volunteered and told the Khmer Rouge that they had been educated or that a member of the family had been a military officer or a clerk in the Lon Nol bureaucracy. The cadres gathered them all up in trucks—the ex-government men and their families—and hauled them away.

Radha was too sick to pay much attention. He also accepted some treatment from a kru Khmer, a traditional medicine man, who applied a concoction to four spots on his belly, which seemed to help ease his symptoms. Amma also traded some clothes for quinine tablets, an effective malaria treatment.

One evening Radha fell into conversation with a neighbor near his hut. "Whatever you do," the neighbor said quietly, "don't let them know you worked with the government. I was out gathering some wild vegetables and saw some bodies in one of the B-52 craters. They were all dead, and I recognized some of them—they were those who had been taken from this village."

Radha was shocked and not quite sure whether to believe him. But it was, in fact, not just plausible but almost certainly true. The Khmer Rouge were murdering people all over the country. Cadres started with calls for military personnel and soon appealed for civil servants and business leaders. Many responded out of a desire to help rebuild their devastated country, while others believed Khmer Rouge propaganda about Sihanouk. Almost all who trusted the Khmer Rouge paid for that mistake with their lives. Those who volunteered were asked to write out their personal biographies; these became the "evidence" of their reactionary views and justified prompt and secret executions—deaths in the shadows.

In Battambang, for example, shortly after the April 17 evacuation, dozens of officers who had turned themselves in assembled wearing their finest dress uniforms with medals, as instructed. The six truckloads of officers were told they were going to Phnom Penh to greet Sihanouk. At a crossroads not far outside the city, they were instructed to get off the trucks for a rest and after doing so, the trucks promptly drove off. A line of Khmer Rouge armed with machine guns stepped out of the forest and mowed them down; four escaped to tell the tale.[2]

In early June, cousin Saravanan, seven, died after a night of diarrhea and vomiting. It was probably a combination of starvation and disease—but who could know for sure? The medicines dispensed by the Khmer Rouge weren't helping. A few days after the funeral, Amma's birth pangs hit. The village leaders sent along a midwife to help, and she gave birth to Murugan, the newest Manickam brother. A few days after that, the family's other young cousin, Chandara, who was five, died after being ill for several days. At this point, the Manickam group was down to ten: Appa and Amma, the seven remaining children, and Grandma.

Radha, recovering from malaria, was still too weak to return to the fields, but one day in early July, he had a powerful reason to recover: the cadres came back. They said Angka needed everybody in Water Buffalo Island to go to Battambang province in the northwest to work in the rice fields. Those who were too sick or weak to go would be allowed to stay behind, and Angka would "take care of them."

Radha prayed for strength. No sane person would let the Khmer Rouge "take care" of them. The next morning he woke up and felt better. He walked with his family and the hundreds of other villagers to the shore of the Bassac, where the river formed a small lake. Soldiers herded the crowds onto several large, beat-up old boats, packing them onto the decks like catches of fish. It was the beginning of a massive forced migration into northwest Cambodia, mainly to grow rice, that would in less than a year move 1.8 million people into a region whose population had been 900,000 a few years before.[3]

The Manickams had not yet given up hope that they might be allowed to leave Cambodia. They approached some soldiers who seemed to be in charge and asked when they would be able to leave for India.

"Oh," a soldier said, "the tracks have been fixed. Get on the boat with everybody else, and then trucks will take you to the railway. You can stay on the train all the way to the Thai border and get back to your country from there."

"Ask about our passports," Appa murmured to Radha.

"And our passports?" Radha asked.

"Your paperwork is waiting for you at the border," the soldier said.

Radha and Appa looked at each other. This was not a good sign; nothing about these people suggested they were capable of keeping records, let alone moving paperwork to the border. The Manickams, though, still hoped that maybe, somehow, they might be able to leave. Anyway, what choice did they have? So they got on a boat and settled in.

The boat was so crowded they could barely sit down, but Grandma had cooked up some rice and packed some dried fish before leaving, so they at least had a bite to eat. Radha's heart was heavy with memories as the boats chugged past the Royal Palace in Phnom Penh. He had spent most of his life in the city. He felt like an exile, banished for life.

"I don't think I'll ever see you again," he said to Phnom Penh. "Good-bye."

The small flotilla steamed for about four hours to Kampong Chhnang, which means "Port of Clay Pots," and the Manickams got off with the hundreds of other people. The city was deserted. The crowds bunked down in the abandoned houses.

Early the next morning the travelers assembled at the city square where a long line of trucks was waiting. The Khmer Rouge lined up everyone and searched them before loading them on. The Manickams obediently got into line and waited. Suddenly Appa turned to Radha. "Do you have your Bible?" he asked. Radha felt ill; he did. He had kept it in the suitcase through all their travels, despite the extra weight. Appa read his face. "Son, you're going to kill us all," he said with a growl. Radha began praying, fervently but silently, for protection. The soldiers searched some of the Manickams' bags but passed over Radha's suitcase.

With a group of comrades, the Manickams boarded a truck, a military-style troop transport, and their convoy began an hours-long ride northwest. Some of the women were pregnant, and the trucks were so jam-packed that everybody had to take turns sitting down. As they drove, they occasionally saw the bodies of people who had died on the journey and been tossed out the back or over the sides of the moving trucks in front of them. The convoy certainly was not going to stop to get rid of a few dead New People.

Finally, the trucks stopped at a village beside some rail tracks in Pursat province. The tracks pointed toward the northwest. Rice fields, scraggly bush, and thinning forest stretched out in every direction. The soldiers emptied the trucks, and the Manickams settled down for the night in one of the empty huts.

8

Angka the Idol

Love the Angka, sincerely and loyally.

—Khmer Rouge saying in
Pol Pot's Little Red Book

At six o'clock in the morning, Radha stood at the doorway of the rickety wooden boxcar, hustling his parents, grandmother, and young siblings up into the dark interior. Each carried a sack containing their meager possessions: some clothes, maybe a few pots or cooking tools, plus some rice or other food. Appa was first, and then Grandma and Amma, carrying two-month-old Murugan, and then the rest of Radha's siblings followed. The train was already chuffing forward when he pushed the last of them into the car, so he had to run alongside for a few steps and then jump and clamber inside.

Dozens of people—some sitting, most standing, and all huddled over their belongings—were packed into the boxcar. The air was hot and humid. The car had no windows or lighting and smelled of pigs and cows—its usual cargo—besides the stench of tired, sweaty, hungry ex–city dwellers long past their last change of clothes. The train was perhaps fifteen cars long.

The ride felt painfully slow to Radha. He knew only that they were heading toward Cambodia's northwestern border with Thailand. He clung to the doorway near his family, leaned out of the car, and watched the countryside edge past. The train clacked toward the border, past mountains and fields and endless rice paddies and canals, and toward freedom and escape from the entire insane mess that was the Khmer Rouge regime.

Water was everywhere Radha looked. During the wet season beginning in late spring, the Tonle Sap, Cambodia's largest lake and river system, reverses direction and floods thousands of acres of countryside around the lake. The Mekong River and the Tonle Sap River meet in Phnom Penh, and then the Mekong continues south and east, while the Bassac splits off to the south. These rivers are so flooded in the spring from rainwater and runoff from the snows melting on the Chinese Himalayas that the Mekong cannot hold it all, forcing the silt-laden water back up the Tonle Sap River into the lake. Once the rains end in the fall, the Mekong goes down, the pressure eases, and the Tonle Sap again flows south and east to the coast, slowly draining the lake. Throughout the centuries, the annual flooding has made the Tonle Sap area one of the most fertile in Southeast Asia.

About noon the train rumbled into a clearing on the east side of a mountain and ground to a halt. They were several miles south of Battambang and less than forty miles from the Thai border to the west.

Squads of children around fourteen years of age, wearing black pants and tunics and carrying assault rifles, surrounded each rail car and began screaming at the passengers. "Out! Out!" they shouted in their shrill young voices. "New People off the train! Now!"

The situation made no sense. They had not yet reached the city of Battambang, let alone the Thai border. But it was clearly foolish to provoke angry children carrying AK-47s, so Radha hurried his family out of the car and stood under the hot sun with the thousand or so other people who had been on the train. The Manickams all had their sacks because he had instructed all his siblings to hang onto them, whatever happened. They waited anxiously.

Radha looked around. A clearing was on the west side of the railroad track, and away from the rails ran Oxcart Road, a dirt track heading west toward a mountain. He would later discover its name was Phnom Tippedei (*phnom* is the Khmer word for mountain). Along the road were several local villagers, Old People with empty carts, who had come down to meet the train. They stared impassively at the newcomers, waiting. Radha tried not to stare back. He was tired, it was hot, and he hoped they would soon be on their way again.

A Khmer Rouge officer got up to address the group. "You have three days to settle yourselves. Three days to build shelters for yourselves and your families. This is where Angka needs you. Go up there," he told them, pointing west at the forest covering the mountainside. "Build your shelters up there. After three days, you will go work for Angka. But until you work, you will receive no food. After you work, then Angka will feed you. From now on you will serve the Glorious Revolution." Then he turned and walked away.

Radha listened, confused at first, and then shock set in. "There must be some mistake," he told his father, who was just as bewildered. So Radha hurried after the officer, who was still at the edge of the crowd, and cautiously approached. His heart was pounding; he had always hated guns, and the officer had with him a couple of armed "messengers"—aides who would at his command beat or even kill anybody he chose.

"Please, comrade," Radha said, "there must be some mistake. We are supposed to keep going to the border."

"No!" the officer screamed at him. "Nobody goes farther than this point!"

Radha turned away. He felt angry and tired and scared—and powerless. He knew at that moment that his family was going nowhere. Hope began to drain from his soul.

He noticed the people heading to the mountain in a line and didn't think his father would be able to keep up, so he approached one of the Old People with an oxcart to ask for a lift. The villager dismissed him curtly, saying, "It's not for people to ride."

So the Manickams picked up their sacks and began to trudge along the path toward the mountainside, his father hobbling on two canes and his mother clutching the baby. They joined the scraggly line of city dwellers heading west. Some of them tried to get back onto the train to collect their meager belongings, but the soldiers shoved them off and pushed them down the path.

Radha watched the Khmer Rouge screaming at the tired, sickly, and frightened people. They fired shots into the air and, if anyone stumbled, kicked them until they struggled back to their feet. Radha, one eye on the soldiers, kept urging his father and siblings to hurry up.

Those who fell usually dropped their sacks, and before they could pick them up the soldiers would shove them onward down the trail. Soon one of the Old People would come along, scoop up the sacks, and toss them into one of the carts that traveled along with them.

That was another step in the Khmer Rouge strategy for separating the New People from their capitalist pots and watches and spare shirts—rush them off the train and down the path so fast that they dropped their belongings. New People wouldn't need their things in the new revolutionary society anyway.

It took a couple of hours to travel a mile down the path and then slowly make their way up the mountainside into the forest where the Khmer Rouge said they had to build a new village.

The site was a few hundred feet above the road in the midst of dense forest. As soon as they arrived, some Khmer Rouge officers came by, assigned each family to a group of ten families, and appointed one person from each group as the leader. They would work in these groups to clear the land and then build their huts. Radha spotted a Buddhist temple perhaps a quarter mile farther up the mountain.

They all soon got to work on their shelters. They were city folk, so tasks like building a small hut, which would have been easy for a farmer, took them hours. But a few families had axes or knives they were willing to share, and slowly the structures took shape. They cleared sites for the huts on the steep slopes by chopping down bamboo thickets and forest vegetation, dug postholes with sharpened sticks, and filled in the frames by thatching leaves and branches together. They smoothed floors and piled thatch together for beds.

Despite this bit of initial cooperation, the newcomers generally kept to themselves in their families or small groups of trusted friends. Some may have wanted to be friendly, but any camaraderie they might have found was swallowed up by despair and fear. Many were former government workers, businessmen, and ex–military officers, but as long as they could pass themselves off as factory workers, taxi drivers, and cooks, maybe Angka wouldn't notice them. Maybe they could just hang on until this terrifying reality went away. Radha hoped so.

Grandma, however, wasn't easily cowed. At one point during those first two days, she noticed a few Old People who had come to the edge of the site to watch. She went over and greeted them, struck up a conversation, and then returned satisfied.

That first evening on the mountain a Khmer Rouge cadre banged on the steel rim of a car wheel, summoning the village to the first of many nightly propaganda sessions. His name was Phan, Radha learned later. He was a tall, lean man in his forties. With his AK-47 and harsh manner he looked every inch the revolutionary soldier. Like almost all the Khmer Rouge officials, Phan had cold, hostile eyes.

The New People gathered at the center of the village where a fire was burning and sat down on the ground in rows of ten as instructed. Phan stepped to the fire, faced them, and began to lay out the principles of Democratic Kampuchea. It seemed to Radha that he would never stop.

Phan told them that Angka had permitted them to help build the new society. "You are all equal now," he said. "Nobody is any better than anybody else. If you think you are someone special because you used to drive a car and eat in fancy restaurants, you are not. One water buffalo to plow a field is worth fifty of you New People. One ox to pull a cart is worth fifty New People.

"You must work hard, very hard, and you must be patient. The Glorious Revolution is still new, so there might not be as much food now as there will be one day when the excellent principles of Communism have been fully applied to society. One day you will have all the rice and fish and fruit you can eat—and more! In fact, one day there will be no more spoons! Angka will build machines that will feed you, so we won't even need spoons to feed ourselves!"

Radha stifled a chuckle. *A society so advanced it had machines to feed people?* The idea was ridiculous. He had an image of a feeding machine bashing out a few of this officer's teeth because he hadn't opened his mouth quite wide enough. Maybe ignorant peasants would swallow this nonsense, but why did they think educated people would buy it? It was infuriating. It was insulting.

Phan continued. "But for now you must bear with Angka during this temporary shortage, which was caused by the capitalist oppressors who destroyed our country. It will take time to rebuild, but the fact that the brave soldiers of the revolution have driven out the Americans with all their airplanes and weapons proves that nothing can hold us back.

"In the meantime, if you work hard, you can eat. Those who do not work will not eat. When Angka gives an order, you must obey it with complete discipline! You must learn from the Old People how to grow rice and build your own homes."

Phan then delivered Angka's rules for the New People's cooperative, and they had a depressing similarity:

- There is no private property. Everything belongs to Angka. If a person is caught stealing from Angka, they will be crushed. ("Crushed" doesn't do justice to the Khmer word translated here: *kamtech*. It's a farming term that means to destroy completely, to smash into a thousand pieces and then wipe away any trace that might remain; to reduce to dust.)[1]

- No lying to Angka. If a person lies to Angka, they will be crushed.

- If a person will not work, if they are lazy and live off the work of others, they are betraying Angka and will be crushed.

- If a person tries to fake illness to avoid going to work and is caught, they will be reeducated. Or crushed. (Radha would soon realize that when the Khmer Rouge took you away to be "reeducated" at one of the many prisons dotting the countryside, in practice it often had the same result as being crushed: a short walk to a mass grave.)

- Angka will provide for all the people's needs, including all their food. If people try to gather their own food apart from what Angka gives them, they will be crushed for betraying the trust of the community.

The list was punctuated by warnings not to do anything stupid because "Angka has eyes like a pineapple."

Eventually the officer returned to his original theme.

"The Khmer are strong people," he said. "They don't need food like those soft, weak capitalists. Me and my Khmer Rouge comrades fought the Americans for ten days straight on one banana! One banana! Ten days!"

Radha sat in the dark and thought, essentially, *Yeah, right*.

"Now," continued the officer, "you are free! We are all free, and we are all equal! You are free from Lon Nol and his corrupt regime, free from the material possessions that once enslaved you! Free from your cars and fancy clothes and gold and books. Free from your worthless schooling, free from all the corruption and oppression of a capitalist society. We do not need the things you used to have—your schools and churches and businesses. Do not think of such things, or you will not be able to work hard. Only the enemy needs or wants such things. We are all the same now. There is no rich or poor. You are happy here. We all work for Angka, for the community, for the revolution. Comrades, you are very free."

Radha realized that, happy or not, he better not complain or mention anything about life before the Khmer Rouge takeover. That suggested dissatisfaction, which implied both disloyalty to the revolution and that Angka had in some way left itself open to criticism.

"The Khmer need no economic or cultural connections or dependence on other countries; we will do things the Khmer way!" the officer continued. "We must launch an offensive with revolutionary zeal! We must achieve independence-mastery! We must, with courage, win a great victory over the rice fields, over the floods, over the lack of roads. We must never cease our struggle to take our destiny in our hands! We must struggle, always, to reorganize society along revolutionary lines. Correct revolutionary understanding will allow all good comrades of the revolution to work to their utmost!"

The indoctrination sessions happened most evenings for the next three years. They went on for hours, usually until after 10:00 or 11:00 p.m., and the main ideas were always the same—an endless recycling of rhetoric.

All through that first meeting, as the sun went down and the air cooled, Radha sat peering at the speaker in the firelight, trying to swat inconspicuously at the mosquitoes that swarmed out of the forest. The more his limbs hurt, the more incredulous he became. No private property? The cadre obviously had been a poor farmer just months before. He probably couldn't even read. He was spouting socialist slogans and sayings and ordering people around, but who was he? Radha couldn't believe that a crowd of ignorant peasants and children with guns would run society from then on. The Cambodian proverb "The dry gourd is sinking, and the clay pot is floating" came to mind. A rough English equivalent would be "The world is turning upside down."

In Democratic Kampuchea, many words no longer carried the same meanings. According to one of Angka's slogans, for example, "Liberty means the absence of discipline, the absence of morality!" Radha and the rest of Tippedei's New People were just discovering the meaning of "revolutionary freedom."

They weren't alone. Across the country, the Khmer Rouge were in the process of sending millions of people into the countryside as part of its plan to "reorganize" Cambodian society into a classless agrarian utopia.

The group sat and listened, trying to look attentive. Revolutionary freedom seemed unlikely to include the liberty to whine about long meetings or mosquitoes. When his speech was over, the officer shouted, "Long live the revolution!" three times. The New People echoed it back to him each time, copying his salute of a raised fist thrust into the air. He also had them repeat "We are committed to obeying!" and "Long live Angka of the revolution of Kampuchea!"

Then they all headed to their makeshift beds under the trees. Their huts weren't finished yet.

―――――――

The first morning after the New People's arrival was a festival day for the Buddhist monks at the nearby temple, which, likely due to its remote location, had not yet been shut down. Radha, Indira, Dhanam, Selvem, and Ravy walked over with a few dozen other New People and sat down on each side of the walkway going to the temple with their heads bowed and held up their bowls. Two or three monks came by and ladled out some rice and fish, and then the Manickams returned to their site. It was the last celebration at that temple for several years. Some days later, the Khmer Rouge forced the monks out of the temple to join the New People; Angka, of course, had abolished religion. Monks were parasites, according to Angka, "tapeworms gnawing out the bowels of society."[2]

Later that first morning, Indira disappeared. The family was frantic, but she returned after a few hours with a sack of wild mushrooms. She had gone up the mountainside hoping to find some vegetables or fruit. She ran into some kindly Old People who showed her how to look for mushrooms under leaves and on tree trunks, and which kinds were safe to eat and which were poisonous.

The family talked it over for a while; they ached with hunger, but what if the mushrooms made them sick? What if Indira had made a mistake? There was no medicine, let alone a decent doctor. Finally, Appa said, "Let's just eat it. If we die, we'll all die together." So they added the mushrooms to their skimpy pot of rice that evening, and it was good.

They worked on the huts all that day and all the next. The huts were hard to see from the bottom of the hill because of the forest covering, but dozens were scattered across the slopes. When they were done, each family had a structure about ten feet by ten feet, enough to offer a bit of shelter at night and hold a fire pit. That was Tippedei, the village.

When the family got back to the hut after the third night's propaganda meeting, Grandma pulled Radha aside and handed him a sack with some of his extra clothes. They slipped off into the dark and down the mountain. They were going to get some food, Grandma explained. The supplies they had brought with them on the train were gone.

They stumbled down the hill through the blackness, over the rocks and roots, across the shallow valley, and then a little ways up the far side into the village of Phnom Tathok. They soon spotted an oil lamp; the farmer she had met earlier had told her he would leave one burning in his hut. The villagers may have mouthed Communist slogans and welcomed the Khmer Rouge initially, but why should that stop them from doing a little business for the right price? As long as the cadres didn't find out, of course. And maybe the New People had medicine, something Angka seemed unable to produce.

In whispers, Grandma and the farmer negotiated a deal, and then he took them out to a stable near the couple's rice field, where Grandma and Radha slept on the floor until about 4:00 a.m. Then they got up and headed down to the rice paddies to check the wicker traps farmers used to catch crabs and fish. The farmer came out to help. They found about fifty small freshwater crabs, two or three inches across, which thrive in the paddies.

Grandma gave up a solid pair of trousers made of "Canadian material" (a brand of tough denim) and one of Radha's long-sleeved silk shirts in exchange for the crabs and a three-foot-long chunk of banana tree stalk, which villagers usually chopped and boiled for use as filler in pig feed. As Radha and Grandma left, the farmer's wife grumbled that the New People were "taking food out of the mouths of our hogs."

Radha and Grandma hurried back to their settlement, struggling painfully back up the hillside over the rocks and roots. They had to get back unnoticed before it was time for the first day of work in the rice fields. They stumbled bleary-eyed into their new hut a few minutes before someone banged on the tire rim that served as a bell to get the New People's attention. The rest of the family had been waiting anxiously. They now had the crabs and the banana wood to supplement their supplies, but there was no time for breakfast. Radha and Indira, the two siblings who had been designated for work crews, dragged themselves to the door and headed down to the meeting place. The sun still wasn't up.

In the firelight, the cadres separated the New People into male and female work parties, splitting up families. That too was part of the Khmer Rouge's strategy—separate families as much as possible to weaken family bonds. The soldiers also wrote down who was in each work party and which family they belonged to so they knew who should get food at the end of the workday.

Radha's group of ten set off south through the forest in single file. The idea was to gather the workers before dawn and get them to the rice fields just as the sun was coming up so they had the longest possible workday. Groups of Old People, dressed in black and looking properly revolutionary, were busy planting rice as their families had for generations. Rows of New People, mostly hatless and some still dressed in colorful city clothes, were sloshing through the fields. Young Khmer Rouge soldiers, carrying their assault rifles, were sauntering around atop the dikes that divided the fields into flooded sections, eyeballing the workers.

Radha felt like a prisoner. Up until this point, he had worked for a few days at Prek Long or Koh Krabai, but their stays had been brief, the work fairly light, and the sites hadn't been guarded. But at the edge of the rice paddy, the reality was clear: this was a prison camp.

"Get to work," their group leader said. He pointed out the water-covered field where the rice stems were growing and the paddies to which the stems were to be transplanted. "Make sure you plant correctly," he said. "Do not betray the revolution."

Radha was close to tears. He knew next to nothing about farming rice, and the implication was clear: do it right or die. He could hardly admit that he didn't know how to plant rice. Even worse, if the soldiers killed him in the fields for some imagined offense, what would happen to his family? Another Khmer Rouge saying came to mind: "When you want to kill a weed, you must destroy it all the way down to the root." He began to pray like he had never prayed before. He prayed that God would show him what to do, that his family wouldn't be killed, and that the cadres wouldn't drag him into the forest and kill him because he didn't know how to plant rice.

Radha, struggling to keep his composure, stepped into the seedbed along with the others in his group, bent down, and began to work. He peeked at the others in his group and the Old People working nearby and tried to copy their motions.

Rice farmers plant seeds close together in beds—much smaller than fields—so they can more easily manage the weeds and water levels. After about a month, the farmers pull the stems, which are five to seven inches long at that point, gently out of the muddy beds and then transplant them into flooded paddies. The idea is to give the rice plants more room to grow by planting the stems several inches apart and thus produce a bigger harvest.

That much Radha could figure out. He tugged out plants a few at a time until he had a large handful. He cleaned off the roots by swishing them through the water and then wrapped up the stems in a bunch weighing a few pounds. But he couldn't easily tell the difference between the rice stems growing out of the beds and the tough, sharp blades of grass growing up between them, so he pulled everything in front of him. Sometimes he cut his fingers on the grass, and the dirty water stung his cuts. He had the feeling he wasn't working fast enough.

When he collected a bunch of handfuls, he tied them to one end of a bamboo pole. When he had four or five bunches on each end, he hoisted the heavy pole onto his shoulder and headed to the freshly plowed paddy about three hundred yards away.

Then the work got a bit tricky. Rice stems not planted properly soon float to the top of the water. When he dared to glance around, he could see the soldiers watching carefully, making sure that everybody was working hard in Angka's service and that the rice stayed planted.

Rice farmers have a technique for planting quickly and properly: bend from the waist, hold the stem in three fingers, push the roots into the mud with your thumb, and then tamp down the hole with your forefinger. It should take no more than a couple of seconds to pick a stem from your bunch and plant it, forming nice regular rows; plant three or four in front of you, step backward, plant three or four, step backward.

But Radha knew none of this on that first day; he did realize that if his rice began drifting to the surface, the soldiers could quickly figure out who was at fault. They would execute the counterrevolutionary who had betrayed his people with a brazen yet futile attempt to sabotage the rice crop. He kept hurrying and prayed harder.

All that bending and reaching was backbreaking work, even for those who knew what they were doing. Radha was soon exhausted, but the only water he had to drink was from the rice field or canal. He had no hat. When the group leader called a break in midmorning, he slogged to the edge of the forest and sat down under a tree, leaving his sandals on the dike. A minute later, he was sleeping.

That was a mistake. He woke up after about fifteen minutes and groggily shuffled back into the paddy. Not until his feet hit the water did he look around and realize that someone had stolen his sandals. For the rest of the day (and for a long time afterward), he went barefoot.

When the sun was almost down, his group lined up for an hour-long hike back to the village. The ground was mostly clay, and in open spaces, the sun had heated it up so much it burned his feet as he walked. But he dared not step too far out of line for fear that a soldier would shoot him, so he tried to step from one shaded spot to the next, hoping to attract no attention.

Finally, his group got back to the village. Radha lined up with the others to receive the rations for his family of ten: three fourteen-ounce condensed milk cans filled with rice dust—*kantouk*. This was the family's rations for the next five or six days.

When rice is ground, the husk or skin is removed, leaving brown rice. Then you grind the brown rice again to remove the *kantouk*, leaving white rice. Husks go onto the fields, and normally the *kantouk* becomes animal feed. *Kantouk* resembles brown flour and usually has pieces of broken rice and husks. It makes a tasteless porridge, but with some salt, it can fill your belly. Farmers won't eat it, and giving it to the New People was an insult. The Khmer Rouge people, of course, had lots of white rice, of which the Old People got a share.

Radha took the *kantouk* back to his mother at the hut, who cooked some up and dished out tiny helpings. It was hard to eat, but they choked it down. Appa sat on the ground and wept.

9

Don't Let Them Count One

The scenery of rice-fields in checker-boards, networks of irrigation, canals, dikes, and water reservoirs coming into view
everywhere in the countryside shows that, thanks to the cooperatives, the peasants have acquired a great mastery of the
water and have attained a high political consciousness.

—Khmer Rouge propaganda booklet,
Democratic Kampuchea Is Moving Forward

After about a week of transplanting rice, the village leaders
came by the Manickam hut to say that Radha and Indira,
along with the rest of the healthy young workers at Tippedei,
would be sent away to a nearby project—a levy at Chhay Balang.
The next morning they got up early. "Don't say anything against
the revolution," Appa warned them before they left. "And be careful
what you say at night—there are spies all over the place." Amma told
them to come back to visit when they could and gave them each a
bag with some fish and a few vegetables they'd found or traded to
get. The two Manickam siblings joined a line of workers following a

108

cadre to a site about a half mile away where they were to help build a dike around a new rice field.

Hundreds of men and women worked in separate teams of ten. The workers in Radha's group were given long-bladed hoes resembling mattocks, the kind used by Indochinese farmers for centuries, and woven baskets to carry dirt. Each member of the team had to build a section of dike three feet square and three feet high each day. They worked in pairs; one dug a channel beside the dike and lifted the dirt into a basket with the hoe, while the other hauled it to the top and dumped it. It was hard work but manageable—or it would have been if Radha had known how to hold a hoe. He grasped it too tightly and soon had massive blisters all over both palms and some of his fingers. Nobody told him that you loosen your grip when you swing a hoe so it doesn't pull your skin when it hits the ground.

The pairs of workers couldn't head back to camp until they had finished their own sections of dike. The new field was on dry land, so the work could have been heavier, but for a bunch of city folk, it was still quite a shock. Radha finished with everybody else, and they headed back to camp. There cadres handed out fourteen ounces of rice for each worker to cook for himself; compared to what the nonproductive families got back at the village, it was a feast. Radha also had the fish from his mom. He hadn't seen Indira all day.

Radha's name had been shortened, in Khmer Rouge fashion, to one syllable: "Dha." The Khmer word for comrade is *mit*, so he became "Mit Dha." He wasn't allowed to speak with his sister or anyone else in the women's camp. That first night a cadre called the workers together and repeated the Khmer Rouge line about how independence-mastery requires victory over the fields, all-seeing Angka requires much hard labor, blah blah blah. Then he got down to the rules for this camp: They were not to mix with the women from the female camp, or they would be crushed. They were not allowed to go to the women's area or attempt to communicate with them, or they would be crushed. If they tried to plow on other people's backs like the capitalists (that is, shirk from work), they would be crushed. They could not speak of their former life—movies or songs or food or anything else about the old society. They could not talk about what they had experienced since the Glorious Revolution. If there was any sign of a relationship between one of them and a woman, they would be brought before a special meeting of the group, judged, and then crushed.

Radha watched him and then headed to his mat when the meeting ended. It had been a long day, but the extra rice helped. It was dangerous to try to slack off because of the guards with assault rifles and there was little point in trying to malinger. You had to finish your section in order to go back to camp to eat, so you might as well just get it done.

So that's what Radha did. The workers were up well before six, worked until noon or so when they ate a bite and rested, and then hoed and hauled again from one until they were done. Supper and a meeting ended each day. It was hot, so you couldn't work too fast, but you couldn't stop either. Time dragged like a plow behind a water buffalo in an endless field. The Khmer Rouge didn't want him to think about his previous life—well, right then he didn't want to think about it either. He swung the hoe, scooped dirt, swung the hoe, scooped dirt. His hands stung like crazy during those first few days, but eventually it was evening and then morning, evening and then morning, day after day after day.

After he had been at the camp a few weeks, Grandma became ill and died. By the time he got permission to visit Phnom Tippedei, she had already been cremated. All he could do was stand at the edge of the pit and look at her remains.

Chhay Balang was just one small part of a massive construction effort going on all over Cambodia. The main effort was put into expanding the system of canals, dikes, and dams to provide water for new rice fields, but the Khmer Rouge also attempted to build bridges, roads, and some buildings. Human labor instead of heavy equipment was used to do a majority of the work. One Khmer

Rouge booklet proclaimed, "Ten thousands, twenty thousands, thirty thousands people are working in each worksite for building up reservoirs, canals, dikes . . . the works are rapidly going forward. The rural areas of Democratic Kampuchea are undergoing deep changes."[1] The booklet was published in English so the capitalist American dogs could read it and know that they had failed to stop the unleashing of the Khmer people.

Once, while he was working in the rice paddy, Radha paused for a moment to lean on the hoe while another team member carried up a basket of soil. A harsh young voice barked at him a second later. "Why don't you get the dirt ready for the next basket while you're waiting?" the guard said. His stomach grew tense. He lifted the hoe and started chopping at the ground. The guard moved on.

One evening the cadres banged on the tire rim. All the workers assembled in the central area, and the cadres hauled out one of the comrades. The man had been accused of leaving the camp and returning to the village at Tippedei.

"He has betrayed Angka!" a cadre yelled. "What do we do with traitors?"

The man's fellow comrades knew the correct answer; all such questions had the same answer. "Crush him!" they shouted with enthusiasm, because a lack of enthusiasm for Angka's whims and suspicions was dangerous.

"Very well," said the cadre, who then sent them all back to their cooking fires.

Radha returned to his camp and set about grilling his bite of fish and boiling his rice. Later that evening some fellow workers—he didn't know their real names—came by as he was sitting around a fire with some comrades. They started talking quietly. The soldiers had killed the man they had accused of going to Tippedei. "They killed him, and then they cut out his liver, sliced it into little pieces, and then cooked it. And they all ate some! Some people saw it with their own eyes!" said one of the men.

111

Radha nearly threw up his fish and rice. He had never heard of such a thing. But those who lived in the country or had been around the military knew of the practice. He couldn't believe it. *Eat human liver? That's crazy*, he thought. Soon after, he left the fire and went to bed.

The next morning while tramping out to the dike-in-progress, a fellow worker caught Radha's eye and nodded toward a ditch near the dike—there was a hand sticking out from under some dirt. Radha knew then that what the man had said was true. He kept walking, then he started hoeing, and then he tried to stop thinking.

Radha's crew finished the levy at Chhay Balang, and in August, the cadres announced that the work crews would be sent to the front lines of the battle for independence-sovereignty for mastery over the roads. That is, they would with hoes and baskets build a road to Koas Kralar, which would run north-south over to the west of Phnom Tippedei. Hundreds of workers hiked to the new campsite, dumped off their stuff, hoisted their hoes to their shoulders, and followed the cadres down to the project. It did not look good.

The last project had been hard work, but working in teams, a comrade could reasonably hope to finish his three-foot section of dike in a day and get back in time to cook his rice before enduring the propaganda meeting. This time Angka in its wisdom had decided that Democratic Kampuchea required a road through flood plains and rice fields. Many sections of the route were either thick mud or thick mud covered in water.

The crews set to work. Where it was reasonably dry they carried on as before. Where it was wet they slopped the mud into baskets, carried them to the supposed site of the road, and sloshed the mud onto the directed spot. Sometimes the mud was simply too thin for the hoes and they had to use their hands to get it into the baskets. Slowly the road was built up; even under such harsh conditions, hundreds of comrades working together can make some progress.

But because of the water, they often had to work far into the night. They slept on high ground, either on railroad beds or one of the many termite mounds that rose up out of the plain. The termites stayed deep inside the hill and didn't attack them.

The workers sometimes lit fires after the sun set so they could see well enough to work, but the fires would burn out eventually. On one especially dark night, Radha was standing in water, swinging his hoe. He could hear the grunts and splashing of the comrades working next to him, perhaps ten or fifteen feet away, but couldn't see them. He heard his neighbor line up a hard swing with the hoe, and then a sickening clunk as the man accidentally buried the hoe blade into the face of a Khmer Rouge guard who had wandered too close.

With a splash, the guard collapsed into the muddy water. Radha could tell the worker was just standing there, probably frozen with fear. Amid shouting, the other guards rushed up and shone their flashlights on the fallen man. It was hard to see, but Radha thought the man's whole face had been whacked off. He looked dead. Guards grabbed the worker and dragged him to the top of the road. Radha heard what seemed like an eternity of screams, thuds, crunching, shouts, pleadings, kicks, heavy breathing, and then footsteps and muttering, and then silence.

The comrades went back to work and finished their sections. The next morning Radha saw the unfortunate worker still lying atop the road, beaten to a pulp, with a dark stain spreading out onto the ground from a gash in his neck.

The day after that Radha noticed a young Khmer Rouge, perhaps thirteen years old, walking around carrying a long bamboo pole. A woman was standing near the base of the roadway waiting for her basket to be filled with dirt. She was dirty all over, from her sandals to her hair, which was cut short in the only approved style, and she looked tired. The boy walked up behind her and without warning slammed the pole into the small of her back—and then again and again.

"I count one," he shouted, as she cried out and staggered but somehow remained upright. He yelled in his angry teenage voice that that was her first warning and after three, she would be crushed. She must not waste time just standing, doing nothing. She must always be working. Angka had a saying for just this lesson: "On the work site until death!"[2]

Radha did not want to be beaten. He did not want his throat cut. He did not want to die of starvation or disease or fatigue. He wanted to survive, and so while watching this woman suffer he determined that he would never allow them to hit him; he would always work hard enough that they would have no reason to hit him. "Don't let them count one," he sometimes said to himself.

Others adopted similar strategies of survival and ways of turning inward, shutting out the horrors of daily life as much as possible. In his memoir, Pin Yathay writes about an ancient Buddhist prophecy that declared that one day Cambodian houses would be empty, the priests would be persecuted, the ignorant would rule over the educated, and only the deaf-mutes would survive. Pin Yathay became a deaf-mute: "I had found my method of survival."[3]

To Radha, the phrase "Don't let them count one" became something more; it was his form of resistance. He didn't believe that opposing the Khmer Rouge meant refusing to submit and work for Angka. That was simple suicide. Radha had no real hope of a future and saw no way to escape, yet he did not give in. His Christian faith was real, but to say that his faith kept him strong would give the wrong impression; he certainly didn't feel strong. To oppose the Khmer Rouge was simply to live while keeping within himself the knowledge that he was not one of them. At the time, it was enough.

After building the road, Radha was assigned to crews that built canals, dikes, and reservoirs at Chromouk and Koy Chetdey. Some weeks later, Radha's crew was granted permission to travel back to the village of Tippedei to visit their families. But when Radha got there, he found his family had been moved to a village about a day's walk northwest of Tippedei. So, with permission, he set out for Kok Porn. In northwest Cambodia, the rounded, tree-covered mountains rise suddenly out of the plains so that the rice fields run almost up to the base of the mountains. Kok Porn was on a plain surrounded by paddies and small stands of trees.

Once there Radha asked around for the Indian family and soon found them settled into a hut. A kindly man with an oxcart had agreed to carry Appa and the small children from Tippedei to Kok Porn. After a few days, Radha returned to the work site with his crew.

Simply surviving became more and more difficult as the fall continued on. Radha had a piece of plastic to help keep him dry when it rained, but plastic didn't fill his stomach as the cadres steadily cut back on the rice rations. The Khmer Rouge were already basically starving all nonworkers, but until then the regime had provided enough food to the productive people—meaning those healthy and strong enough to do manual labor—that they could manage.

The workers became so hungry that they started secretly eating whatever they could find. Angka's provision was never inadequate, so anybody seeking extra food was attempting to undermine the revolution and must be crushed. In the fields and at the sites, Radha and the other workers sometimes stooped to pick up something from the ground and slip it into their pocket or under their hat or into a fold of their clothes. Back at camp, Radha would slide a snail—or maybe a crab—he had found into the fire. He knew other workers were eating small lizards and sometimes even put into their cans of boiling rice the earthworms that grew as long as chopsticks.

10

A Strange Dance

Massacres are part of revolutions. Those who call for society to be upended know this fact very well and never condemn violence. Their argument is always the same: only new violence can drive out previous violence. The previous violence is hideous and cruel. The new violence is pure and beneficent; it transforms (not to say transfigures).

—Rithy Panh, *The Elimination*

By late fall of 1975, the Khmer Rouge had divided the country into seven administrative "zones" centered on Phnom Penh. The regime also continued to establish the cooperatives that supposedly were to produce the rice to finance the rise of Democratic Kampuchea. Pol Pot and his Central Committee did not acknowledge the existence of the Communist Party of Kampuchea. Nor did they acknowledge they were setting up a Communist regime or reveal the identities of the individuals running it. Angka was still mostly a mystery—even to those living under its rules.

In January 1976, Angka did, however, release a new constitution for Democratic Kampuchea. A windy preamble claimed that the

Khmer people, 95 percent of whom were peasants and laborers, had unhesitatingly sacrificed their children and husbands by the thousands on the battlefields. They just wanted a society "informed by genuine happiness, equality, justice, and democracy without rich or poor and without exploiters or exploited, a society in which all live harmoniously . . . to do manual labor together and increase production for the construction and defence of the country."[1]

The constitution called for the establishment of a legislature representing peasants, workers, and the military, as well as various administrative bodies. But neither the legislature nor the various bodies were set up. The document formalized the "collective principle" and declared that every individual "enjoys full rights to a constantly improving material, spiritual, and cultural life." It guaranteed absolute equality and zero unemployment, an idea one journalist more literally translated from the Khmer as "worklessness is absolutely nonexistent in Democratic Kampuchea."[2] That much was true.

The constitution declared that "Glorious Seventeenth of April" was the national anthem. The song begins, "Glittering red blood which blankets the towns and countryside of the Kampuchean motherland! / Blood of our splendid worker-peasants! / Blood of our revolutionary combatants, male and female! / Blood that was transmuted into seething fury, into fierce struggle / on 17 April, under the Revolutionary Flag! / Blood that has liberated us from slavery!"[3]

A few refugees by this time had escaped from Cambodia and informed international aid organizations that Kampuchea was indeed covered in blood, but their stories did not end with liberation. Their horrendous reports of mass executions, forced labor, and starvation were largely ignored. Some in the West found the refugees' accounts too incredible to believe, while many of those on the political left in media, government, and academia were sympathetic to the oppressed peasants rising up against the imperialist Americans and their capitalist lackeys in the Khmer Republic. They rejected the refugees' stories as the exaggerations and complaints of the losers.

117

There was no way to verify the stories either way; shortly after the evacuation of the cities the Khmer Rouge had expelled almost all foreigners and severed almost all communication with the outside world, except for some trusted Communist allies such as China and North Korea.

Another factor was that Prince Norodom Sihanouk left exile in Beijing in September 1975 for a multicontinent propaganda tour on behalf of his new but unacknowledged masters, the Khmer Rouge. It began with the United Nations in New York. Sihanouk, who still enjoyed much credibility with foreign governments and observers, told delegates that the evacuation of the cities had been carried out without bloodshed and refugee reports of mass executions and other atrocities were unfounded. His aides, however, complained to reporters that the Khmer Rouge were trying to get rid of him and that privately he was "appalled" at what was happening in the country.

In early December 1975, Radha was sent to Kraleung Dom to help with the rice harvest. Knowing nothing about how to harvest rice (you have to grab and bend the stalks in a certain way so the sickle can cut them properly, and it's easy to slice your hands), Radha struggled to keep up. He was often cold. "Get to work!" soldiers, wearing their comfy pajamas and scarves, would scream. "Are you a capitalist? Is that why you're cold?"

Radha suffered some cuts on his hand at first, but his bigger problem was that he was slow. If he didn't rush, the five or six harvesters in his line would soon leave him behind and vulnerable to a guard's kicks and abuse. They would taunt him, saying, "You used to hold a pen, well now you'll hold a sickle in the rice field—that's your pen."

The harvest, unsurprisingly, was not going as well as the Khmer Rouge had predicted. Rumors that Angka was already preparing for a purge spread among the workers. Radha believed that the two chief cadres of his new camp had heard the same rumors. Their names were Leap (pronounced Lee-ap) and Moha, and both were feared as brutal killers. Moha was later executed by the cadres imported from eastern Cambodia, but Leap, who was maybe five foot one with pale skin and vaguely Chinese features, managed to survive. This was perhaps in part because Moha gradually became more kindly over the months Radha knew him, while Leap maintained a reputation for working people to death.

The relationship between local Khmer Rouge officials and the workers, especially the New People, was a strange dance. Everybody had to behave as if the propaganda coming out of Phnom Penh were true (for example, the rice fields were sure to yield a bumper harvest and the workers were happy, healthy, and fully committed to serving Angka with all their strength), even though it was obviously nonsense. When talking to superiors one had to speak and act as though the Constitution of Democratic Kampuchea was a daily, living reality.

This dynamic extended up the chain of command as well. News from the field to the Central Committee in Phnom Penh was always positive because bad news was evidence of treason. During the early years, this created a false optimism at the top even as the countryside degenerated. The workers could see that the canals, constructed by forced laborers with few tools and minimal knowledge of engineering, were giving way. The rice crops were failing, the workers were dying of starvation and disease, and Cambodia's Great Leap Forward was in reality a leap into the abyss.

In day-to-day interactions, Leap could be vicious and capricious one minute and act like an arm-around-the-shoulder confidant the next. Leap and Moha came to regard Radha as a friend—sort of. To protect himself Radha pretended he couldn't read or write, but he would offer to help them out with various projects, suggest improvements, and generally be helpful in managing the cooperative. Despite this, or perhaps because of it, Leap mercilessly teased Radha by yanking hard on his beard. Radha could only laugh. He burned with anger on the inside, but outwardly he was compliant.

Once Leap decided to punish a comrade named Mao who was accused of stealing some vegetables. Radha decided to vouch for him. "We need this guy," Radha said. "Don't kill him, just give him a tough job." In a rare display of leniency, Leap sent the worker out to a field to clear the brush from the top of a termite hill that was several feet high, covered in thorns, and infested with poisonous red ants. He sent Radha with him and told them not to come back until they were done.

For a while Radha sat off to one side and watched Mao struggle with the thorns and slap at the fire ants swarming onto his bare arms and up his legs. The bites were painful; occasionally the Khmer Rouge would tie prisoners atop fire ant hills to torture or even kill them. The ants get their name from the burning sensation caused by the poison they secrete from their abdomen and place on top of their bites. Radha soon realized that at the rate Mao was working, neither of them would get dinner that night or possibly the next either, so he stepped in to help.

A bit later Moha showed up. He watched them a few minutes, and after Radha explained the situation, he began helping too, hacking at the bushes with his machete. Moha habitually wore a grim expression, but Radha sometimes wondered if he sensed in Moha a touch of remorse at how it all turned out—at the things he was forced to do.

Others, however, such as Comrade Kha, seemed suited to Khmer Rouge society. He talked constantly in an attempt to ingratiate himself with the workers, but they called him "Leach" behind his back because he sucked up to the cadres and hung out with the *chhlops*—the spies. Radha noticed that Kha was watching one day when another worker, Vy, took off his shirt while washing up in a canal before lunch, displaying a skull-and-crossbones tattoo on his left shoulder. It was a memento of the military training he had received from US forces when he was in the Khmer Republic's army. Vy knew taking off his shirt was an invitation to be executed, but that day he either forgot or just didn't care.

120

Later that afternoon a handful of soldiers turned up at the field. They stripped Vy, tied his hands behind his back, and marched him across the fields, beating him from behind with bamboo poles as they went. When they got just inside a stand of trees, they hammered him across the back of his neck, broke it, and left him there. Later he might well have been dragged away to one of the B-52 craters that dotted much of the countryside. The craters filled with water in the rainy season and over time became impromptu mass graves, depending on how close they were to a village or one of the hundreds of small bamboo or concrete prisons scattered throughout Democratic Kampuchea.

Radha was shocked but pretended not to notice Vy's execution. He looked down or to the side or focused on what he was doing—anything to keep him from looking at the brutal scene as it unfolded. *Who was next?* he thought. Radha never became so jaded that he stopped being shocked, but over time he taught himself how not to see certain things—even when his eyes were open and looking right at them.

However, one evening in December 1975, he had nowhere else to look. Leap and Moha gathered about one hundred younger workers, men and women, for a firelight meeting near Kraleung Dom. Leap came to the front and opened with the usual exhortations to obey Angka, becoming louder and more forceful as the night dragged on. Eventually Leap turned to the question of traitors. "What do we do with the enemy?" he roared. "Crush them!" the workers shouted back.

Leap and Moha took their flashlights and began strolling up and down the rows, shining the beams onto the comrades' faces, one at a time. Radha was near the front. He could hear the leaders work their way down the rows behind him. They grabbed one of the workers and hauled him roughly toward the fire. "This traitor has stolen rice from the cooperative! He has betrayed Angka! What do we do with the enemy?" Leap shouted again.

121

"Crush him!" Radha called back with all the others. So, in the flickering firelight, Leap and Moha dragged the terrified worker to a tree about twenty feet away from Radha. They tied the worker's hands together in front of him and then to the tree above his head so his chest was exposed to the crowd. Radha could feel his heart pounding but couldn't pull away his gaze.

Leap picked up a rifle, ripped off the worker's shirt, and then began poking at the guy's torso with the tip of the bayonet. Suddenly Leap plunged the blade into the guy's midsection and ripped open a big wound, exposing his organs. Then Leap reached in and pulled out the man's liver with his hand, using the bayonet to cut it free.

Radha somehow knew the worker was screaming the whole time, but for him the world went strangely silent. He couldn't believe what was happening. The image persisted in front of his eyes—Leap, standing in the firelight glow, holding up the man's liver in a dripping red hand as the victim shrieked in terror and agony. Radha clenched his jaw so tightly it felt locked, and his arms and legs seemed frozen in place.

Leap separated the gall bladder from the liver and then put the liver in a pan and placed it over the fire. He held the bladder over the drinking cup of a canteen and began to squeeze. Bile trickled into the cup. He took a sip, and looked out over the faces of the workers while he waited. The fire crackled behind him. After a few minutes, Leap cut off a piece of the prisoner's liver, put it into his mouth, and chewed. Moha had some too. Radha could see the prisoner was still alive, barely, behind Leap. "This," Leap shouted, "is how you treat enemies of the revolution!"

Eating an enemy's liver wasn't unique to the Khmer Rouge, nor would Leap have regarded it as cannibalism. In Khmer culture, the liver has connotations similar to "heart" or "spirit" in English. Someone who has a "big liver" is insolent, rude, and willing to cross boundaries; someone who is evil has a "black liver." Khmer warriors for centuries have eaten human liver as a battlefield ceremony, believing that eating an enemy's liver is a sign of domination, and by doing so they absorb his strength and courage. Some have said it provides talismanic protection and even invincibility. Others say eating liver "detaches" the heart and, like alcohol, removes inhibitions and makes the eaters bold, resolute, and detached, and thus able to do otherwise unthinkable things.[4]

During the civil war, Khmer Rouge soldiers would rush into the battle against hopeless odds, believing they were protected by the livers they had ripped out of prisoners or corpses on the battlefield and eaten. Some Khmer Rouge cadres carried around with them human gall bladders they had extracted from their victims, sipping the bile from time to time. It was bitter but good once you got used to the taste, some said, and it cooled the body. You could tell who was drinking the bile by their eyes, which turned either red or yellow.

To Radha, the rest of the assembled workers had faded away. He saw Leap and the blood and the prisoner still tied to the tree. That's all. Then Leap picked up the bayonet again, walked over to the prisoner, and cut out his heart. The comrade finally died.

The meeting ended soon after. Radha went back to his sleeping area, lay down on his mat, and tried to forget what he had just seen. But he couldn't. Most nights since the revolution had begun, Radha had prayed before going to sleep, *Lord, thank you for letting me live another day.* And when he woke up in the morning he had prayed, *Lord, thank you for letting me live another night.* But after what he'd just witnessed, he wasn't so sure he wanted to live anymore. That night he prayed instead, *Lord, I don't want to go through that. Please don't make me go through that. Take me home, Lord.*

11

Something Rotten

It was almost normal for people over thirty to be frightened of their own children. And with good reason, for hardly a week passed in which the *Times* did not carry a paragraph describing how some eavesdropping little sneak—"child hero" was the phrase generally used—had overheard some compromising remark and denounced its parents to the Thought Police.

—George Orwell, *1984*

Later in December 1975, Radha was sent from Kraleung Dom back to Kok Porn to visit his family. He and Indira went out daily with sickles to the rice harvest, joining hundreds of people strung out in lines through the fields.

In Kok Porn, Radha discovered that he knew a man in his work crew—a former airline employee from Phnom Penh. Sometimes they'd talk about their time in the business world. The man tended to be morose. He'd lost everything to the Khmer Rouge, including his children. They hadn't died; they were becoming devoted followers of Angka. One day Radha listened as the man's oldest boy, a lad in his teens, called to his father, "Comrade, come and eat."

The man was furious. "Don't you dare call me comrade!" he shouted at the boy. "I'm not equal to you!" That's about all he could do. Children were already encouraged to report their parents for deviation from the party line, and it was risky even to challenge a youth who had embraced the system. Angka was the ultimate authority, not parents, and the Khmer Rouge had set up systems of education and indoctrination that were pathetically ineffective in one way and diabolically potent in another.

Many thought the Khmer Rouge were antieducation, a misperception fed by the widespread belief that the Khmer Rouge killed everybody who wore glasses because it proved that they were educated. Many of those wearing glasses were targeted, especially in the early years of the regime as the Central Committee tried to root out all the ex–government bureaucrats, scholars, and teachers.

But the Khmer Rouge were not opposed to all learning; they just intended to exterminate anyone whose education left them with a hint of Western individualism. Many local leaders were illiterate, but party members had to be able to read to rise through the ranks, partly to communicate and partly to be able to absorb Communist doctrine. That's why the regime's "Four Year Plan to Build Socialism in All Fields" called for universal literacy and for schools for children to be set up all over the country; the Central Committee saw children and youth as the blank tablets upon which they intended to write the future of Democratic Kampuchea.

Whatever schools Angka did set up were for Old People only and taught little except Communist slogans. Many survivors later recalled no schools at all. A few schools in Phnom Penh offered more formal education for the Central Committee members' children or taught technical skills, like operating machinery. Children in some schools did get slightly better rations than those in other schools.

The Khmer Rouge indoctrination programs, however, transformed children. Lacking strong ties to the old society and taught to resent its inequalities, children were vulnerable to the lessons of class warfare. "It is the youth of today who will take up the revolutionary tasks of tomorrow," Pol Pot said in a 1977 speech, for youth are the "most receptive to revolution."[1] The Khmer Rouge yanked children as young as twelve, most of them from poor rural areas, away from their families to live in camps where cadres taught them discipline, hatred, and obedience to Angka alone. The kids believed the cadres who told them their parents didn't love them but Angka did. "Angka is the mother and father of all young children, as well as all adolescent boys and girls," went one saying.[2]

"They ordered us to attend meetings every night where we took turns finding fault with each other, intimidating those around us," reported one young survivor. "We survived by becoming like them. We stole, we cheated, we lied, we hated ourselves and each other, and we trusted no one."[3]

They became the fiercest and most brutal members of the Khmer Rouge cadres and soldiers. Youth became "the dictatorial instrument of the party," as Pol Pot put it. A particular sign of loyalty to Angka was to turn in or even beat one's own parent for the slightest violation of Angka's rules, and Radha occasionally saw children denounce their parents. Cadres usually preferred to eliminate enemies during the night, as it amplified the sense of terror, but when a child helped beat a parent to death the cadres held the execution during the day. "I'm not killing my parents," the child would shout, "I'm killing enemies of the revolution!"

In January, Radha turned twenty-three, and he and Indira left Kok Porn with different crews on a "youth work force." Radha spent the first half of 1976 traveling on these "work brigades" for projects involving dozens or even hundreds of people in various regions of northwest Cambodia. This was typical Khmer Rouge strategy: identify a problem or project and then throw as many bodies at it as possible. They had waged the civil war in much the same way, shoving troops into battle zones regardless of casualties. People were expendable, and the Communists attempted to rebuild Cambodia with the same militarized approach and language with which they had fought the civil war. Everything was a "battle" or "struggle" to "achieve an overwhelming victory" over the countryside or the rivers or the latent capitalist tendencies of the people. "Every work site is a fiery battlefield," said Angka. "Transform your anger [against the enemy] into enthusiasm to launch an attack on work!"[4]

For one project, hundreds of single men and women were to go work on a canal and dike about two days' walk away from Kok Porn. The area, called Koy Chetday, was in the middle of nowhere, it seemed to Radha, a plain southeast of Battambang with little water and few trees. The workers were all New People, selected because the job was a miserable one. The ground was too hard to use a hoe or shovel, so the cadres handed out picks—one or two per group of ten. Those who weren't swinging a pick had to scrape up the dirt with their hands.

The youth crew worked on the project for about a month. They complained and grumbled incessantly but never openly. They muttered to themselves about how the Khmer Rouge were obviously idiots and cruel and starving the workers to death.

Most of their project supervisors were young male or female cadres in their twenties, soldiers and farmers with no construction experience. When one of the leaders realized he had made a mistake, he would say, "Angka has made a great leap forward," and give the workers new and contrary instructions.

Radha eventually got to know another young worker named Phon. He used to be a weightlifter back in his town near Phnom Penh and somehow had kept a photo of himself among his possessions. Once he took it out and showed it to Radha. He peered at the image of a very fit, muscular young man eyeing the camera, then over at Phon, who was as gaunt as the rest of them. "This is not you!" teased Radha.

"What do you mean?" insisted Phon. "That's me!"

"No, it can't be," Radha continued. "I see here a guy who has big muscles, but you don't."

"It's because of the porridge," Phon said.

They chuckled a little but dared not laugh aloud. Plus, they were too hungry to laugh.

Throughout his travels with the work crews, Radha hung onto his Bible. It hadn't been easy. When he had left for his first work crew, Amma had given him a knapsack like the Khmer Rouge carried—a bag with a strap and a drawstring on top—and he put in it his Bible, a few extra clothes, a blanket, a spoon and pot for cooking, and a couple of photos of his parents and siblings.

The Bible was heavy, and he rarely had time to read it. Reading of any kind was dangerous for New People. He certainly couldn't carry a book around the work sites, but sometimes he would sneak it along with him when he went off into the bush to relieve himself or glance at a page or two during a midday break. Radha loved to read, and despite the danger, it was comforting to have a real book. It was like having God along with him and a reminder of life with his fellow believers at Maranatha Church. "The Lord is my shepherd, I shall not want," he read repeatedly. When reality became overwhelming, he recited John 3:16.

He still hungered to know God, but it was difficult to reconcile God's love with watching a cadre cut out somebody's liver. *Why would God allow this?* he wondered. *Why would God allow Lakshmi to die? Why would God allow all those other people to die?*

When he did get a chance to read his Bible he often found himself in Old Testament passages that described God's judgment on Israel. When people don't believe in God, it seemed to him, God just got rid of them. Eventually Radha concluded that God had allowed the rise of the Khmer Rouge as a punishment for the sins of the people. *I guess this is how God gets rid of people in Cambodia,* he thought.

In February, the cadres let the workers go back to visit family at Kok Porn. When Radha and Indira got there, Radha was disturbed. None of the Manickams looked healthy—nobody did, so no big surprise—but Appa was in worse shape than ever. Back in Phnom Penh he had been a big man, more than two hundred pounds, but after months of near-starvation and illness, his belly looked taped to his backbone. The skin on his face seemed papery. Loose flesh hung down all over, and Radha noticed how wrinkled skin dangled from Appa's upper arm. His arthritis was so bad he could no longer walk at all, even with canes. Amma or another family member had to help him outside, dig a hole for him a few yards from the house, help him sit down so he could relieve himself, cover it up when he was done, and then carry him inside. "So man wastes away like something rotten," lamented Job, "like a garment eaten by moths."[5]

Of course, the stay was much too short. After a few days, the cadres came by to select another district work force of especially strong young people, half women. The cadres said Angka would provide better food and living conditions than they could get in Kok Porn. They picked twenty from Radha's village, including Radha and Indira again. But Indira refused to leave Appa and Amma in such a state. She feigned illness and convinced the cadres to take her name off the list. Ravy, the next in line, was still too young to go, and he was small anyway. Dhanam, Selvem, Annapoorani, and baby Murugan were all skinny and undersized, with their skin and hair showing the discoloration of malnutrition. The children spent their days either doing small chores they'd been assigned around the village or hanging out by the Manickam hut.

Just before Radha left, Appa said to him, "Give me your watch. We might need it to trade for food." But Radha refused. It was gold, Swiss-made, and beautiful—a gift from Appa's father to him and then to Radha. He had kept it hidden all this time, sometimes in his sack but usually in a small pouch he had sewn in his tunic under his left arm. He hoped, unreasonably, that one day he might wear it again. That was, at the time, a ridiculous excuse not to give it to his father.

On the work crew, he would get more food than the unproductive people in the village. However, a gold watch might be the difference between life and death for his parents and siblings. Despite Angka's best efforts to stop them, black markets operated in every corner of the country. Throughout the revolution, people swapped gold and jewelry they had hidden or buried for bits of food or Western medicine that comrades and Khmer Rouge officials siphoned out of the system. Few dared to collect food or possessions openly in defiance of Angka, but it was easier in places where the cadres themselves did a little surreptitious trading. Some did a lot of trading, stockpiling supplies and food. Even for them, though, it could be risky.

But Radha couldn't bring himself to give up the watch. When he picked it up or saw it among his things, it always reminded him of better days. "No," he said to his father. "You gave it to me. It's mine. I'm taking it."

He came to regret that decision.

———◆———

The district work force that Radha joined that February, about fifty male and female workers, was sent to Svay Sar, which was near Phnom Tippedei. Near the sleeping area was a pond surrounded by trees, so the waters were shaded and cool. When he went to sleep he could hear what sounded like wolves howling and it scared him. Radha thought that the animals were probably scavenging corpses in shallow graves. He suspected the wolves would attack a live person, and he was in no shape to fight off a pack. Now the nights, as well as the days, seemed long.

Their leader was a man everybody called Pok ("Father") Prom, a Khmer Rouge officer in his fifties who walked around with an AK-47 on his shoulder. He wasn't exactly friendly, but he was determined that his crew would be fed; he arranged for every worker to get two meals that included fourteen-ounce cans of rice every day. His crew seldom worked late into the evening, but they earned that rice clearing bush and trees from rice fields with hatchets and hoes.

Radha worked with the bush-clearing crew from February 1976 until the beginning of the rainy season in June, often sleeping on the top of termite hills or in hammocks slung between small trees. The termites tend to stay inside their mounds even when people are cooking or sleeping atop them, but they swarm out of their hills during the warm, wet days of early summer and fill the air. Once, as Radha lay on the ground next to a fire, a winged termite flew into his right ear. He screamed and tried to dig it out with his fingers. Termites don't bite people, but they don't have a reverse gear either—it just kept pushing farther into Radha's ear canal.

Radha yelled and moaned all that night; his ear hurt desperately and nobody had tweezers to pull out the termite. He asked God to let him die, but over the next few days the bug stopped moving, and a month later he realized that he could feel it no longer. He guessed it had just died and eventually the parts had fallen out.

In June, Angka merged the people of Svay Sar with a village called Tuol Mateh. Everybody in Svay Sar grabbed their packs after work one day and walked over to the new site. It was in the middle of a large plain where rice fields were dotted with stands of trees and sugar palms, and foothills lay a few miles to the west.

Tuol Mateh was a large village with well over one thousand people, Radha guessed. The settlement housed single males on one side and females on the other. A few of the families had small homes, but most workers slept in long huts in rows with their heads toward the middle like two lines of hot dogs on a grill. The huts were organized around a central area that had a communal dining hall. Stables, storage huts, and a few other buildings also peppered the area. Radha and the others staked out some spots in one of the huts.

Radha and his crew now had a new boss. Instead of Pok Prom, who at least recognized that workers needed to be fed, they were under a particularly nasty piece of work named Vouen. He was slightly chubby, unusual even among the Khmer Rouge cadres at that time, and had light skin. He screamed a lot, and the story was that he had ordered young men and women executed because he suspected them of immorality. Radha believed it. He later heard that Pok Prom had been executed in a purge.

Soon after the newcomers arrived, a loud "bong, bong, bong" filled the air. It was the sound of a bar hammering on a cylindrical oxygen tank with the bottom cut off. Vouen was calling the workers to the big dining hall, where he assigned them all to work crews.

Vouen also invited the comrades to use the goods that they still had with them from the old life. "Don't hide them," he said. "We know you have them hidden away in your packs and buried outside your huts. It's OK. Angka wants you to use and enjoy whatever you have with you."

After being under the rule of the Khmer Rouge for a year, everyone should have known that this was obviously a trap. But some people apparently wanted to believe Angka was finally relaxing a little. The next day people wore their bracelets, watches, and rings. They showed one another their crumpled photos and took tiny whiffs of perfume. Radha couldn't believe it. He kept his gold watch in the pouch under his left arm.

The next day Vouen and his cadres went through the camp and confiscated everything they had seen. They emptied perfume bottles, turned them into kerosene lamps, and used gold chains to connect the caps to the bottles. They also dropped rubies, emeralds, and other gems into the bottles so the lamps had a little color. The garish result seemed rather unrevolutionary to Radha, but he didn't point that out.

In July of that year, 1976, a cadre named Proeun selected five New People, including Radha and a friend named Pho, to collect some water buffalo from another village. "Just leave your stuff here," Proeun told them. "You'll be back soon." That also was a lie.

The procession headed off through the fields and soon turned through a marsh full of stiff young reeds. The sharp leaves cut Radha's bare feet. "Are you a capitalist? Don't you know how to do anything?" Proeun jeered when Radha was forced to edge painfully along. Proeun, of course, had rubber-tire sandals.

It took all day to hike to the village where the animals were kept in a square corral. Each worker was assigned a pair of water buffalo to bring back. However, none of the buffalo had been broken to the plow. Radha stood by the rails next to the other workers and stared at the enormous creatures, unsure of what to do next. Water buffalo are normally fairly docile, but Radha didn't know that. He had never been that close to an ox, let alone a buffalo, and he was afraid of their massive horns.

Proeun ordered Radha to go get his buffalo, but Radha wasn't even sure which two were his. Somebody had pointed them out, but now they all looked alike to him. *Are they kidding me?* Radha thought to himself, and he started to pray silently as he climbed into the corral. Pho, who grew up on a farm, leaned over and told him to grab the rope—one end went through each buffalo's nose ring and then wrapped around the horn to make a sort of bridle. Radha still wasn't sure which two buffalo were his, so he grabbed the rope that was tied to one of them and waited until everybody else had theirs. Then he took the only one left.

They walked back to Tuol Mateh with the buffalo and dropped them off at the stables. They'd been gone three days. When Radha got back to his mat in his hut, he picked up his sack and found it was suspiciously light. He looked inside; gone were his photos and his clothes. All that was left of his Bible was the cover—all the pages had been ripped out and were gone. Vouen had set them up. The only possessions he had left were the clothes on his back (which still contained his gold watch), his spoon, and a blanket that was only three feet square. Later he saw some of the Khmer Rouge smoking cigarettes rolled with the red-gilded pages from his Bible.

Radha was soon sent back to Svay Sar to begin his new job: water buffalo plowman. One of his animals was a mean-looking female who had once torn her nostril when she yanked on her rope, so she was hard to turn. The first morning of the job, he hoisted his plow over his shoulder, took up the ropes, and joined his crew of nine other plowmen heading out to the rice fields. He carefully watched the plowmen already out working their paddies as they guided their animals through the muddy ground; it didn't look that hard.

When they arrived in the field, Proeun delivered a typical Khmer Rouge motivational speech: "Angka needs you to take care of your water buffalo and your plows. Each water buffalo is worth fifty humans, so don't lose yours. Make sure yours are watered and fed properly! They will be fed better than people. If you break a plow, you are an enemy of the revolution and must be crushed! Now go to work."

Radha, eyeing the others around him, carefully hooked up his plow to the yoke between his animals. He guided them toward his assigned paddy. His left hand held the rope to guide the buffalo, while his right was on the plow handle. He would later realize that you can't plow too deep, because if the animals startle, they'll jerk the blade out of the ground and probably break it, which explained Prouen's threats on the first day.

The basic pattern was easy: head down the middle of the paddy and then turn left, following the perimeter around to the starting point and then back up the middle just to the right of the original furrow. Keep doing this counterclockwise loop until you work your way across the whole field. Still, Radha was nervous. Prouen made him go first. Radha figured he was looking for an excuse to kill him. (Radha wasn't aware of it at the time, but in some places in Cambodia, the Khmer Rouge put teams of about eight New People under the yoke and forced them to pull plows. It's not clear how often this happened, but it was obviously intended to work them to death.)

Radha guided his buffalo up to the edge of the field, stepped into the water, and started up the middle, with the others behind. He got to the far end and was about to turn left when he noticed some workers standing atop a nearby dike waving and calling for him to go right. His group leader hadn't bothered to tell him that the first lap goes clockwise to shove the mud on the edges toward the middle of the field, instead of pushing it out. Those workers had probably saved his life.

On the way home that first night, the workers left their plows in the fields. Pho showed Radha how to ride the buffalos home but neglected to warn Radha to sit near the beast's hind end. The buffalo, trying to scare off flies, swung its huge head around and slammed its horn against Radha's calf. He fell off the animal's side and collapsed to the ground, moaning. Pho chuckled, but it was good-natured—and, thankfully, Radha wasn't seriously hurt.

12

A God of Disorder

Because the regime is captive to its own lies, it must falsify everything. It falsifies the past. It falsifies the present, and it falsifies the future. It falsifies statistics. It pretends not to possess an omnipotent and unprincipled police apparatus. It pretends to respect human rights. It pretends to persecute no one. It pretends to fear nothing. It pretends to pretend nothing.

—Czech dissident Vaclav Havel, "The Power of the Powerless"

Radha had been plowing near Svay Sar for a few weeks when he developed an infection on the second-smallest toe on his left foot. Soon it got so bad he could see a hole in his skin, right through to the tissue underneath. He couldn't step into water and walking was painful. So in early September 1976, his group leader sent him to the hospital at Daun Ba.

Everyone avoided the Khmer Rouge hospitals if possible. People went there expecting to die, not to be healed. Survivors later described them as full of broken people lying curled up amid feces, bloodstained bandages, and rotting clothes.

But Radha went anyway—what else could he do? He limped over to Daun Ba and found the converted Buddhist temple where patients lay suffering on the floor in rows. He lay down on a mat and tried not to pay attention to the people dying around him. Sometimes they lay quietly; sometimes they moaned.

Every morning a youth "trained" by the Khmer Rouge as a nurse came by to clean Radha's infection with tamarind leaves (a common ingredient in herbal remedies), change the bandages, and maybe sprinkle a little powdered penicillin on it.

On the bed next to Radha was a man with an infection on his shin about three inches long and much worse than Radha's. Every morning the nurse reached into the man's infection with a pair of tweezers to pull out the five or ten maggots that overnight had grown large enough to see. The man would clench his teeth and sometimes scream with pain, and for Radha that was almost as bad as the stench of the man's rotting flesh. Radha was afraid that his own wound would soon be that bad, so every day he covered his foot with a piece of cloth to keep off the flies. After a week, he could stand it no longer and left the hospital to go back to Toul Mateh. He still limped and dared not go into the water.

When he got back, Voeun was gone. Supposedly, he had been "reassigned," but the workers assumed he'd been executed in a purge. As the revolution progressed, Pol Pot and his chief officials became increasingly paranoid, so the purges became more frequent and unpredictable, sweeping like brush fires through the ranks as cadres turned on one another in desperate bids to save their own skins. "Eliminate, eliminate, eliminate, again and again, ceaselessly," exhorted the Khmer Rouge magazine *Revolutionary Flag*, "so that our Party forces are pure, so that our governing forces at every level and in every sphere are clean at all times."[1]

"The sickness must emerge to be examined," said Pol Pot in a speech in December of 1976. "As our socialist revolution advances, however, seeping into every corner of the Party, the army and among the people, we can locate the ugly microbes. They will be pushed out by the . . . socialist revolution. . . . If we wait any longer, the microbes can do real damage."[2]

The particular purge that got Voeun may have had to do with the size of the rice crop that fall. The region around Battambang, where Radha was working, was Cambodia's major rice-producing area. Throughout the previous year, Khmer Rouge officials in the northwest had been sending a certain amount of rice on to Phnom Penh. But in August 1976, the Central Committee came up with the "Four Year Plan to Build Socialism in All Fields."[3] It wasn't officially released to the comrades until the next year, and Angka never even tried to implement large parts of it, but many of the policies it proposed filtered down as orders to the cadres almost immediately.

One major part of the Four Year Plan was that the rice crops would yield an average of three metric tons per hectare per year. The one ton per hectare per year that most paddies produced simply would not generate enough revenue from rice exports to continue the revolution. While a few individual paddies might have hit the target, to expect it as a national average was absurd. To reach it, Pol Pot and his comrades proposed that some paddies, particularly in the northwest where Radha was working, would generate six, eight, even ten tons per hectare, mainly by tripling the number of crops grown through irrigation. According to the Four Year Plan and other documents historians have recovered, the Khmer Rouge believed victory over the rice paddies was inevitable if the farmers had proper revolutionary consciousness.[4] According to Khmer Rouge doctrine, it was irrelevant that no region in Indochina has ever produced such rice harvests.

When local Khmer Rouge officials realized how much rice they'd need to meet their quotas, many cut the rations of workers back to almost nothing. They told the workers in Radha's group that Angka needed the rice to pay back China for aid during the civil war. Meanwhile, officials in Battambang continued to tell officials in Phnom

Penh that the crops were good. In effect, they falsified their reports to save their own lives and starved their workers in the process.[5]

The sham couldn't go on long. In the fall of 1976, the Central Committee realized that, despite the rosy reports from their subordinates out in the zones, there wouldn't be nearly as much rice as they needed for export. Pol Pot and his inner circle may have heard that the New People out in the cooperatives were starving, but they wouldn't have been too concerned.

Pol Pot concluded that the problem must be that traitors, spies, and capitalist counterrevolutionaries were sabotaging the rice harvest. He transferred whole corps of cadres and soldiers whom he trusted from the eastern and southwestern provinces into the northern and northwest regions. There they ousted the current cadres and officials with little explanation and much behind-the-scenes bloodshed.

That may have been why Voeun disappeared; regardless of the reason, his removal probably saved Radha's life. Instead of executing the thirty or so Tuol Mateh workers (including Radha) who for one reason or another could not go into the water, Voeun's replacement, Von, found another job for them: clear off the side of a mountain, Cheung Tinh, to make a place for a cornfield.

Von was a seasoned Khmer Rouge officer who came from the tiny Arabic minority that lived in southwestern Cambodia. He was over six feet tall, a good-looking man who oversaw the cooperative from atop his large horse. He could neither read nor write but seemed to have more common sense than his predecessor. Despite the bloodthirsty reputation of the cadres from the southwest, Von was the best of the Khmer Rouge officers Radha met in those years.

Where other Khmer Rouge leaders seemed to delight in making humans do labor that machines could have done easily, Von didn't. He arranged for a bulldozer to come push down the trees on the lower levels of the mountain. Radha's crew then cleared off the bush, dug up the ground with hoes, and planted the spring corn.

As they planted, the crew members furtively nibbled on the raw seed corn. They were so hungry and ate so much that they were soon short of seed. Von had to know, but instead of executing the crew, he simply ordered more seed corn from Phnom Penh.

Despite the corn, Radha felt hungrier and hungrier. He was served only rice porridge seasoned with fish paste. Only the luckiest comrades got a piece of vegetable or a bite of fish in theirs. The stuff tasted the same, every day, twice a day. The kitchen workers often used dirty water from shallow canals, especially in the fall dry season, because the sources of clean water were farther away. Radha often tasted sand and grit in the porridge. Sometimes, when a horse died, the kitchen staff put that meat in the pot, but no one got more than a few pieces.

Near the end of September, a man passing through from Kok Porn, where the Manickams lived, delivered the news that Radha's father had died. Radha asked his group leader, Comrade Proeun, for a three-day pass to go home. "No," Proeun said. "You can't help your father anymore. He's gone. We need people to work." Radha pleaded, begged, and finally offered his gold Swiss watch, the same one he had refused to leave with his father ten months before. Proeun wasn't interested. The Khmer Rouge knew only the Japanese brands like "Orient," so "Swiss watch" meant nothing to him. Radha begged and begged. Finally, Proeun took the watch and gave him the pass.

Radha hiked all day, arriving in late afternoon. So many people had died since he had left that Kok Porn looked like a ghost town. He stopped in front of his family's hut, and a scrawny, misshapen girl crawled out. She was so weakened and diseased that her legs no longer worked; she edged out on her backside in a kind of a crab walk. She was pale and nearly bald from malnutrition. If he hadn't been so concerned about finding his family, he might have wondered who she was.

The girl struggled forward, grabbed his hand, and pulled. "Brother," she croaked. He looked down, eyes widening in horror. "I am Indira."

The once pretty, healthy young woman who had stayed behind to look after their parents now couldn't even walk. Radha just stood there sobbing.

Amma soon heard that her son was back and hurried home from the rice fields. She and Radha just stood looking at each other for a moment. "Where's your dad?" she finally asked. It was a strange question, but Amma didn't know how to break the news of Manickam's death to her oldest son. They went inside the hut and began to talk and weep.

Besides Appa, Radha's two youngest sisters and youngest brother had also died of illness and starvation: Annapoorani, six; Dhanam, thirteen; and Murugan, just one year old. Ravy, the second oldest brother, was away working in the fields. The other brother, Selvem, who was eight, was out with a children's crew but would come home later that night.

Just days before, Amma and Appa had traded for food a pair of emerald rings, family heirlooms they had kept securely hidden all this time. Each ring had a five-carat stone that had once been a very light, delicate green. As they were passed down from generation to generation, they had darkened to a rich, deep green, which made them more valuable. Amma's gem was cut square, and they exchanged that one for four field rats. For Appa's round-cut stone, they got ten fourteen-ounce cans of rice.

They never got a chance to eat any of it. From the beginning, Angka had decreed that nobody eat any food that Angka did not provide, as it implied criticism of Angka and opened up a sliver of opportunity for independence. But families still living together in a hut continued to eat together. Then in the early fall of 1976, the Central Committee announced that even families eating together in a place they regarded as their own was a "capitalist framework" that hampered the revolution. Engels, among other Marxist thinkers, had noted the connection between families, private property, and counterrevolutionary ideas. Families and property created buffers between the individual and the state and undermined the collective spirit.[6] Pol Pot declared, "We will follow the collective path to socialism. If we do this, imperialists can't enter the country. If we are individualists, imperialists can enter easily. Thus eating will be collectivized, and clothing, welfare and housing will be divided up on a collective basis."[7]

It's doubtful whether many Khmers, even among the cadres, quite believed this, but one did not question Angka's word. Plus, it was an easy way for the cadres to increase control over the people.

Therefore, the directive came down from Phnom Penh that everyone in the cooperatives would eat all meals in communal dining areas called "cuisines." All food in every village was collected in the collectivist kitchens, cooked in collectivist pots, and distributed in the collectivist cuisines. When the orders reached the villages, cadres and soldiers went from hut to hut confiscating whatever food and pots and utensils the comrades had left. Comrades were allowed to keep only a spoon each to bring with them at mealtimes.

The soldiers came to the Manickam hut on the very day Amma was cooking the rice and rats for which they had just traded their emeralds. Cadres came into their hut and seized their pots, the food in their pots, and everything else edible. The cadres also ransacked the hut and found the family's photos, including one of Radha's paternal grandfather, the one who'd saved a French general, proudly sporting a chest full of medals. That alone almost got them killed, but Amma frantically explained to the suspicious cadres that Grandfather had not been a Republican soldier and the medals were from a much earlier time.

"Give me some rice!" cried Appa as the cadres were walking out with the food, but they ignored him and went on to the next hut.

Appa could take no more. He died a day or two later.

The day after hearing this, Radha noticed Selvem, the fifth Man-ickam sibling, come up from behind as he sat eating his porridge on the floor of the cuisine. Selvem, a smart and endearing boy, had already finished his food. He stood looking over Radha's shoulder at his bowl. Radha had sometimes shared his ration with Selvem, but this time he refused to look back. Radha hastily drained his bowl, got up, and left, leaving the boy standing there. It was the last time he saw him.

Radha also received one more piece of bad news: a friend had committed suicide. Sine, like Indira, had faked an illness to remain behind at Kok Porn with his sister. Sine and Radha had traveled and worked together in 1975 before Radha was sent off to Svay Sar. Amma explained that while Sine was out in the fields some months earlier a poisonous green snake bit his foot, and he ended up with a serious infection that kept him from working. The cadres shouted that he was lazy and living off the labor of his comrades. They cut off his food. Sine was so angry that he just gave up. In Indochina grows a potato-like root called *kdouch* that if not soaked and cleaned well causes serious nausea and vomiting but isn't necessarily fatal. Sine purposely ate so much bad *kdouch* that he died.

That day, as it all sank in, the anger and frustration that had been building in Radha welled up. Appa and three more of his siblings were dead. He couldn't look after himself, let alone the remaining members of his family. *I believed in you,* he silently raged at God. *I even disobeyed my parents to follow you. And now look at what you've done to my family. Why are you punishing me? Why?*

Radha's Bible was long gone, but he recalled 1 Corinthians 14:33, a familiar passage: "For God is not a God of disorder but of peace." The Khmer word for "disorder" is also the word for "war" or "con-fusion." Focusing on this helped him to feel connected to God once again—for a while. In those days, it seemed, he often argued with God.

143

13

Super Great Leap Forward

I suck in the brown water through my lips; it smells like old,
wet straw. You who believe in a better world, a world without
classes, without currency, a radiant world that wishes everyone
well, have you tasted the rice field gurgling in your throat? Do
you know the savor of pools where eels have slept?

—Rithy Panh, *The Elimination*

When you starve to death, soon after the supply of food ends your body begins to burn through the reserves of fat in your liver and then elsewhere in your body. When those are gone, the protein in your muscles begins to break down. To save energy, noted a *Time* story on Cambodia that described the process, your pulse rate and blood pressure drop. Women stop menstruating and children stop growing. You become exhausted, obsessed with finding food, and edema, a swelling in the joints and abdomen, sets in.

You can survive this way for months, but eventually your body collapses. When the end comes, your intestinal walls suffer damage, often causing severe and constant diarrhea. Your circulation system malfunctions due to the loss of body fluids that control the heart, and your immune system falters, leaving you vulnerable to diseases such as typhoid, cholera, tuberculosis, and malaria. Even if they survive, children under two will be permanently scarred by prolonged starvation.[1]

This process was well under way for many Cambodians by late 1976. Radha returned from Kok Porn to his work site near Svay Sar and was soon staggering under the workload. After finishing with the cornfields, his crew was sent back to the rice fields and canals. The workers joked, with a weary gallows humor, that they ate anything that moved, but it was little short of the truth. All their thoughts revolved around food. "We eat anything," went another saying, "except the table legs and the nail heads." At different times during the four years of the Khmer Rouge regime, Radha ate bark, tree roots, and leather, so a table leg might not have been out of the question.

Given that so many of the New People were starving to death, it was more than galling that the Khmer Rouge cadres and soldiers seemed always to have enough to eat and not enough to do. Field workers who came back into Tuol Mateh for, say, a new tool might see cadres lounging in hammocks and enjoying some coconut or pineapple.

Open rebellion was useless, but almost everybody tried to get away with finding food outside the cuisine. It was the only thing that kept them alive. And it was possible only because the rice fields were large and the workers were spread over wide areas. Besides, the Khmer Rouge officials, ruthless on patrol in the villages, were less-than-disciplined supervisors if it meant they had to go out and slog through muddy fields.

One time after Radha had been standing waist-deep in water all day passing baskets of dirt, he pulled up his leg to find an enormous black leech fastened to his foot. It was as thick as his toe and swollen tight with his blood. A co-worker yanked it off for him and then glanced around. All the cadres were out of sight, so the comrade quickly built a small fire, toasted the leech, and ate it. One day that same worker got so hungry he went into the kitchen at night, stole some food, and then fled into the countryside. Radha never saw him again.

Another day during the midday break—it wasn't "lunch" because it seldom involved food—Radha tried to fill his empty stomach with water from the pond near the sleeping area. *Lord*, he prayed, gazing into the waters, *I'm so hungry. Where can I get some food?*

Right then he saw a huge field snail floating toward him. It weighed at least half a pound, he guessed. He had never seen such a snail. He grabbed it up quickly, trying not to let his comrades see what he was doing, and wandered over to a nearby fire pit. He squatted by the fire, just a worker taking a few minutes to stare idly into the flames, and stealthily slid the snail in among the coals. He let it cook for a while, then fished it out, pulled off the shell, and put the whole thing in his mouth—or he wanted to, but he couldn't; it was that big. He needed a couple of bites to stuff it all in. It was delicious, kind of sweet and juicy, but the main thing was that it filled his stomach.

Water was everywhere, so Angka instructed the workers to plant small vegetable crops hidden on the tops of termite hills, which were the only places dry enough to grow anything other than rice in the wet seasons. Workers often sneaked a few bites of raw vegetable when nobody was looking. They also collected wild tubers they found in out-of-the-way corners.

Radha often buried a pot in the mud in a far corner of a field he was plowing, usually near a termite hill so he could find it again. When his group leader was out of sight, he hunted field crabs. He made cooking fires by banging two stones together to spark kindling made of the pods from silk-cotton trees. The pods, which are a little larger than a banana, are very flammable when dry. He would also scare up small fish in the paddies by stirring up mud with a rake. He'd whack the fish, put them in his pocket quickly, and cook them as opportunity offered. If he saw a group leader from a distance, he hurriedly put out his fire, hid his things, and got back to work. He still had to finish the two hectares of plowing or whatever else he'd been assigned. No one brought food back to the huts; if you found it in the field, you ate it in the field.

Some of the vegetables were poisonous. Radha began by just tasting plants he found that looked edible. If it was bitter, he spat it out, but if he could possibly choke it down, he did. He also kept an eye on the birds because they would drop things, such as ironwood tree seeds. They were chewy when raw but better when cooked. He also learned how to distinguish between plants that looked alike; one tree had smooth leaves that were edible, but the leaves with a light fuzz on them from a different kind of tree were potentially fatal.

It was also possible to pop raw rice with the husk still on into your mouth, but the husks were rough as sandpaper. Many Cambodians who came to the United States after 1979 had appallingly bad teeth, blackened and worn down in part from chewing unhusked rice and other raw plants that were never intended to be eaten.

Radha managed to follow the plow during the day, but if he walked into deep mud, it was hard to get out on his own. When walking along the tops of narrow dikes, it was an unwritten rule that the men had to step aside into the muddy fields to let women going the other direction pass.

One day Radha saw a female worker coming toward him along the top of a dike and realized that, if he did step off the dike, he might get stuck. But if he knocked a woman off a dike in full view of any cadres or soldiers, he might be executed. He was incredibly tired and at that moment didn't really care if he lived or died. So he put down his head and just kept walking, and the woman did the same. They bumped gently and then collapsed together into the mud beside the dike. Leap came by a few minutes later. Radha thought it might be the end, but Leap just laughed and pulled them out. Radha later came to regard it as the first time he tried to commit suicide.

Radha believed by then that the Khmer Rouge were deliberately working the New People to death. He weighed less than ninety pounds, he estimated. He felt like a ghost. His eyes were sunk deeply into his head, looking out on the world from dark caverns. He found it hard even to walk and was, like most workers, often covered in dark and white lice. The dark lice lived in his hair; he could get rid of those by shaving his head and then diligently picking the parasites out of his scalp and crushing them with his fingernails. The white lice or body lice, however, were much harder to find. They lived in the seams of his clothes and came out at night. They would wake Radha with their bites, and he could feel them crawling across his body and in the folds of his skin—behind the knees, under the arms, near the groin—but they couldn't easily be killed. Sometimes Radha, even though he knew it was pointless, in frustration would pick a few out of his clothes, place them on a rock, and crush them with an ax.

The Four Year Plan called for the comrades to achieve victory over the paddies and make a "super great leap forward" by planting two, three, or even more crops per year in selected areas. In Radha's region, the cadres doubled down on the New People to get it all done. The gong rang at 3:00 a.m. to signal them to report in for work. Radha's crew of plowmen spent their first hours of work in darkness carrying bundles of rice stems out to the fields for replanting. Then they came back to the stables to pick up their animals to get ready for the day's plowing. They worked all day, and after eating their evening bowl of rice gruel, they had to go back out to pull and bundle more rice stems for transplanting. They worked by firelight, if somebody bothered to build a fire, until midnight. Three hours later, they were up again.

Some evenings Radha's crew had to pump water from the canals into the fields using a pedal-powered waterwheel. The moveable wooden wheels, with blades attached, were about ten feet high and connected to a crude stationary bike. The thing was designed to splash water over a dike from one field or canal into the next, so the worker had to pedal pretty hard to move any water at all. A single worker could handle about ten minutes of pedaling, at most, so the comrades took turns. They had to keep at it until they had covered the field to a specified depth, usually a couple of inches or so. Sometimes in the evening they built dikes or dug canals. The occasional evening propaganda meeting came as a relief.

The Khmer Rouge who supervised the fields were mostly ex-soldiers. They came up with several techniques to discourage malingering. In the middle of Svay Sar was a shallow fish pond that became increasingly cool as the fall wore on. When a comrade claimed to be sick with fever or diarrhea and unable to work, the Khmer Rouge shoved the sick person into the pond. Those who came up nearly chilled to death were excused from work. Of course, they also received no rations that day. Those who survived the cold water with less difficulty were cheating Angka and punished. "You shiver with fever," went one of Angka's sayings, "you shake like a tractor, you vibrate like a motor car, you ache for food, you quiver from laziness, you've caught an imaginary disease."[2]

The Khmer Rouge would also force those who claimed to be "chicken blind," or unable to see well enough at night to work, to run through thickets of thorns. Those who avoided too many thorns could clearly see well enough to work—those comrades got double work assignments for shirking.

The cadres searched everybody who came into the cuisine to eat and if they caught you with food, well, look out. Radha watched one day as a worker sneaked a field crab into the dining hall. He slipped it into his empty bowl and then held out the bowl to the cooks, hoping that the hot water of the gruel would partially cook the crab. The servers saw the crab in the bottom of his bowl, so the soldiers dragged him outside for a beating.

Pho, Radha's friend on the plowing crew, was a cheerful guy, considering the circumstances, always talking and joking, but his judgment was poor. One day Pho got so desperate for something to eat that he stole some raw rice still in the husk. That night it began to pour, and over the din of water on the tin roof, Radha could hear a tiny fire burning next to him and the rice grains popping as they roasted. Radha pretended to be asleep. He had warned Pho not to do it, but Pho hoped that the rain would cover the sound of the fire and maybe even keep the *chhlops* away. He was wrong.

Suddenly a handful of the young spies appeared out of the darkness and rain and pounced on Pho like skinny little hyenas. They beat him with their fists and kicked him with their rubber sandals, screaming and cursing at him for betraying Angka. Radha rolled out of the way—there was nothing he could do. He watched, horrified, as the children kicked Pho in the face until his left eye popped out onto his cheek. Pho screamed and shoved it back into the socket. The *chhlops* tied him up and dragged him off, blood on his face.

Radha thought that was probably the last of Pho, but he came back to the hut the next day. He was from the country, so the village leaders let him live. He was blind in that eye from then on. "I'm going to kill those kids," Pho grumbled, but Radha cautioned him against trying. "They'll kill you, and they'll kill your whole family," he said.

14

Rebels Within

In this revolt the [rebel] steps out of living within the lie. He rejects the ritual and breaks the rules of the game. He discovers once more his suppressed identity and dignity. He gives his freedom a concrete significance. His revolt is an attempt to live within the truth.

—Czech dissident Vaclav Havel, "The Power of the Powerless"

The 1976 rice harvest began in early December. To thresh the rice, workers in most of the country spread the stalks on a hard piece of ground, stomped on or drove oxen over it, flipped it with pitchforks, and then threshed it again. Parts of Battambang province where Radha was working were under the direct control of officials in Phnom Penh. Radha was in "Region 1," and the workers had special "privileges" such as more equipment. Radha's crew threshed with tractors.

Radha used to look wistfully at the huge piles of unhusked rice heaped into big barns, which held tons of rice, mountains of rice, enough rice to drown in. The workers regularly shoveled rice into wagons and then watched as tractors hauled it away. When the rains made the dirt roads impassable for the tractors, oxcarts did the job. They got more rice in their bowls during the few weeks of harvest but never enough to fill their stomachs.

During a break one afternoon at Savy Sar, Radha walked into the cuisine to get a drink of water. It was empty, so he sat down and picked up an official Khmer Rouge magazine one of the cadres must have left lying around. He began flipping through the pages and reading some of the articles.

"Can you tell me what the magazine says?" said a voice behind him. Radha froze, and his heart started pounding. It was Leap, whom Radha had assured many times he could not read.

Radha struggled to look casual as he turned around. "Oh, no, I don't know what the articles say, comrade," he said. "I can't read."

"Can't you read?" Leap demanded. "You looked like you were reading."

"Oh, no, I'm looking at the beautiful pictures here," Radha said. "Angka has done a fine job putting all this together in this magazine—all these pictures of meetings of important comrades and everybody working. It's very good."

Leap left without saying anything more.

The magazine was only one of Angka's cultural achievements. Many work sites and cooperatives had loudspeakers that continuously blared songs extolling Angka's wisdom and superior provision. In addition to the national anthem of Democratic Kampuchea, a variety of patriotic songs were played over the loudspeakers. One featured children's voices: "Because of Angkar, we have a long life ahead, / A life of great glory. / Before the revolution, children were poor and lived lives of misery. . . . Now the Glorious Revolution supports us all." After his siblings died, the song struck Radha as much worse than a cruel irony.

Radha hated one in particular that seemed to loop endlessly. The gist was this: The winter is so cold, but our hearts are warm because we are working hard to rebuild the country; we are happy because we are no longer under capitalist control. Radha especially hated that stupid song on chilly mornings when he stepped for the first time into the cold waters of the rice paddies. "My heart's not that warm," he'd grumble to himself.

He wasn't alone in mocking Angka quietly to himself. Even the Old People muttered their displeasure through satirical revisions of Angka's favorite slogans. "Before, we cultivated the fields with the heavens and the stars, and ate rice / Now we cultivate the fields with dams and canals, and eat gruel," went one takeoff on a Khmer Rouge saying. "Be masters of your own destiny! The dead must bury themselves!" said another. Also, "Since Angka has enlightened me, I have become more and more of an idiot" and "Angka has the many eyes of a pineapple, but none of them has an iris."[1]

One evening Radha was threshing with his work group, flipping rice stalks with a pitchfork for the tractor to drive over. As he worked, he heard the young soldier who was supervising the threshing improvise some words to the tune over the loudspeakers. Roughly translated, the soldier's new lyrics went something like this: "Living under Angka's leading is painful. Living with Angka's ration is painful. We are starving. It's like being in hell."

Apparently the soldier had simply had enough; something inside him snapped. Radha could hardly believe his ears. *I hear you, brother, and I agree, but are you serious?* Radha thought, keeping his eyes on his work. The soldier, who was sitting on the edge of the threshing area, got no more than a couple verses into his song before several *chhlops* gathered quietly behind him. Then one clobbered him on the back with a bamboo pole, and the rest joined in with fists and clubs. "You're a traitor to Angka!" they screamed. "You have betrayed Angka's trust!" They tied his elbows behind his back and hauled him off to the cadres. The next day he ended up buried on a termite hill.

People didn't have to believe Angka's lies for the revolution to continue. As long as they acted as if Angka really was all-knowing and infallible, as long as people lived the lie, totalitarianism continued.

153

But with a few mocking verses this soldier had shattered Angka's facade and exposed the system for what it was—a fabrication, a deceit perpetuated by thieves and destroyers. When he could no longer live within the lie, when he dared to act and speak according to reality, he showed that it is possible to do so. By saying what everyone was thinking, the soldier threatened Angka itself. So he had to die. "Truth is nowhere to be found," writes the prophet Isaiah, "and whoever shuns evil becomes a prey."[2]

In January 1977, Radha spent his days plowing rice fields and his evenings working on dikes. He had just turned twenty-four. Across Cambodia, the Khmer Rouge water systems were generally weak and ineffective, tending to either drown the rice crops with too much water or give way in the rainy season under the pressure of high water. Having executed almost everyone with any technical education, including their engineers, the Khmer Rouge had to figure out how to build dams, roads, and canals from scratch. But in Battambang province, the systems worked reasonably well, as far as Radha could see.

Failures were largely caused by the ignorance or stupidity of the Khmer Rouge supervisors. For example, one field had good soil that needed little or no fertilizer. The cooperative leaders, however, had a fertilizer crew as a punishment detail whose job was to empty the latrines, mix it with other waste, and spread it on the fields. Radha often saw these workers, under the glares of their supervisors, dip their finger into the feces and put it on their tongue—supposedly tasting it to make sure it wasn't too salty for the soil.

Apparently this test wasn't very effective. Some fields got far too much fertilizer, making the soil too rich and too deep. Radha often had to march behind his plow through knee-high feces-laced mud. The rice plants in those fields would have big stalks and small yields of rice. Radha heard that the farmers who had owned the fields before the revolution tried to point this out to the cooperative leaders and were executed for their candor. "Are you more educated than Angka?" they demanded, according to the story. "Angka gave you the plan and you didn't follow it, and now you tell Angka that it was wrong?"

In February, Radha went to a meeting for all the youth work leaders at Koh Kralor, about a half-day's walk south of Phnom Tippedei. He marched into the square in line to find perhaps a thousand other comrades from all over the region. Khmer Rouge music playing on the loudspeakers lauded the virtues of Angka and the glory of living in such a wonderful Communist society. He saw, for the first time, the Khmer Rouge party flag, red with a yellow sickle and hammer, flying higher than the national flag, which was also red with a yellow profile of the towers of the famous temple, Angkor Wat.

And then he saw his mother, who had walked all the way from Kok Porn in the hope of finding Radha. She seemed to him unbelievably thin. They hurried toward each other and, although they dared not hug or express much emotion, managed five minutes of hurried conversation. Amma had tragic news: Selvem had been beaten to death. His body had become swollen, and he couldn't work, but the leaders had said he was lazy. They just kept beating him until he died. Ravy had run away from Kok Porn to another village, but she believed he was still alive.

Indira had died of disease or starvation or both. Amma had slept with her daughter's dead body on the same mat for three or four nights. Simply burying Indira's remains would have been almost impossible for Amma in her weakened condition, but really she just found it impossible to let go. To bury Indira would have been to acknowledge that she was truly gone.

Radha was devastated. His mother was on her own, and he had one sibling left. But he could do nothing and had to return to his place at the assembly. He hurried back and sat down on ground covered with a powdery dust. He was cold.

Over loudspeakers, Khmer Rouge officials formally announced the Four Year Plan to the comrades in the northwest. From then on, the workers of Democratic Kampuchea would raise seven tons of rice per hectare per year! Their indomitable spirit would allow them to triumph over the rice fields. They must work harder to rebuild the country and so defeat through hard work and independence-mastery the capitalists and colonialists who sought to overturn the revolution. Then, in a festive gesture, the Khmer Rouge distributed to everybody a bowl of thin rice stew.

Radha hardly noticed the speeches and then walked back to the cooperative. The news wasn't exactly unexpected, but it was still hard to hear that his family of ten was now down to three—all the result of Khmer Rouge policy. He was being worked to death, and what did he get? Rice porridge—a spoonful of rice twice daily in warm salt water. Once per year the workers got a couple of oranges and maybe a tablespoon of palm sugar. The more he thought about it, the angrier he became. And then they made him sit through this ridiculous charade calling for seven tons of rice per hectare per year. The whole thing was . . . words failed him.

Also in February, Radha and some comrades spent a couple of weeks on a lumber-harvesting crew not far from Tuol Mateh. They worked in teams of three, cutting down and trimming three large trees per day. They sawed the trees down in the morning, before the rising sap made the saws sticky, and then whacked off the branches and sawed the logs into boards. One comrade stood on top and the other worked the saw from underneath. It was brutal work; some of the trees were five feet in diameter.

They hauled the logs through the rice fields using ropes twisted out of cowhide but started eating them when they discovered that the leather swelled up and became soft and chewy after being in the water all day. They told their supervisors that the ropes had broken.

The crew leaders quit believing them after a couple of weeks and gave them regular rope from then on.

Radha was sent back to Tuol Mateh in late February and put in charge of breaking buffalo to the plow—one pair per day. *They're still trying to kill me*, he thought when he got this assignment.

He quickly learned a few basic techniques. The animals could be herded into the enclosure and then caught, but they usually refused to let him put the guide ropes on their necks. So, first, he led them to a field with mud up to their knees. Sometimes they would charge him, but he learned how to jump out of the way at the last second and whack them with a pole on one horn as they passed. Apparently it stung, because they seldom charged more than two or three times. Then, if they refused the rope harness, he'd whack them again, and they'd settle down and submit. If they persisted and tried to run, well, they quickly tired of dragging a harrow behind them. After that, he'd hook them up to a plow, and they didn't object so much.

Radha was on buffalo-training duty for the rest of February and March. Then he was sent back to the rice fields in April. About then the Khmer Rouge leadership tried to train their local-level crew leaders in their version of the latest rice-growing techniques. Radha was among those assigned to sit through classes with Chinese officials who explained to them strategies for managing water levels and methods for harvesting. These strategies would supposedly allow them to bring in three rice crops per year, one every four months. Radha listened and nodded, but even a city boy like him knew it wouldn't work.

April 17, 1977, was the second anniversary of the Glorious Revolution. It was a holiday all over the country, so to celebrate the cadres held a propaganda meeting from 7:00 to 11:00 a.m. (instead of the late evening). At that time the Central Committee in Phnom Penh also sent down another directive to the cooperative leaders—Angka needed the workers to produce more loyal revolutionaries.

15

The Plan

[If the only] possible passion was revolutionary passion, match-making was the province of Angkar.

—Rithy Panh, *The Elimination*

In the spring of 1977 in the cuisine at Tuol Mateh, Radha ran into an acquaintance, a young woman named Phy. "Angka just married me to that old man," she said, pointing. "There he is." Radha looked. The guy was old, a peasant, and likely a loyal soldier of the revolution. He was very dark (an undesirable trait in Cambodian culture) and missing his front teeth. One leg was shorter than the other. Phy told him that the cooperative chiefs just went into the rice fields, picked him out, and matched them up. She had just come from the ceremony. Radha was appalled.

Similar pairings were going on all over the country. In the aftermath of the Four Year Plan, the Central Committee had realized that the Super Great Leap Forward required even more labor than the inferior New People, who were unable to work with true revolutionary enthusiasm, would be able to generate. Besides, they seemed to be dying like flies out in the cooperatives. So infallible Angka set up a series of mass weddings across the country, the fruit of which would be the next generation of the new socialist man.

In some cooperatives, males who were Old People could request permission to marry a particular woman or perhaps set up a match for a child, but Angka usually took care of marriages in Radha's villages. The Khmer Rouge themselves, of course, picked their own spouses.

Not long after Radha learned of Phy's marriage, the youth brigade leaders pulled him in from the rice fields for a chat. "Comrade," Noeun said, "we want you to get married."

Radha did not want to get married. Comrade Noeun had mentioned this to him some months earlier, and now the cadres were back with an order. He recalled from his days at church in Phnom Penh the words of 2 Corinthians 6:14, "Do not be yoked together with unbelievers." He objected mildly to the cadres, despite the risk. "He who protests is an enemy," went one of Angka's sayings, "and he who opposes is a corpse."[1]

"Comrades," Radha said, "I can barely walk. I am too weak. I cannot look after a wife."

The officials were unimpressed. They told Radha he was getting married whether he liked it or not.

Radha went back to the rice fields and complained bitterly to the Lord. He began to pray while plowing. *Lord, I don't want to get married. You let my father and my siblings die, and my mother is in desperate shape. I don't know whether Ravy is even alive. I have lost everything that mattered, and here I am stuck in a rice field waiting for Angka to marry me off to some girl from the Old People.*

He felt that God owed him a break. The more he thought about it, plodding along behind the buffalo through the rice paddy, the angrier he became. Finally he said, "Lord, if you make me do this, I'm not going to be a Christian anymore. I'm through."

In late June, the village of Tuol Mateh, perhaps two thousand people at that time, gathered around the communal dining hall for

159

the wedding ceremony. Radha was one of seven young men lined up to walk into the hall beside a row of young women. Somberly, they filed into the cuisine, turned, and faced their new spouses. But when the girl opposite Radha saw him, she let out a shriek and dashed from the hall. "I don't want that one!" she wailed on the way out.

Radha was relieved, although perhaps also a bit slighted. He stood there awkwardly while the cadres conferred among themselves and then sent him back into the crowd. The wedding continued without him.

There was another ceremony in July. Again, the young woman opposite Radha flatly refused the match. "He's too dark!" she exclaimed. "Give me another guy!"

If Radha or any other New Person had defied a direct order, he would have been summarily executed. But these two women were Old People, still officially loyal. The cadres conferred again and then ordered Radha out of line.

In late July, Angka arranged yet more weddings. Radha found himself opposite an attractive young woman with very light skin, probably a city girl from Phnom Penh or perhaps Battambang. Her name was Vy. *Oh, thank you, Lord*, he thought to himself.

But at the last minute, the head female cadre stepped forward to object. "No," she said, "Vy must marry this other man." She pulled Vy out of line and gave her to the ugliest, darkest Khmer Rouge farmer they had available, probably as his reward for loyal military service.

The officials had one more ceremony lined up that year in August and another girl in mind for Radha. She was from Phnom Penh, and Radha thought she would be a good match. But on the day of the wedding, no one could find her. Later Radha learned that she had fled the village the night before, right after hearing he was to be her husband. Apparently the Lord was answering his prayers after all, at the expense of his ego.

Radha continued with life as Angka's plowman. The rainy season ended in late summer, bringing the next cycle of planting and harvest. Radha lost himself in the routine—up early, work all day on almost no food, sit through a propaganda meeting, and then try to catch some sleep. He hardly ever dreamed in those days; he just sank into oblivion until being roused by the inexorable "bong, bong" of the wake-up gong.

He did have one bright spot. In late 1977, he asked for and received permission for Amma to move from Phnom Tmey, the village where she'd been sent, to Tuol Mateh. Ravy had left Kok Porn months earlier and neither of them knew where he had ended up or even if he was still alive.

Then in January 1978, Radha heard that Ravy was in the area, having managed to join a work crew. So Radha arranged to "lose" his buffalo and got permission to go look for it where he thought Ravy's crew was working. Radha didn't find his brother, but he left a message with a couple the Manickams knew from Kok Porn. "If you see Ravy," he said, "tell him I'm at Tuol Mateh."

That month Noeun again called Radha in from the fields. "Comrade," the cadre said, "we want you to get married." Another mass wedding ceremony was planned for April 18, the day after the third anniversary of the revolution. "And if you don't get married this time," Noeun added, "we're going to give you your own plot of ground—three feet by six."

He was to marry a girl named "Men," pronounced "Main." Radha later found out that her name was Samen, but in Khmer Rouge fashion, it had been shortened to one syllable. Radha had seen her around but never spoken to her. All he knew was that she seemed quiet.

Radha went back to his place in the field and began to pray; only this time he was praying desperately that the girl would be there and the marriage would happen. He no longer cared how weak he was or whether he would be "unequally yoked." In Democratic Kampuchea, everybody was equally yoked—to Angka.

161

Lord, he prayed, *keep her here. My life depends on it.*

But at times during those weeks before the wedding Radha didn't care much if he lived or died. It was during this period that he almost committed suicide atop the termite hill by singing "This World Is Not My Home" in English, deterred at the last second by the promise of a "plan."

About a month later while plowing, Radha saw a boy walking across the fields toward him. Radha paused as the child approached. When he got close, they stood looking at each other for a few seconds, and Radha could see the tears in the boy's eyes. It was Ravy. He jumped at Radha and grabbed him around the back of the neck in a tight embrace.

"I was looking for you," Radha said.

"I heard you were getting married," Ravy said. "That's why I came."

Ravy had given up hope of ever seeing his brother and mother again. He'd been working on a youth brigade in a different part of the province, building canals and planting rice. Only once had he nearly been killed; he was standing guard while some younger comrades secretly cooked and ate some rice, but the soldiers let him off with just a day without food. He never saw his comrades again.

Radha talked with Noeun and Leap, and they checked with Von, who agreed to let Ravy stay in Tuol Mateh with Radha's plowing unit. Ravy decided that God must have had a plan for him to find his family.

About two months later, on April 17, Radha came to a meeting with all the young men and women set to marry the next day. One of his water buffalo had escaped the day before, and he found the beast and made it back to the meeting just in time. If he had lost the buffalo, he likely would have been executed.

At the meeting, cadres delivered the usual message: be faithful to Angka, do not betray Angka, always be committed to Angka. *This is the Khmer Rouge version of premarital counseling*, Radha thought.

On the morning of April 18, 1978, Radha and eighteen other young men filed into the large dining hall and lined up across from nineteen young women. The women did not have intricately patterned gowns, jewelry, or makeup. Instead, they had Angka-approved hair and wore the gray pajama uniforms of the Khmer Rouge, while the men wore blue pajamas from North Korea. Officials had selected and matched the young people, with the plan for the couples to become the nucleus of a new model village called Tuol Samnal about a mile away from Tuol Mateh. Most kept their eyes on the floor. Samen simply went through the motions of the ceremony, as did Radha. She was New People too.

All of Tuol Mateh was present to watch. A cadre got up and exhorted the couples for more than an hour to "join together to build a glorious new Cambodia" under Angka's infallible guidance. "Angka needs you to produce more children," he said, "and you must help the Khmer people achieve victory!" The newlyweds, coupled off, all came up to the front of the hall and individually pledged to their fellow villagers and to Angka that they would teach their children to honor the courageous Khmer Rouge revolutionary fighters and raise at least seven tons of rice per hectare per year. Those were their wedding vows. Each person took five or ten minutes, trying to fake as much revolutionary enthusiasm as possible.

No dancing, singing, or feasting followed the ceremony. Village leaders gave Radha a red and white krama, but he hated it because it was the color of the Khmer Rouge. Samen agreed to swap it for her blue krama. Radha, Samen, and the other couples went out through the rice fields to Tuol Samnal, where most of the huts had been built over the previous few weeks. He was twenty-five, and she was twenty-three. They had one small backpack each. It was a quiet walk.

The cadres had chosen Radha and Samen to be the leaders of Tuol Samnal. He was in charge of a ten-man group plowing rice fields;

she was in charge of ten families and responsible for planting rice in the plowed fields. They dropped their belongings—a mat and a couple of pillows—in their tiny hut. It was just big enough for two people to lie down with a bit of space at the foot of the mats. The huts were on stilts made from the branches of nho trees; when shoved into the ground, the poles would take root after a few months and start growing twigs that would need to be trimmed occasionally.

Part of Radha's job as unit leader was to spy on the other new couples. Late in the evening, a cadre would meet him on the outskirts of the village, and they would prowl quietly underneath the huts. They were supposed to listen to what the couples talked about for indications of counterrevolutionary leanings, for the sound of cooking or eating unauthorized food, and also for evidence that the couples were doing their best to produce the children Angka expected.

The idea of listening in on another couple's intimate marital relations disgusted Radha, and he didn't want to catch anybody at anything. He wanted to protect them, not get them arrested. Whenever the chance arose, he would hurry on ahead of the cadre and whisper up through the thatch walls, "Hey—be careful! We're coming. Whatever you're cooking, put it away!"

Radha and Samen themselves were not exactly close. They were living as a married couple—it would have been dangerous to do otherwise, because he certainly was not the only spy around—but they seldom spoke, and never about anything personal.

One morning, after about a month in the new village, Radha fell ill. He could barely walk and had serious diarrhea. He felt exhausted and dehydrated and wondered if his malaria was coming back. Samen had already gone out to work. He staggered out of his hut to find his supervisor and asked for the day off. The cadre reminded him of the rules—no work today, no food tonight. "Yes, comrade," Radha said. He doubted he could keep anything down anyway. He went back to his hut, lay down, and fell asleep.

Samen unexpectedly came home at noon. She went to her corner, picked up a few small rice-dust cakes wrapped in a scarf that her sister had given her recently, and brought them over to his mat, her eyes looking down. He was desperately hungry—and desperately weak. "Thank the Lord," he whispered under his breath.

Samen looked up sharply. "Are you a Christian?" she exclaimed.

Radha started to shake, panic rising in his chest. Angka had forbidden all religion, and Samen would surely turn him in.

Then he heard a quiet voice, the one he had heard weeks earlier, say, "Tell her."

So he did. He asked Samen to sit down, and he urgently confessed in whispers because spies were everywhere, that yes, he was a Christian. He begged her not to give him away. "Please, please do not tell anyone!" he said.

Then he looked into her eyes, really for the first time. They were wet, and tears rolled down her cheeks. She leaned close. "That's OK," she whispered. "I am too."

Radha looked at Samen, and right then it hit him like a water buffalo: *that's the plan.* Radha suddenly felt light, and somehow Angka didn't seem quite so ever-present anymore.

They went outside the hut to see if any spies might be passing by, and when the coast was clear, they began to really talk to each other for the first time. Samen's full name was Nget Samen, and her father was Nget Choy, a Cambodian pastor with the Christian and Missionary Alliance. Her grandfather had been one of the first Cambodians to accept Christ through Western Protestant missionaries back in the 1920s. The family had been one of the most prominent in Christian circles in Phnom Penh and Kampong Cham province.

Radha and Samen also prayed together that someday God would open a door and allow them to see the other side of the world.

16

The Other Plans

He will rescue them from oppression and violence, for precious
is their blood in his sight.

—Psalm 72:14

Radha heard more of the details of Samen's story over the
next several months. She was the sixth of nine children born
to Nget Choy, pastor of the Khmer Evangelical Church in
Phnom Penh. Pastor Choy was very strict—the children weren't
allowed to listen to secular music or watch secular movies, and
they were always at church. He was also very generous and took in
many nieces and nephews who had come to Phnom Penh from the
countryside for university or work.

Nget had not always been so proper. His father, Nget Try, a devout
Buddhist, had been a Chinese immigrant to Cambodia in the early
1900s. He and his wife became Christians in 1923 after hearing the
gospel from a missionary whose car broke down outside his house
in the Mekong Delta near the Vietnamese border. The Nget family
was among the first generation of Christians in Cambodia; several
family members became evangelists and pastors.

Nget Choy, the youngest of six children, did not take easily to his family's faith. His children later told stories of a man who was smart (he spoke several languages) and charitable but, before he became a Christian, possessed a violent temper. When Nget was a young man, the head of a martial arts school refused to take him as a pupil. According to the story, the instructor told him he was the kind of person who, after he learned how to fight, would kill his own teacher. This so enraged Nget that he taught himself the skills by peeking through holes in the school's wall and then practicing the moves in a nearby forest. Nget even said he thought about murdering the teacher in his sleep with a long knife but never went through with it.

When Choy was in his early twenties, his father asked him to study the Bible. He didn't want to, but he had to obey. He studied with some missionaries and, one day, prayed that God would make Himself real to him. That night, he later told family members, he had an experience very similar to the calling of the prophet Samuel. He was awakened three times by a voice calling, "Choy! Choy!" After the first two, he ran to his Bible teacher's hut, but the third time he said, "Lord God, I'm Your servant. Please speak to me."

A bright light filled the room, and God promised Nget that he would serve God the rest of his life and that God would bless him because of it. "You and your generations to come," God told Nget. Nget got up off his mat, rushed over to the light, and tried to hug God. Instead, he ran into the wall and bruised his fingers.

Nget and his wife, Eng Say Heang, later settled in Phnom Penh. He went on to become the first Cambodian staffer for the International Bible Society and worked as an editor on the first Khmer Bible. He was also a professor and administrator at Takmoa Bible School, a ministry of the Christian and Missionary Alliance, and pastored the denomination's church in Phnom Penh. As members of a tiny Christian minority, they faced some persecution at times, but their ties to a foreign mission agency gave them a certain status among believers, along with a bit of financial stability.

The first of nine children, Sameth, a daughter, was born in 1947, and the others arrived over the next two decades: brothers Chan SaKhun and Sichan, sister Samoeun, brother Saman, sisters Samen and Samith, and brothers Sidore and Credy.

When the Khmer Rouge rolled into Phnom Penh in April 1975, seven of the nine Nget children managed to evacuate with their parents. Sameth was married and living in western Cambodia—her parents had no idea what happened to her family. Chan SaKhun, a soldier in the Republican Army, had recently returned to Cambodia from Texas, where his unit had been training with American troops. He and his wife were living in Phnom Penh, but the evacuation happened so fast that they lost touch, and the Nget family never saw them again. They heard later that Chan SaKhun had tried to escape from his village and been caught and killed.

When the Nget family heard that the Khmer Rouge were ordering everybody out of the city, Say Heang told the family to go pack. Samen collected some of her nice clothes, including her favorite yellow and green silk blouse. Her mother told her to get rid of it and go pack old clothes, work clothes, because she would be working in rice fields.

The Nget party consisted of thirteen people: Choy and Say Heang and their seven children still with them, ranging in age from twenty-six to six, plus Samoeun's husband, Taing Vek Huong, and their two-month-old child, Wiphousana, along with Grandfather Try and his youngest son Sreng, who was Choy's half brother. They stuffed all their belongings and Grandfather into a small car and walked out of the city, with the siblings pushing the car.

The first village they were assigned to, Pey, was in Takeo province just south of Phnom Penh. Samen and some of her siblings were conscripted for work crews that would go out to dig and plant for a few weeks at a time, come home for a few days, and then return to the fields.

All the women had their hair cut short in the approved style. Samen hated the look but could hardly protest. She thought it was because the Communists wanted people to spend all their time digging, not fixing their hair. Khmer Rouge soldiers and cadres occasionally flirted with Samen and her sisters, but the girls weren't interested.

One night Grandfather, who usually needed help to get outside to relieve himself, left the hut on his own and passed away. They found him outside the next morning.

At the end of June 1975, the Nget family was part of the massive transfer of New People from the southern part of Cambodia to Battambang in the northwest to raise rice. The Ngets, like the Manickams, endured several hours on a packed truck to reach the rail crossing in Pursat province. There they boarded a train and were then dumped off at Oxcart Road. They also were given three days to build shelters before the real work began. The name of their new village was Sophy. As soon as the family was by themselves, Choy and Say Heang began praying fervently. As city people, they had no idea what to do next.

They spent the first night huddled on a termite hill but within a day found sympathetic Old People who, in exchange for clothes, showed them how to weave leaves into thatch for roofs and walls, sink posts, and build beds to get themselves off the rain-soaked ground.

Nget Choy was appointed as a group leader. One of his responsibilities was to ensure that his group sent enough workers out to the crews to meet its quota. The other families argued with him and refused to send their children, although they would have never dared to oppose Old People. So Choy sent his own children in their place.

The Nget siblings resented this, but Samen soon realized that she got more rice on the work crews than her family members were receiving in Sophy. She often managed to save some food to bring back to her family. When she was home, she saw how many people were already dying of starvation and how desperate families were ill from eating anything they could chew.

Shortly after the family arrived in Sophy, Samen's brother Saman and Uncle Sreng tried to escape to Thailand. One morning the family woke up and they were gone. Samen heard nothing of what happened

169

to them until years later. They had been caught and sent to a jail in nearby Battambang, where Sreng was soon executed. Saman likely would have suffered the same fate, except he was mistaken for a relative of a Khmer Rouge official. He was released and sent to build dikes, and after that he worked on a unit that turned human waste into fertilizer until the Khmer Rouge fell.

Later that fall, the Taings (Samoeun and her husband and child) disappeared. Perhaps the cadres had hauled them away, but the family suspected instead that they had made a run for the Thai border, so they kept quiet. The Khmer Rouge wouldn't know if a given family was missing a few members.

In Sophy, Samen's mother planted some cucumbers and squash (the Khmer Rouge were not yet cracking down on people who grew their own food), but before they ripened the Ngets were sent to a new village not far away called Khlengchour.

At Khlengchour in early 1976, Nget Choy died. He had grown steadily weaker with hunger and malaria and likely other diseases as well. On his last day, all his remaining children gathered around his mat, and he called them each by name. Then he raised his hands and said, "I'm happy." "Do you see God?" his wife asked anxiously, but he just kept repeating, "I'm happy."

Suddenly, in a moment of clarity, he moaned and said, "I should not die on the ground like this!" before passing away. The family was devastated. Samen's mother slept with the corpse for three nights. People had done much worse things with deceased relatives. According to one rumor, a woman was executed because she started to eat her husband's corpse.

After Nget Choy died, the family couldn't find anyone willing to carry his body out into the field and bury it. They offered his clothes as payment, but the comrades all insisted on rice, so the family had even shorter rations than usual for a few days.

Old People mourned openly when a loved one died; they wept and wailed and vented their grief. New People were denied that luxury;

it displayed a loyalty outside Angka and that was not permitted. So at the grave the Ngets shed a few quiet tears and felt the sorrow building up inside them.

Within a month, Samen's mother and brother Sichan also died. Malaria, dysentery, tuberculosis, and meningitis were likely raging through the village, but it seemed to Samen that her mother really died of a broken heart. Now the Nget family was down to four: Samen, twenty-two; Samith, twenty; and two younger brothers, Sidore and Credy, who were about sixteen and nine. Samen didn't just miss her parents and other siblings; she longed to pray with them, to gain strength and courage from their encouragement and support. They had brought her hope even in the darkest days, and now they were gone. Samen wondered whether she was the oldest living member of her family.

She was not. Two of Samen's older sisters were still alive and would soon make it to the United States. She also eventually would be reunited with her older brother Saman. But before then, Samen would face many trials and much more grief.

The oldest Nget child, Sameth, had been living in the city of Pailin, on Cambodia's western edge, with her husband, Savin, when the Khmer Rouge took over. The couple had six children, including a six-week-old infant, and had narrowly escaped being separated on the first day of the Khmer Rouge regime.

They too were forced into the countryside to build huts and dig canals. Their children were soon sick and starving from eating green bananas and ground-up banana stalk. "There's no future here," Savin told Sameth. "If we stay here, we're all going to die."

In December 1975, after months of prayer and near despair, Savin got permission from the village leader to go visit a brother in Battambang. He left with his Seiko sport watch and a diamond ring and headed north and a little west, planning to pass through the mountains to the Thai border.

He found a way out and made it across Cambodia's northwestern border into Thailand after a seven-day hike, dodging Khmer Rouge patrols and living on wild potatoes and the bit of rice he brought.

He found himself in a refugee camp. The Thais were unwelcoming to the Cambodians trickling across their border, all bearing tales of horrible deprivation under the Khmer Rouge, but they allowed international aid agencies to provide for basic needs and medical care.

Savin needed that care; he arrived with a bad case of malaria and ended up in bed for weeks. He'd told Sameth to expect him home in a month, so when that day passed Sameth figured her husband was probably dead. Cadres often intimidated villagers with stories about how many fugitives fleeing Angka's wisdom they had caught and executed.

Finally, Savin recovered somewhat. He left his bed and sneaked out of the camp to nearby Thai villages, where he could find what he wanted in a thriving black market. His watch and ring he bartered for about ten pounds of dry rice, two pounds of shrimp, five pounds of sugar, tennis shoes for everybody, sleeping pills for the baby (an infant crying at just the wrong moment could cost them all their lives), and just in case, one rifle and two grenades. Loaded down with his supplies, he made his way back through the mountains and forests and sneaked into his family's hut. As far as his village leader knew, he had gone off to Battambang and never come back.

Sameth and Savin planned to leave with another family, but somehow word got around and thirty-six people, mostly women and children, showed up when they met just outside the village shortly after sundown. Savin was scared; such a large group would surely be caught and probably executed. They left anyway. They traveled at night, hiding from Khmer Rouge soldiers, sneaking through tall grass, and hacking through heavy bush. They often heard shots and slipped past Khmer Rouge camps close enough to hear Angka's music.

After five days, they ran out of food. Water was always scarce; once they drank water that had collected in an elephant's footprints. On the seventh day, they came across an abandoned sugar cane farm; the fiber was sweet but hard to chew and made their mouths terribly sore. Once they stole papaya from an untended Khmer Rouge camp.

On the eighth day, they got to the border, which was marked by a creek. Savin hid in the woods for hours, watching patrols go by, and figured they had a thirty-minute window to cross the waist-deep waters. They made it—all thirty-six.

Thai officials at first refused to register them as refugees because they didn't believe such a large party of mostly women and children made it that far on their own. They said that just a day or so earlier, two Cambodian men had arrived after setting out with a party of twelve; the other ten had been killed on the way.

Finally, they were allowed into the camp and registered as refugees—the first step in immigrating to a safe country. Savin applied to come to the United States. He had worked at the US embassy from 1960 to 1963, which made him eligible for a visa, but of course he couldn't prove it. They were stuck.

Then Savin met a missionary who knew the American embassy chief back in Georgia. After a series of letters and applications and processes, Savin, Sameth, and their six children landed in New York on July 14, 1976.

As the Nget family had suspected, Samoeun and her husband, Vek Huong, and their son, Wiphousana, had sneaked out of the village with a friend in an attempt to reach Battambang on October 15, 1975. The three of them spent the next three years at different villages in the northwest. Despite the danger, on a few occasions Samoeun and Vek Huong, who had been staff members with Campus Crusade for Christ, witnessed to fellow villagers—usually those going through loss or deep anguish—about Christ. Vek Huong even admitted to Khmer Rouge officials that he was educated, had worked for an American organization, and had a brother in the Khmer Republic's army who had become a Christian evangelist. He was often under suspicion, but remarkably, Angka never got around to killing him and Samoeun.

They, like every other Cambodian, suffered serious deprivation but managed to stay reasonably healthy, considering the circumstances, for the next few years. Vek Huong secretly fished in the rice paddies, and in one village, the leader selected Vek Huong to harvest coconuts for his personal supply. He learned to easily shinny up the trees, and his reward was a coconut or two each day, which he and his family either ate or traded for other food.

———— ·◆· ————

Samen knew none of this. She just knew that Khlengchour's leaders kept sending her out to work in the fields, and she kept going because refusing would mean death. She was angry, but at the Khmer Rouge more than at God. She didn't think much about God in those years; she felt like she had left Him behind.

And then one day in early 1976—perhaps February, but it was hard to be sure because the days ran together—her group leader brought her an offer. She had caught the eye of one of the cadres in Khlengchour. He wanted her to know that he had much food available, and he could take good care of her. He wanted to marry her.

Samen remained calm while listening to this marriage proposal by proxy. "Which one is he?" she asked. Three or four bosses were always walking around, and she wasn't sure who was who. Her group leader couldn't describe him well enough to clear it up. Samen, however, wasn't interested and politely declined the offer.

Refusing that offer took ferocious courage or deep despair, or perhaps some of both. Samen more than half expected to be dragged off and executed, but a few days later she and her sister Samith were assigned to a large party that was sent to a different village called Chromouk. Samen arranged for a family to look after her younger brothers Sidore and Credy and left with the group.

Samen was relieved. She wondered at first how she escaped so easily, but realized later that her suitor might not have known of her refusal. Perhaps her group leader did not deliver her response, or perhaps she told the official Samen was thinking it over. Had she stayed in Khlengchour, she would have had to marry the cadre. *Perhaps*, she thought, *God is protecting me after all.*

Chromouk brought its own set of problems. It was so short of food that the Khmer Rouge told people that Angka required them to go out and forage for wild vegetables in the forests. Worse, after only about a week she heard from someone who lived in Khlengchour that the family looking after Sidore and Credy had left for another village, taking the boys with them. She had no way to track them down. Her family of thirteen was now down to her and Samith.

A few months later, perhaps in June 1977, Angka ordered that Chromouk merge with Tuol Mateh. The two sisters trudged over with everybody else and found a couple of spots in one of the long huts. She got to know a kindly older woman in her group, Heang, and began to regard her as a godmother.

In Tuol Mateh, Samen became ill for a long period—that is, even more ill than was normal under the Khmer Rouge. When Angka started arranging marriages to build up the revolutionary strength of the people, her group leader kept her out of the lineup. She was too weak and sick. *Thank God*, Samen thought.

Then in early 1978, Samen was eating her thin rice porridge in the cuisine when her group leader instructed her to come to her quarters after the meal for a chat. Samen was scared. The leader sat her down and said, "Comrade Men, we want you to get married. His name is Comrade Dha."

Samen knew who Comrade Dha was and protested that she was too weak and sick to marry, but her group leader insisted. So Samen asked for a few days to think it over. She prayed about it, privately, and went to Heang, who she discovered later had been talking to Radha's mother, Ve Meenachi.

175

"You should do it," her godmother told her. "It's time. You need someone, and you can look after each other when you're sick."

"Look after each other with what?" Samen asked. "All we have is our spoons."

She agreed to the marriage but was scared. She also was resentful about having to marry an unbeliever and sad that of her whole family, only Samith was there for the ceremony. She said the vows, promising to raise the rice and the revolutionary offspring, all the while thinking that nobody could do that. It was ridiculous.

A month later when she learned that Radha was also a Christian, she was very, very relieved.

17

Equally Yoked

The man said, "This is now bone of my bones and flesh of my flesh; she shall be called 'woman,' for she was taken out of man."

—Genesis 2:23

In Tuol Samnal, where Samen was in charge of the women and Radha managed the plowmen, the comrades worked nine days straight with the tenth supposedly a day off. The cooperative leaders, however, always turned it into a day of propaganda meetings and planning sessions followed by some dismal chore, such as hunting the rats that ate enormous amounts of grain. The workers would find the two holes of a nest, close up one, drown the rats out the other, and then club to death those that showed their little snouts. The comrades were supposed to report how many rats they killed and turn them in to the kitchens, but instead they cooked and ate them out in the field.

Radha couldn't stand the rodents and never actually killed one. When his plow would burst through a nest in the fields, he would yell and jump back as they scurried past his bare feet. In such moments, Radha was perhaps more scared of the rats than of the Khmer Rouge.

Samen would playfully tell him that the others teased her for marrying "the comrade who is afraid of rats." She, however, was a pretty good rat hunter. She liked the change from the backbreaking work of tending to the rice fields. She was also adept at killing poisonous snakes, which were common.

Given the pitiful rations and overwork, Samen and Radha were thankful to be alive. And they had family around. Ravy lived in the youth camp section of Tuol Mateh, Amma in the adult quarters, and Samen's sister Samith with the youth.

Radha and Samen got along pretty well with the people they supervised, particularly a man named Bich and his wife. Radha sometimes would play with their son. Bich was a hard worker and funny. He was also quite short with very fast hands and knew how to snatch fish out of the canals, which he often shared with Radha and Samen.

As Radha got to know his crew better he realized, despite their best efforts to hide it, that some of them were educated and several had come from Phnom Penh. Radha also discovered that people can work harder and longer with a bit of time to rest during the day. His crew seemed to appreciate the rest, and Radha, for the most part, kept his bosses happy.

Most important, Radha and Samen had each other. Their love was planted in the rice paddies, so to speak, and although it took a long time to blossom, it continued to grow. In a totalitarian state, it's not safe to trust anybody—not friends, parents, children, or even spouses. Anyone might turn you in, not because of a lack of affection or even love, but in a panic to save their own lives. Revealing an intimate truth to another person during the Khmer Rouge rule meant putting your life into someone else's hands.

But over time, Samen became his confidant, and he became hers. He told her all about his education, his family's former wealth, his faith in Christ, his support of Lon Nol. She told him all about her family's history of ministry: that her grandfather had been one of

Cambodia's first Christians, that her father and uncle were both prominent pastors, and that her cousin had been a major in the Republican Army and a Christian evangelist.

They prayed together, furtively, and often talked about one day leaving Cambodia. Privately he called her *Oan*, which is literally "little sister" but might be translated something like "sweetie," and she called him *Bong*, which is "older brother" but in the context of a marriage is the normal term of affection. They talked and dreamed, dreamed and talked. It kept them going.

In the eyes of someone from the West, their marriage would not have seemed very affectionate. In traditional Cambodian culture, relationships between husbands and wives are reserved and proper. No touching in public. Some Cambodians of Radha's generation might have held hands and perhaps even hugged, but Radha and Samen had not grown up in those kinds of homes. And the Khmer Rouge continued to enforce this reserve, although for different reasons. For a comrade with true revolutionary consciousness, family ties are a weakness, not a strength.

Knowing these things about Samen made Radha trust her more and feel protective of her. So when one day Samen told him that he had yelled at her in the hospital, Radha was taken aback. Near the end of 1977 and some months before they were married, she had come to the hospital near Tuol Mateh with horrible pain and cramps, probably a combination of illness and starvation. She had been moaning and screaming when across the hall some jerk hollered at her to shut up and go to sleep! It was Radha, who had been in the hospital because he'd been coughing up blood. He had had no idea who was screaming, just that it was a skinny guy with short hair who'd been brought into the room across the hall. Radha didn't quite know what to say.

When Radha was single and found food in the fields, he cooked and ate it in the fields, but now he always brought it home to share with Samen. She did the same. While standing on a dike one evening,

Radha turned around and saw a massive frog, weighing at least a pound, sitting on the dike about ten yards away, right next to the water. He was so hungry he ached, but he knew he could never catch it. So he prayed, *Lord, I really, really want that sucker*, closed his eyes, and flung the stick he used for guiding water buffalo at the frog as hard as he could. When he opened his eyes, he saw that the stick had punctured the frog. He scrambled over and scooped it up, covered it with his shirt, and then brought it back to his hut where he quietly cooked the legs in the fire pit and brought the meat in to Samen. It was delicious.

Another time, while coming home from a meeting of community leaders on a dark night, he cut through the back garden of an elderly couple—Old People and ex-fighters for the Khmer Rouge. They had earned the enmity of all the comrades because the only work they ever did was tending their own vegetable patch, keeping all the produce for themselves. Radha absentmindedly kicked at a plant on his way through, and then his face fell when he realized he had booted a pumpkin off its vine. He grabbed the gourd and ran home, terrified that someone had seen him.

He and Samen knew they had to get rid of it as soon as possible. It was a terrible risk, even in the dark, but they cut up the pumpkin, slipped outside to the fire pit, and baked the pieces in the coals. They were sticky and sweet. Something about eating together brings people together, especially when eating together is a matter of life and death.

Meanwhile, Radha had been getting to know Von, the chief official for the area around Tuol Mateh, a little better. Von rode all around the fields near Tuol Mateh on his horse, checking on this and that, and he seemed to trust Radha's advice and suggestions. Von also ordered the kitchen staff, who usually had evenings off, to work after dinner just like the field crews. The kitchen workers resented this. Von even arranged for the cooks to prepare food in the evenings so the field workers could get a bit of rice when they returned in the evening.

Once a large centipede bit Radha on the little toe of his right foot as he walked across a dike; insect and scorpion bites were common. Radha moaned all night and could barely walk in the morning, but he prepared to go out to work as usual. Von heard about it and came to Radha's hut. That itself was a breach of etiquette, because Von was head of the cooperative; Radha's supervisor was responsible for handling such matters. Von told him to stay home that day—and because it was on Von's orders, Radha still got to eat.

One day that summer at a meeting for all the workers, the bosses warned everybody not to let the oxen and water buffalo get loose to graze and trample the rice fields. The comrades had been getting sloppy about this during their nap and dinner breaks. Anyone who allowed this to happen would be crushed! It was the usual promise.

The day after the warning, as Radha was taking his buffalo to his field, he saw Von atop his horse on a dike. He waved Radha over. "Would you like to follow me?" he asked pleasantly and took Radha across a canal to a field near the edge of the cooperative. All the young rice stems, freshly planted, had been trampled and grazed down to the roots. The wrecked field and the incriminating buffalo tracks were in plain view of the cuisine. "Do you see this?" Von asked. Radha could barely choke out an answer. "Yes, comrade," he said.

Plowmen were supposed to sleep in the fields with their animals to avoid making the beasts walk back and forth. But every evening Radha had been letting four or five of his plowmen take turns sneaking the half mile or so from their campsite back to Tuol Mateh or Tuol Samnal to spend the night with their wives and children. Radha assumed that if they got back before the workday started at daybreak, no one would be the wiser. Their comrades could keep an eye on their animals while they were gone, but some of them had apparently slept through the debacle.

181

"Your animals did this!" Von barked. "Do you recall the meeting yesterday? I don't know whose animals these were, but they were from your camp. I don't know what you told your men, and I don't care anymore." At this point Radha was plainly terrified, quaking and praying silently. Von got off his horse and stepped over to Radha. "Comrade Dha," he said, "I don't know what you're going to do, but just make sure that those hectares grow rice." Radha said he would do everything possible. Von squinted at him and then got back on his horse and rode away. *Thank you, Lord, for saving me again*, Radha prayed.

Radha hurried back to his crew, called a meeting, and began to yell at them. "Whose buffalo were those?" he demanded. "Who was supposed to be watching them? I almost lost my life over this!"

Nobody said anything. They just looked back at him with expressionless faces. Gratitude for overnight trips home only went so far. Finally, Radha took a deep breath. He had learned in the rice-growing classes he had attended taught by Chinese officials that it was possible to save trampled crops because the roots were still in the ground. He gathered three volunteers and had them replow the field and break up the ground by hand; some weeks later the rice plants came up, as thick as usual, and the land produced a good crop.

But even before that crop ripened, as Radha was plowing one day, Von came up on horseback. "Do you want to die or something?" he demanded. Radha did not. "Why do you keep allowing your people to do this?" Von snapped. He had been out riding and spotted another trampled field. Radha apologized profusely. "I am so sorry, Comrade Older Brother," he said. "My workers do not intend to do this. We really do want to rebuild the country. We all want more food for our people." Von just rode away. It was another close call.

18

Inevitably, Angka

Torture is inevitable. The question is, a little or a great deal?

—Khmer Rouge interrogation manual for the
prison Tuol Sleng, quoted in the documentary
S-21: Khmer Rouge Killing Machine

Life under Von was too good, so to speak, to last. Von was fierce by any reasonable human standard, but compared to most of the other cooperative heads he was a complete pushover. His days were numbered—even without the purges that Pol Pot sent raging through the ranks of his own cadres in 1978. Sure enough, one day Von disappeared. His wife and son somehow avoided arrest.

The purges were related to the fact that in 1977 and 1978 Pol Pot became increasingly provocative with Vietnam, his much stronger neighbor to the east. Khmer Rouge units raided Vietnamese villages across the border where they massacred the residents, sometimes disemboweling them, and burned the huts to the ground. Pol Pot cut diplomatic relations with Vietnam on December 31, 1977. In early 1978, he promised to stir up hatred for the "contemptible Vietnamese" and make them "shriek like monkeys screeching all over the forest."[1] He regarded a war with Vietnam as necessary to recover lost territory and restore the Khmer empire to its former glory. His "victory" over the imperialist Americans in 1975 encouraged the belief that his forces could defeat the much larger, battle-hardened, and better-equipped Vietnamese military. He was oblivious to the fact that the American retreat from Indochina had far more to do with American domestic politics than Angka's farsighted leadership.

At one point Pol Pot declared, "We absolutely must implement the slogan of one against thirty." He had decided that one Khmer soldier should be able to kill thirty Vietnamese before dying in battle and so, estimating conservatively, "We need only 2 million troops to crush the 50 million Vietnamese, and we would still have six million people left."[2] It was a brilliant piece of arithmetic.

It was also delusional, but not in the usual sense of the word. Such ideas flowed out of an ideology that held Angka as infallible and "revolutionary consciousness" to be the most important factor in any human context. One Marxist fan gushed in a Socialist periodical ironically called *Alive* that Pol Pot's genius was his creative ability to transform "existential reality into historical projects" through materialist dialectics.[3] George Orwell more accurately explained in the words of Big Brother that, for the true Communist revolutionary, reality is not something objective and external. Rather, reality exists only in the human mind and "not in the individual mind, which can make mistakes, and in any case soon perishes: only in the mind of the Party, which is collective and immortal. Whatever the Party holds to be the truth, is truth. It is impossible to see reality except by looking through the eyes of the Party."[4]

The Vietnamese evacuated their border regions and retaliated with some cross-border attacks but refrained, for the time being, from launching a full-scale invasion. The Vietnamese weren't prepared to let the Khmer Rouge rampage through their territory, but they preferred to avoid outright war. The Vietnamese understood that Cambodia was rapidly disintegrating, yet they didn't want anarchy in their western neighbor; they wanted a buffer state between themselves and Thailand. Vietnam, which had its own internal tensions, also did not want to draw international condemnation for invading a neighbor. After the 1975 victory of Communist North Vietnam, hundreds of thousands of Vietnamese fled the country by sea, becoming known internationally as the "boat people."

The Vietnamese also worried that an attack on Cambodia would draw retaliation from China. The Chinese had provided much support for the Khmer Rouge, including aid, weapons, and advisors. Pol Pot accepted it despite Angka's doctrine of total Khmer independence; without Chinese support, the Cambodian Communists would not have survived. China as a matter of ideology supported a Maoist-like regime in Cambodia but primarily saw the Khmer Rouge as a client state to advance its interests in Indochina. China and the Soviet Union were at the time locked in a struggle for dominance of world Communism, and the latter was the primary patron of Vietnam. The Chinese, then, certainly didn't discourage Pol Pot's aggressive attitude toward his Communist brethren to the east.

Inside Cambodia, however, Pol Pot's grasp of power had become increasingly precarious by 1978. Angka's program of unlimited victory over the fields, the land, and the class enemies was less than overwhelming. In Pol Pot's mind, spies, traitors, and saboteurs were the problem—a suspicion strengthened by two failed assassination attempts, one by poison. He reportedly moved around to several different residences in Phnom Penh, never sleeping in the same place two nights in a row.

Another reason for the Central Committee's concern was that throughout its regime, the Khmer Rouge viciously suppressed the uprisings that occasionally flared up in different areas of the country, executing tens of thousands of people. Those repressions raised serious doubts about Angka among even some of the most devoted revolutionaries. Perhaps more important, after taking power in 1975, the Khmer Rouge fragmented into a handful of factions vying for control of the party. By 1977, Pol Pot had crushed many of his internal opponents, but his campaign of terror generated much resentment and fear. Top commanders in the western and eastern regions plotted coups, and those in the eastern areas very nearly succeeded in the spring of 1978. Angka put down the revolt only after weeks of brutal conflict.[5]

The rebellions solidified Pol Pot's paranoia and determination to root out anybody with past, present, or future Vietnamese sympathies; such people had "Cambodian bodies and Vietnamese minds." That summer he ordered several villages composed of thousands of people near the Vietnamese border to move into the northwest because they were suspected of having Vietnamese loyalties. Most were sent to desolate, unproductive areas where they were supposed to starve to death quietly, but not all lived long enough for that to happen.[6]

In early 1978, Radha encountered a shaken Ravy, who had just arrived from a field about a half mile south of Tuol Mateh. "I was coming back with the buffalo," he said, "and Khmer Rouge soldiers grabbed some of us and told us we had to go help bury bodies of enemies." In one of the fields, he saw a whole village of people who had been massacred. They were from a village in the east, near the Vietnamese border, that had been moved because it was under suspicion. While Ravy watched, a crying baby, maybe a year old, crawled onto the breast of his mother lying dead on the ground and tried to nurse. One of the soldiers came over and smashed his head with the butt of his rifle. Another child was calling, "Wake up! Wake up!" to its unmoving mother until a soldier walked up and crushed its head with a hoe. "These are the enemy," one of the soldiers yelled out.

Ravy was frozen with fear at first, but eventually he started walking, and then running, and he hurried the buffalo all the way back to Radha. "Don't tell anybody," Radha advised him. "Just don't tell anybody."

186

By the summer of 1978, Pol Pot had the whole country in a near-continual state of purge. New People and even Old People working the fields knew very little about the larger picture, but they knew when purges hit their villages. By June of that year, Radha and Samen had been living for several weeks with an official named Mao and his wife, Khon, who had also been a soldier. Radha and Samen moved into their hut when Khon was pregnant and helped look after their place and the baby when it arrived. Radha and Samen got along well with this couple, and although Mao was known as a hard commander, he and his wife even shared some of their food with Radha and Samen.

When word of a coming purge filtered through to Tuol Mateh that summer, Mao fled, leaving his wife and child behind. His chances of surviving on the run were grim, and he may have thought his family had a better chance of surviving by staying home and hoping they were overlooked. However, a common Khmer Rouge saying was that "a weed must be pulled out by the roots." Angka rarely let the families of the suspected escape. The Manickams went back to a small hut of their own in Tuol Samnal.

When the Khmer Rouge in Radha's region decided to arrest a traitor, they would summon the doomed man after work and inform him he was going "to the Upper Village" or "to cut the bamboo." The victim was then supposed to go home to his family to say good-bye and report in the next morning to be hauled away for execution.

But sometimes the traitors got no warning at all. Late one evening shortly after Mao's disappearance, Comrade Noeun and a handful of other new cadres gathered up Radha and about four other field workers. Noeun had been one of Radha's youth force leaders; he had avoided the purges and ingratiated himself with the new leaders by spying on his comrades.

187

The cadres told Radha and the other workers to get their hoes. The cadres then took their helpers and arrested three Khmer Rouge officers in their fancy military hammocks—the kind mosquitoes can't bite through. Radha had worked with all of them before: Yun, Moha, and Toeung. "Why are you doing this to us, Older Brother Noeun?" Yun asked plaintively. "We are loyal to Angka. We have done nothing wrong." The cadres tied the prisoners' hands behind them, and the whole group marched from Tuol Mateh across a canal and through a muddy field to the top of a termite hill dotted with small bushes.

Dig a hole, the cadres told the workers. Radha and the others set about chopping through the hard surface of the mound with their hoes. When they had dug a man-length hole about twenty inches deep, the cadres forced the prisoners to kneel. A cadre stepped forward, grabbed the first prisoner from behind and, with one hand over his mouth, used the other to saw through his throat with a large palm branch, which are tough and have sharp, rough edges.

It was dark, so he didn't see much, but Radha could hear the prisoner gurgle on his own blood as he died. The cadres did the same to the other two prisoners. The world seemed to go silent again for Radha, and his head was pounding. He tried not to look and leaned on his hoe, clinging to the handle lest he collapse. Then the cadres shoved the bloody bodies into the hole with their feet, leaving the termite hill stained red.

"Cover them up," a cadre instructed. So the workers scooped the dirt back in and returned to their huts.

The next morning Radha and the other workers headed back out to the fields as usual. He believed he and the other workers had been chosen specially to view the execution as an object lesson in loyalty. Workers noticed the freshly turned earth on the termite hill the next morning and that Yun, Moha, and Toeung were missing. Mao's wife, Khon, and her two-month-old baby were arrested, along with Moha's wife and children. Toeung's wife was recognized as a loyal worker for Angka and spared. Yun had no family.

About noon that same day, Radha was with several buffalo at a mountainside near Cheung Tinh—it was his turn to take them into the hills to graze. There he noticed an oxcart carrying the two families of Moha and Mao drive up with several cadres. He ducked behind some trees but kept watching. The two women and most of the children were clubbed to death; one of the cadres swung the baby by its feet and smashed its head against a big rock. Radha could see the blood splash.

By that summer, almost everyone who had been associated with the previous set of village bosses in Tuol Mateh—from Von on down through Mao, Moha, and the rest—had been replaced, including low-level supervisors like Radha. Not all of them just disappeared or were executed. Some were merely demoted, but none of the New People retained any authority. Pol Pot trusted only the southwest, a region famous for the fanaticism and brutality of its cadres.

A man named Ros—a dark man with curly hair—showed up about then and started issuing orders to Radha's plowing crew; he was Radha's replacement. He often bragged about how much he loved and served Angka, and he tried to give the impression that he had been a soldier. Radha was happy to be done sneaking around the huts at night listening for the sounds of treason and the smells of unauthorized cooking, but it also meant he could no longer offer even a shred of protection for the other workers.

Although at some level everybody was suspect, Radha initially thought he was under no particular suspicion. He had earned a reputation as a hard and reliable worker, and if he was not quite as consumed with revolutionary fervor as Angka would like, at least his people finished their work.

But a few weeks after Ros showed up, Radha was sitting on a dike with several other plowmen, chatting during their break. One commented about that night's upcoming meeting, and the word he used for "meeting" was *metinh*. Radha, still playing the loyal servant of Angka, corrected him. "No, comrade," Radha said, "you shouldn't use a foreign word like *metinh*. Use the Khmer word, *prachum*."

Just then Radha looked up and saw one of his plowmen standing in the water and looking past Radha's shoulder. He glanced behind him to see Ros eyeing him suspiciously. Then he realized his error—*prachum* was a word only an educated Khmer would use. The countrified way to pronounce it was *pachum*. Radha went back to his buffalo and resumed plowing. He hoped Ros hadn't heard him.

That was the first of several instances where Radha later realized he had betrayed himself through a slip of the tongue. Even the words he had used in his wedding vows had given off the whiff of an educated vocabulary. Soon he started hearing rustling and footsteps under his hut at night—spies were listening. Later he heard that both he and Samen were on the list of people to be executed.

The execution list in most cooperatives was long, which is perhaps why Radha had not been arrested immediately. Many were executed right away, but others were hauled away to one of the 167 "security offices"—the euphemism for "prison"—the Khmer Rouge set up all over the country. Some security offices were converted Buddhist wats built of stone, but many were just thatch huts with corrugated metal roofs. A nearby clearing or B-52 crater usually served as a mass grave.

One day in the fall of 1978, cadres arrested a friend of Radha's named Sân, a short, dark man with thinning hair and a tendency to talk too loudly and too much. He apparently let slip he had been to school in Phnom Penh. Radha saw soldiers pushing Sân down the path, his arms tied behind him, with his wife standing watching and trying to hide her tears. She knew that if she showed remorse for a traitor, Angka would regard her as an accomplice, and they had three small children she needed to care for.

A month later, Sân came back, much to Radha's surprise. He'd been taken to nearby Banân Prison, he told Radha, and whipped with electrical cords and otherwise tortured. He lifted his shirt to show

Radha the wounds on his back. The cadres wanted him to confess to being a colonel in Lon Nol's army, but he had not been and refused to say otherwise. He insisted to the guards that in Phnom Penh he had made bicycles for Angka and served Angka loyally.

Day after day Sân suffered through the interrogations, and at night they locked him with shackles into a long row where he heard the screams of his fellow prisoners. Often he woke up to find his neighbor had disappeared. He saw cages filled with centipedes and scorpions that the guards placed on the prisoners. He witnessed them pull out prisoners' fingernails with pliers and then pour alcohol over the victims' raw wounds.

Guards elsewhere tortured prisoners using a variety of methods. They tied prisoners atop red-ant hills, sealed plastic bags over people's heads, hacked off digits with hatchets, and sliced babies out of pregnant women, sometimes while exhorting the prisoners to "be sincere with Angka." One survivor, Haing Ngor, writes in his memoir that he was one of dozens of people tied to crosses and then hung from crossbars with their feet above slow-burning fires.

Eventually the guards at Banân Prison let Sân go. Perhaps they believed he really was a loyal comrade, although that was not normally relevant to Khmer Rouge torturers at work. The guards at the prisons were seldom interested in obtaining real, true information; they wanted confessions.

In this regard, the provincial operations were just like the most terrifying of all Khmer Rouge prisons—Tuol Sleng in Phnom Penh. The name literally means "Hill of the Poisonous Tree" and carries a connotation as a place to keep the guilty. More than fifteen thousand men, women, and children passed through the halls of the converted Phnom Penh high school, a three-story complex code-named Security Prison 21. Kaing Guek Eav, known as Comrade Duch (pronounced "Doik"), was in charge. He fit the stereotype of the faceless, soulless bureaucrat who supervised incredible evil without batting an eye.[7]

191

New arrivals were photographed, processed, and then tortured. Former classrooms with white and beige checkerboard-tile floors contained whips, clubs, and hooks, as well as beds, desks, and chairs to which guards manacled prisoners. Interrogators also used electric shock and what is now called waterboarding.

Guards worked over the screaming prisoners and then made them sit at a desk and scribble out an "autobiography," beginning with their childhood. A guard wrote for those too injured to hold a pen. In 1975, Tuol Sleng handled only a few hundred prisoners, and the vast majority were New People and Khmer Republic officials. But by 1978, up to 1,500 were imprisoned at a time, most of them Khmer Rouge cadres and loyal party members caught up in the vortex of the purges.[8]

Prisoners were expected to relate how they pretended to serve Angka while spying for the CIA, the KGB, or Vietnam, including the names of their associates and fellow traitors. Comrade Duch reviewed each confession, made notations in the margins, and sent it back to the guards, who would subject the prisoner to another round of questioning to extract the correct answers. Sometimes the confessions went through many drafts, and the victim endured weeks or even months of agony until Angka was satisfied. Each prisoner, in a futile attempt to placate their tormenters, implicated dozens of innocent friends, family, and acquaintances who, when duly arrested and interrogated, fingered dozens more. This network-style investigation confirmed the existence of ever-widening circles of counterrevolutionaries and justified Pol Pot's paranoia.

Prisoners who had delivered acceptable confessions without dying in the process (Comrade Duch sometimes chided the interrogators for not taking enough care to keep the prisoners alive) were trucked away to a site outside Phnom Penh called Choeung Ek. It became known as the Killing Fields. There the prisoners were slaughtered and dumped into mass graves. Duch, in a macabre pretension to legitimacy, kept detailed files on many of the prisoners, including confessions and photos of the brutalized prisoners before they left, dead or alive.

Unlike the efficient and mechanized Nazi gas chambers, most Khmer Rouge methods of torture and execution had an agrarian feel, like sadistic farm boys slaughtering sheep. Tuol Sleng, with Duch's obsessive recordkeeping, was the exception. Pol Pot wanted Cambodia to export enough rice to purchase modern machinery, but the only thing the Khmer Rouge ever produced on a truly industrial scale was death.

19

Risking Angka's Wrath

Totalitarian domination based on terror . . . turns not only
against its enemies but against its friends and supporters as
well, being afraid of all power, even the power of its friends.
The climax of terror is reached when the police state begins
to devour its own children, when yesterday's executioner becomes today's victim. And this is also the moment when power
disappears entirely.

—Hannah Arendt, "Reflections on Violence"

The piles of Tuol Sleng victims were signs of the regime's growing weakness, not strength. The more the country deteriorated, the more desperately Pol Pot tried to pinpoint the traitors. And the more Khmer Rouge officials and soldiers were tortured and executed, the more control slipped out of Pol Pot's grasp.[1]

The cadres who survived remained as cruel as ever, however. They survived *because* of their cruelty. New People probably could not have explained how or why Angka's aura of invincibility was fading, but over time they grew increasingly willing to risk Angka's wrath. Of course, hunger also made them bold, and by this time many didn't care if they lived or died.

One day in late 1978, Radha and a half dozen other workers were in a thatch barn near Tuol Mateh building grain bins by mixing rice stalks with mud to fill in the sides of a wood frame. One of them, Kan, suddenly announced, "A lot of food coming."

"What are you talking about?" Radha asked. "It's not lunchtime yet."

"Ah, you're wrong," Kan said. "Look at the ground."

Radha looked and saw a fat old dog that had just wandered into the barn. It belonged to one of the soldiers and likely had better rations than any of the New People. "Yeah," Radha said, chuckling, "it's food."

But Kan was serious. "I'm going to kill this dog," he declared.

Radha was scared. Kan was normally a trustworthy comrade, someone who looked out for his crewmates and seldom spoke a rash word. This was completely out of character. "You can't kill that dog," Radha said. "You'll get us all killed."

"Nobody will know," Kan replied, "because we'll do it in here." He picked up a hatchet he'd been using and called the dog over. He petted it, lined it up by his leg, and then whacked it sharply on the back of its head. It keeled over.

Kan quickly cut up the dog, found a pot, piled some big rocks together for a makeshift stove, and made dog stew. When it was ready, the hungry workers pulled out their spoons and started to eat straight from the pot. This was unheard of: to kill an animal belonging to a member of the Khmer Rouge right under his nose, and then to eat it! It was an incredible risk.

Radha had no desire to try dog, but he was hungry too. And he could tell from their sideways glances that he needed to dig in. If Radha didn't implicate himself in the crime, they'd think he might squeal on them and kill him before he could.

The next morning Radha was first into the barn and found the rocks of the makeshift fireplace and the pot still on the floor. He lifted up the lid, and there was the dog's head. "Do those guys want to kill us?" he muttered to himself.

"Older Brother Kan," Radha said when the worker came in, "why didn't you get rid of the evidence last night?"

"I was just so full and tired last night," Kan replied. "I just wanted to go home and go to sleep."

"Yeah, you'll have a nice long sleep when they find this," Radha said.

"OK," Kan said, "we'll just have to finish eating it, and then we'll bury the remains."

In late December 1978, wounded soldiers, usually carried in on hammocks, started showing up at the hospital near Tuol Mateh. Radha was on a crew that had to spend the night once or twice every week waiting outside the hospital doors for one of the patients to die—a likely occurrence, given the lack of medicines, genuine doctors, and clean (let alone sterile) facilities. When that happened, a crew of four would carry the deceased in a hammock to Choeng Tinh and bury them on the side of the hill, taking turns in pairs because they were so weak.

At the time, they didn't realize how close the Khmer Rouge were to the end of their regime. A fellow worker had managed to keep a battery-powered radio hidden. Radha barely knew him, but together they listened quietly to Voice of America when they were away from others or in out-of-the-way spots. At the end of December, they heard that the Vietnamese, risking the wrath of the Chinese, had finally invaded Cambodia.

Radha was really happy, but of course he showed no emotion. That would have been dangerous, even in front of a coconspirator in possession of a banned device. The radio's owner was expressionless, and from then on, he stopped letting Radha listen.

Radha soon realized the significance of the wounded soldiers at Tuol Mateh. His cooperative was in northwest Cambodia, and

Vietnam was to the east. By the time he heard on the radio that Vietnamese troops had "invaded" Cambodia, they had already advanced almost all the way across the country. The "invasion" was simply the start of the battles taking place all over Cambodia as one hundred thousand Vietnamese troops attacked on Christmas Day. Until that point, the Vietnamese had said publicly that the Khmer Rouge were allies, even as the two countries fought skirmish after skirmish on the border.

The Vietnamese captured Phnom Penh on January 7, 1979— Radha's twenty-sixth birthday. Democratic Kampuchea, with its starved populace, half-trained and poorly equipped military, and shortage of resources, had no chance to withstand the Vietnamese forces supplied by their Soviet patrons.

However, the Khmer Rouge were not yet willing to surrender. Even after Phnom Penh fell, group leaders held brief morning meetings on the edge of the rice fields before plowing started. Ros, Radha's replacement, once stood on the dike and warned the workers that the Vietnamese were doing horrible things to Khmer people. "Don't trust them," he said. "Don't join them, they will kill you. Trust Angka, for Angka will take care of you."

The meetings always ended the same way. "Long live Democratic Kampuchea!" Ros would shout, and the workers would echo it back, punctuated by the raised-fist salute. They would also repeat slogans along the lines of "Long live the revolution Angka Kampuchea!" and "We commit ourselves to the revolution and to serve Angka to the end!" They would also affirm that they were opposed to the Vietnamese and the KGB. (The warning against the Soviet secret police had certain logic in Angka's world, since the Soviets supported Vietnam. Radha, of course, had never heard of the KGB. He figured it out months later.)

Radha guessed that this new effort to "reinforce" support among the workers meant the Khmer Rouge were probably losing—plus, he was burying their dead soldiers. He didn't trust Angka, but he

197

didn't doubt that the Vietnamese were murdering and raping their way through Cambodia. He had seen the Khmer Rouge persecution of the Vietnamese and heard of brutal Khmer Rouge attacks on Vietnamese people throughout his time in the cooperatives. Surely the Vietnamese were doing the same.

This made nightly guard duty a discomfiting chore. He and his comrades had no weapons and only their voices for alarms. *This is so stupid*, Radha thought.

One night in mid-January while heading back to his bed after guard duty, he ran into Bich. "Older Brother," Bich said, "I just went past the kitchen, and there's nobody there." "What do you mean?" Radha asked. So they crept back to the kitchen and sure enough—it was empty of even the Khmer Rouge guards. They concluded that the Vietnamese must have arrived, so they eased their way back to their huts, collected their wives and a few others, and hurried back to Tuol Mateh to see if anybody was there.

It was quiet but not quite abandoned. The few people who remained said that everybody had been ordered to a neighboring settlement just over the canal, Tuol Samal, so that's where they headed. The next morning Tuol Mateh's cooperative leader called everybody together. He told them the Vietnamese were coming and everybody had to go to Anglong Mean, "Upper Village," higher ground about a day's march away to the southwest.

So Radha, Samen, Amma, Ravy, Samen's sister Samith, and her brand-new husband, Huoth Try (the cadres had married her off in December), along with a couple thousand other residents of Tuol Mateh, quickly packed up their spoons, mats, and tools and hurried down the trail. It was the dry season and dust puffed up with every step, clogging the nostrils of Radha's two water buffalo. The animals could happily slog for hours through knee-deep muddy rice paddies, but they found the dust difficult. While passing through abandoned villages, Radha's party found and dug up a few yuccas, a potato-like root they ate raw as they walked.

Some of their fellow villagers also found spouses, whether they wanted them or not; the cooperative head matched up several couples as they marched. He'd grab a couple of single people on the way and, while standing in a rice field, perform a very simple ceremony and say, "OK, you two are now married." It was apparently an attempt to reinforce loyalty to Angka and thereby prevent workers from deserting to the Vietnamese.

When the group arrived at Anglong Mean around six that evening, their village leaders handed out rice to the various families, as a communal kitchen was impossible. But after eating in communal halls for years, they had only spoons and nothing in which to cook the rice. The Manickams scrounged around and found a few bowls and metal cups that come with canteens.

After dinner, the village's cadres called another meeting. All the young couples had to go back to Tuol Mateh to the "front lines" and continue tending to the rice—the men had to plow and the women had to plant. They might have been heading into the middle of gunfire and grenades, but without a rice crop everyone would die the next year anyway.

Radha and Samen gathered their mats and buffalo and trudged back down to the trail to Tuol Mateh. They were assigned a place in a long, crowded hut that formerly housed singles, and then they resumed work. They saw no Vietnamese but kept a wary eye out. Samith and Try stayed in Anglong Mean because his job was to deliver supplies from Anglong Mean to Tuol Mateh. A few days later, Try showed up at Tuol Mateh in an oxcart.

A rod connected to the oxcart wheel had broken on the way down. Radha fixed it, and Try asked him to come on the journey back to Anglong Mean in case it broke again. So they left with the cart and got there late that evening. But just after they arrived, a messenger arrived on foot from Tuol Mateh to announce that the Vietnamese had arrived at Tuol Mateh! Everyone had fled!

Radha broke down in tears and prayed. *Lord, You brought this woman into my life. You put us together because we are both Christians. Please protect her. Please. I want to see her again. Bring her back here.*

He stayed up all night pacing. He imagined her running for her life from voracious Vietnamese soldiers and what they might do if they caught her. But he dared not return to Tuol Mateh to look for her—she wasn't there, supposedly, and he had no idea where she might go even if she had escaped. It was agony. He realized afresh in that moment how much he loved her.

When the eastern sky began to lighten, someone called out that people were coming down the trail from Tuol Mateh. Radha went to keep watch. *Maybe she made it*, he thought, peering down the road through the forest. He kept pacing. And when the sun was still low in the east, a party of about one hundred villagers who had fled at the sound of fighting came limping down the road. He caught his breath and started running toward them. Almost immediately he saw Samen, guiding the two buffalo in front of her.

He rushed down the trail to her, and she looked up with a smile when she saw him. They didn't hug, but they did perform the *sampeah* (the traditional Cambodian greeting) and looked each other in the eyes. He came closer and took the ropes from her hand.

"I thought you'd never come back," he told her softly.

"No," she said. "In my mind, I always thought about you and Amma. I always prayed that I would come back."

20

A Killing Field

Son of man, can these bones live?

—Ezekiel 37:3

The Vietnamese invasion ended the Khmer Rouge regime in January 1979, although it would be years before Angka was truly finished. Except for those still loyal to Angka, the Cambodian people welcomed the invading army. Under Pol Pot, nobody could go to bed confident they wouldn't be hauled away to prison or executed during the night. Most people woke up just grateful to be alive—a short-lived relief because it meant another day under Khmer Rouge rule. The people also felt hatred and resentment, not only because of the Khmer Rouge's murderous ways but also because of the sheer pettiness and degrading nature of Angka's constant daily demands.

The end of the regime left many Cambodians feeling relieved yet worried. They had soaked in anti-Vietnamese rhetoric for years. Radha half expected the Vietnamese soldiers to come raping and pillaging through the countryside. After the 1975 victory of the Vietnamese Communists, hundreds of thousands of people fled in rickety boats, risking death from drowning, pirates, and hardship, rather than live under the Vietnamese brand of socialism. Many Cambodians saw a disturbing continuity between the regime in Hanoi and the new one in Phnom Penh. It was a little like being rescued from a street gang by the Mafia; things were going to be more organized, but it wasn't clear they were going to be a lot better.

Vietnam immediately set up a client government—the People's Republic of Kampuchea or PRK—in Phnom Penh. Its chief officials were Khmer Rouge defectors led by Heng Samrin. Ex–Khmer Rouge officers like Hun Sen and other Cambodians who had lived in Vietnam or otherwise proven themselves reliable allies of the Vietnamese held senior posts. The PRK was harsh with political opponents, but initially it allowed many personal freedoms. Khmer society could not have handled much more repression. Over time, the new regime also imported aid from allies of its Vietnamese occupiers; for the first time in four years, Cambodians had a government that might not starve large numbers of its own people to death, at least not deliberately.

When the Vietnamese swept through the country in the initial invasion, Khmer Rouge forces and major Khmer Rouge figures, including Pol Pot and Nuon Chea, fled and hid in a fortified camp in Thailand near the border. Later in 1979, Pol Pot gave a rare series of interviews in which he blamed the Vietnamese for the deaths of "millions" of Cambodians and his subordinates for losing control of the situation when the Khmer Rouge were in charge.[1]

As the Vietnamese slowly took control of the central plains of Cambodia that spring, the Khmer Rouge retreated to malarial mountain hideouts in the west and northwest. Before leaving, they often threatened villagers not to cooperate with the Vietnamese, promising to return and exact revenge on all traitors. Sometimes the Vietnamese would "liberate" a village, abolishing the communal dining halls and letting residents elect leaders. But after the Vietnamese left, the Khmer Rouge would swoop in the next night, seize the food, kill the elected leaders, and reestablish communal kitchens. In the mountains, the Khmer Rouge regrouped and promptly began a guerrilla warfare campaign against the Vietnamese occupiers.[2]

The Manickams saw very little of the Vietnamese at first and gradually less and less of the Khmer Rouge. Radha and Samen were back together in Anglong Mean with Amma, Ravy, and the rest of their surviving relatives, but they and the other villagers had almost nothing to eat. They scavenged for food in the nearby areas and continued to starve slowly over the next few weeks. Once Radha and his brother-in-law Try caught and cut up a stray dog. On another occasion, they found and butchered a stray cow. They needed the meat badly, but they were nervous. After nearly four years under totalitarian rule, they felt like they were risking execution for eating Angka's cow.

The hundreds of villagers staying at Anglong Mean soon realized that staying where they were was hopeless. The whole crowd, including the Manickams, set out through the countryside of northwest Cambodia in a large group, hoping to find food. However, scavenging for food was easier for a small party. As they traveled, families and individuals drifted off to find their own way. The sounds of fighting drew closer, and the number of Khmer Rouge soldiers and cadres grew smaller and smaller until there were none.

Radha's group was one of the fortunate ones in that its leaders just abandoned them. They heard stories from other travelers of how Khmer Rouge had driven comrades—men, women, and children—before them as they retreated into the jungles of northwest Cambodia, deep into the Cardamom Mountains, so they couldn't defect to the Vietnamese. When the hunger-weakened villagers either could not or would not continue to flee, the Khmer Rouge just massacred them, leaving the bodies strewn around the countryside.

Sometimes the Khmer Rouge murdered their comrades before leaving. Radha heard that the leaders of one village called a meeting, slipped from the center to the edges of the crowd as it gathered, and then chucked a grenade into the middle.

By late February, the Anglong Mean group had shrunk to about ten families, including the Manickams. They kept moving in search of food and one day came to a region named for its main feature, Ang Trachak Chet, or "Cool Hard Basin." The Khmer Rouge had turned the pool into a reservoir perhaps one hundred yards across. The basin was about half full and maybe twenty feet deep.

As Radha walked up, he saw a dozen or more corpses lying along the waterline. They were in various stages of decomposition; some looked fairly fresh, while others were swollen and had been dead for weeks already. He felt sick. This was exactly what the Khmer Rouge told them the Vietnamese soldiers would do, except that the Khmer Rouge had done it. There was no telling how many bodies were sunk in the water; he could see some in the middle floating near the surface. He turned away from the reservoir hurriedly, but the Anglong Mean group stayed in the area because the ground was rich in yucca and a few other edibles.

Some days later, Radha headed off into the woods by himself to look for firewood. As he wandered, he saw a bone that looked human. Then he noticed a skull. The more he looked on the forest floor, the more human bones he saw. He had wandered into the middle of a forest of dry bones, a mass grave, a killing field.

Radha had seen much death in the previous four years, but not on this scale. What he saw at Cool Hard Basin was shocking in a new way. He couldn't tell how many bodies lay in this forest, but it was hundreds. He wasn't scared—he had been too close to death himself to be frightened of corpses—but he had a heavy feeling. He wondered how many of these people had been murdered for a ridiculous or petty reason, the result of Khmer Rouge paranoia or an imaginary slight to Angka, and how many had died of disease and starvation.

Outside Cambodia, many international observers believed that conditions in the country were set to go from horrific to catastrophic.[3]

The Vietnamese invasion severely disrupted that year's rice planting and harvesting, leaving Cambodians in danger of even less food than under Pol Pot. Cambodia's major rice crop is planted soon after the monsoon rains start in May and harvested in December and January. The minor rice crop is planted in the fall after the summer monsoon rains end and harvested at the beginning of the dry season in February and March. The four-month December-to-March harvest season, then, had nicely gotten under way when the Vietnamese attacked. The vast majority of the country's food production for the year was likely to rot in the fields, and no one knew how or whether the next major crop would be planted. The Khmer Rouge had gathered large stores of rice in barns and storehouses around the countryside, but they took some with them when they fled and burned much of the rest.

The Vietnamese seized the few remaining crops and storehouses and shared little of it with the Khmers. The Vietnamese needed the food to feed the two hundred thousand troops that by then had been sent to deal with the Khmer Rouge resistance. The fighting made large sections of the country extremely dangerous, and few people wanted to spend time in open fields planting crops. As a result, it appeared the country was going to be short of food through the next planting cycle—at least another year.

The aftermath of the invasion, however, provided a few months of chaotic freedom throughout Cambodia. Many of the people Angka had displaced during its reign, like the villagers of Anglong Mean, were suddenly free to move about the country. They abandoned Angka's rice fields and with the encouragement of Vietnamese soldiers headed home to their villages and cities. Hundreds of thousands of starving people, stick-thin and many with discolored hair and skin infections, traveled in groups of all sizes, crisscrossing the country in a desperate search for food and family.[4]

Meanwhile, the trickle of Cambodian refugees over the border into Thailand was swelling. Thailand limited journalists' access to the refugee camps, but the refugees' emaciated figures, wide eyes, and barely believable stories of life under the Khmer Rouge galvanized the world. The scale of the Khmer people's suffering was hard to grasp—the violence, the hunger, the sheer number of victims—and led observers and many in the media to compare Cambodia to the Nazi Holocaust. Those stories, plus reports from the few international correspondents able to visit Cambodia in the aftermath of the invasion, put pressure on governments and relief organizations to get involved—and the Vietnamese-backed government in Phnom Penh initially turned down all offers of help.

The International Red Cross and UNICEF were the first to offer aid to the People's Republic of Kampuchea in January 1979, but officials in Hanoi and Phnom Penh ignored their proposals. Cold War geopolitics badly complicated the relief efforts of aid agencies and Western governments. The United States was warming to China, a Khmer Rouge supporter, and China itself was battling the Soviet Union for leadership of world Communism. In February 1979, China even launched an invasion of Vietnam, which ended after only two weeks, to "punish" it for taking over Cambodia.[5] The United States, in particular, worried that the Vietnamese invasion of Cambodia might be Vietnam's first step to taking over all of Indochina.

On the other side, Vietnam and the Soviet Union were unwilling to turn Cambodia into a showcase of capitalist generosity. The PRK angrily dismissed widespread publicity of starving Khmers as a "maneuver by the imperialists and international reactionaries" to get supplies to the Khmer Rouge.[6] Cambodia had become a pro-Soviet "socialist" country, and the Vietnamese and Russians intended to keep it that way. Relief agencies quickly found the PRK government hard to work with. Cambodia had suffered through a proxy war between superpowers; it seemed about to endure a proxy famine.

Confusion, conflict, and competition for public attention and donations among the various relief agencies and UN entities complicated the situation even more. Some proposed aid programs were scuttled amid accusations and hostility, leaving the Cambodian people to rely more or less on their own means in a country whose resources had been ravaged. As a result, Cambodians perished daily as they waited months for significant aid to arrive.

This, of course, was why so many Cambodians hoped to escape their homeland. Thailand was the only feasible option for most Cambodians, as the other choices were Vietnam itself or Vietnam-dominated Laos.

But Thailand strongly discouraged any more Khmer refugees. It set up camps for the few thousand newly arrived Cambodians who had crossed the border but attempted to keep journalists and international aid officials away from them. It also patrolled the border heavily. By April 1979, the Vietnamese offensive had pushed at least fifty thousand and possibly eighty thousand Khmers, less than half of them Khmer Rouge and the rest civilians forced to travel ahead of their "leaders," up against the Thai border. That's where most of them stayed.

In early 1979, aid agencies and government observers warned in dire terms that a famine was imminent; some predicted that two million would die by Christmas.[7]

The Manickam group was managing to survive, camping near Cool Hard Basin, until one of their water buffalo died in early March. They got very nervous. They hadn't seen any Khmer Rouge cadres for days, but as they had been told, one water buffalo is worth fifty New People, and there was no way to hide the beast. The cadres could return at any time. They decided to butcher the animal and split up the meat among the families. They needed it—badly.

It marked the beginning of a period in which food, remarkably, became a little easier to get. The buffalo meat didn't last long, but they kept moving and within days came to a village called Kampong Kdei, some miles east of Tuol Mateh. They had heard that cattle and buffalo were wandering around the area. One of the members of

207

Radha's group caught a cow and brought it back so they had meat again. They settled into the abandoned homes and kept scouring the area for food. Compared to life under the Khmer Rouge, they were living high—even if they were still nervous about leaving cow carcasses out in the open.

So Radha's group decided to settle down at Kampong Kdei for a while. A few other groups were already living there, and it looked like a decent situation—until the Vietnamese soldiers showed up.

Radha was hanging around his hut one day in early April when he heard shouts in Vietnamese: "Attack!" He turned and saw a line of soldiers in battle fatigues and helmets break from forest cover and dash into the town. Radha was petrified with fear, along with the rest of the people staying at Kampong Kdei. The soldiers rushed up and began gathering all the men in the village, clearing huts, and storming through the streets while shoving their rifle muzzles into the faces of the Khmers and asking, "Pol Pot? Pol Pot?" Radha believed they were about to be massacred. *I'll never see my mother or brother again*, he thought in the midst of the yelling and screaming and panic.

One man suddenly fled, splashing across a canal. Some of the soldiers chased after him and were about to open fire, when Radha called in Vietnamese, "Stop! He's not Pol Pot!" They lowered their rifles and the commander came over to see the Indian-looking Cambodian who spoke their language. As they gathered around him, Radha wondered whether he had made a mistake.

"He's not Pol Pot," explained Radha. "He's just another Cambodian who was forced to live under Pol Pot." The Vietnamese commander eyed him with interest. He had been looking for someone to translate Khmer into Vietnamese. He then questioned Radha aggressively, shouting and demanding to know who he was and how he had learned Vietnamese. He may have recognized Radha's accent as from southern Vietnam and suspected him of being a refugee trying to escape Vietnam's Communist regime. The officer soon calmed down and took Radha over to where his men were rounding up the Khmer men.

Radha became his interpreter as the soldiers searched through all the men's belongings and questioned them. The Vietnamese arrested two men who had among their possessions photos of themselves with Khmer Rouge officials in Phnom Penh. They were sent away to new Vietnamese-run camps to be "reeducated." Radha wondered if they were executed. He didn't know that the Vietnamese had set up indoctrination camps for political opponents in Cambodia, as they had in their own country, that were harsh but not automatic death sentences. The soldiers let everybody else go back to their families.

Such leniency, which had been impossible under the Khmer Rouge, was like cool, fresh air in the middle of a hot summer. Radha realized that Cambodia was already changing. Prerevolutionary institutions were beginning to reappear—from markets to Buddhist pagodas to family farms—and the Vietnamese were to thank for it. However, he wasn't quite prepared to throw in his lot with the Vietnamese. The commander asked Radha if he wanted to travel with the unit as their interpreter. He told them he needed to go back and ask his mother and wife and promised to return the next day. They gave him some fresh food, and he went home.

"I don't want you to go with them," Samen said when she heard about the offer.

Amma agreed. "I don't know if I'll ever see you again," she said.

Early the next morning Radha's group quietly slipped out of Kampong Kdei and headed into the countryside.

21

Hard Waiting

The bodies stayed where they lay, dressed in their black outfits,
eaten by rats and worms, glazed by the sun, submerged by the
rains. They fertilized fear.

—Rithy Panh, *The Elimination*

When Radha's group left Kampong Kdei in April 1979,
the Vietnamese soldiers were telling people to head east,
back toward the main Vietnamese line and what they
referred to as the "liberation zone" marked by Highway 5, which
connects northwest Cambodia to Phnom Penh in the south. The
soldiers warned that the Khmer Rouge had killed everybody who
fled with them, so it was best to head back to the safe areas they
controlled. Radha was inclined to believe them, in part because he
spoke their language and felt he could understand them and in part
because the soldiers sometimes handed out food. His initial fears
of Vietnamese soldiers rampaging through the countryside were
quickly fading.

They walked about a half day to the highway and kept moving
along it to the southeast. Radha and Samen's "family" included

Ravy, Samith, Try, Amma, and a couple of boys about ten or twelve years old who had attached themselves to her (Radha referred to them as his "adopted" brothers). They dragged their few goods, including a bit of food, behind their buffalo on two poles that had cloth slung between. The ten families from Anglong Mean were still hanging together.

The highway was crowded with Cambodians, not all of them alive. Bloated bodies lay along the roadside and floated nearby in the rice fields. Most of the corpses looked like Khmer Rouge; that is, their black uniforms appeared new, or at least newer. Their clothes were a stark contrast to what most workers wore: threadbare rags crudely dyed black, light blue garments donated by North Korea, or gray ones donated by China.

Some of the Khmer Rouge corpses appeared to have been shot, probably in battles with the Vietnamese army, and others had been mangled and severely abused. Radha guessed they had tried to blend in with the crowds traveling the highway only to have their uniforms give them away. The workers murdered and then hacked them to pieces in revenge for years of brutality. Angka's "eyes like a pineapple" no longer protected them. Some of the dead were New People. Radha suspected that the crowds had identified them as collaborators with the Khmer Rouge.

So many corpses lay on the highway that the flies breeding inside them became unbearably thick. When the Manickams stopped for a meal, they had to eat inside mosquito netting—a luxury they had scrounged in their travels after the Vietnamese arrived. They also had to sleep in the rice fields away from the road.

After plodding down Highway 5 for a few days, they reached a village called Russey Krang and stopped to rest. There they heard about a river, the Svay Daun Keo, east of the village. Radha and some others took a net they had found down to the river, planted a couple of poles on its bed, and then strung the net between them. Radha prayed, *Lord, please give us a fish.* An hour into fishing, they saw the

211

net shake. They jumped in and hauled out a huge catfish—nearly ten pounds. Jubilant, they carried it back to their settlement. It was the first big, fresh-river fish they'd had in years. It was delicious.

The river was a nice spot where they could catch fresh fish every day, so they settled down by it. Radha and some of the other men made one brief trip back to Russey Krang where they found more than two hundred pounds of unhusked rice hidden in the ground that the Khmer Rouge had overlooked when they fled. For the first time in years, the Manickams weren't feeling quite so hungry all the time.

Some days after the move to the river, Radha announced to his family that he intended to go back west along Highway 5 to the city of Battambang to look for a place to stay. He wanted to return to Phnom Penh, but people were saying that the Vietnamese authorities weren't allowing that just yet. In fact, the new PRK government was keeping many of those attempting to return to Phnom Penh in camps just outside the city. But he intended to return to a city—more people meant more possibilities to earn a living instead of scrounging around the countryside and hoping the fishing was good.

By this time, they'd been traveling around Cambodia for about three months and were miles and miles away from Tuol Mateh, where they had started. In the midst of all the chaos, a barter economy sprang up centered around gold and rice. Radha's group had almost no gold, but they did have rice.

So Radha packed up a sackful and hiked back over to Highway 5 and caught a ride to Battambang with a Vietnamese troop truck. While passing through one of the villages he looked out the back and saw the Vietnamese officer who had wanted him to become his translator. Their eyes met. "You chicken!" he screamed at Radha. "You were supposed to come work for me!" Radha ducked, and the truck kept going.

Radha got off at the edge of Battambang. He wandered into the city, looking for a place to trade his rice and came to an abandoned high school, a two-story concrete brick structure. There he ran into Sân—the friend who had survived Banân Prison—who was staying in some of the empty classrooms. "You should bring your family here," he told Radha. So the next day Radha hid his rice and set out, returning to Svay Daun Keo the following morning. Radha brought Samen and others from their group back to Battambang.

The trip took two very long days. Samen struggled as she was guiding the water buffalo; at the time, they didn't realize that she was about a month pregnant. Amma and Ravy, who had traveled separately, arrived a few days later. Samith and Try decided to head farther west.

Sân kindly shared some of his food with the Manickams, and as Amma, Ravy, and the others arrived over the next few days, they settled under the stairwell of the building next door, placing their mats on the concrete floor. It was early May.

The PRK government spread the word a few weeks later that Phnom Penh factory workers should return to the city. Sân told Radha he was going to take his family to Phnom Penh and that Radha and his family should come with them.

Radha wanted to go at first, and Amma really wanted to head back and find out if their house—the two-story row house with the Suzuki showroom—was still standing. She hoped that some of their possessions might still be there, but Radha doubted that. Everywhere he looked, the Khmer Rouge had destroyed what they had found. He and Samen prayed about what they should do: Go south to Phnom Penh? Stay in Battambang? Head west to the Thai border? Radha accompanied Sân and his family to Battambang's town square, where they found a Vietnamese truck on which they could hitch a ride for the two-hundred-mile trip to Phnom Penh. Radha watched the truck rumble off.

Sân was one of several people Radha knew who left Battambang during this period. Radha was torn. People were moving on, either

213

trying to rebuild their former lives or getting out of Cambodia altogether. Most of them he would never see again. He wasn't sure what he should do, but he felt like he should be doing something. It was hard to just wait.

He knew that the Vietnamese had pushed the Khmer Rouge and their unwilling comrades up against the Thai border, so entering that region posed the risk of encountering more Khmer Rouge. Radha didn't realize that waves of Cambodian refugees, willing to take that risk, had already crossed the Cardamom Mountains and found themselves stuck in the border area. In fact, while Radha was agonizing over whether he should head west with his family, the Thais were planning to drive tens of thousands of Cambodian refugees back across the border into Cambodia in one of the era's most horrifying episodes.

Although it was not nearly as strong as the ethnic hostility between the Khmer and the Vietnamese, a long-standing resentment simmered between the Khmer and Thai peoples. From 1975 to 1979, Thailand's right-wing government had maintained civil relations with the Khmer Rouge because, like Vietnam, the Thais preferred a weak buffer state between themselves and the Vietnamese. The sight of two hundred thousand Soviet-backed Vietnamese troops rolling through Cambodia toward their border made the Thais very uneasy. This was exactly why the United States went to war in Vietnam—to prevent the Communists from taking over Indochina—and here they were.

To oppose Vietnam, therefore, the Thai government decided to cooperate with the Khmer Rouge, which meant keeping starving Cambodians inside Cambodia.[1] Thailand even allowed Khmer Rouge forces, driving Khmer villagers ahead of them, temporary safe passage into Thai territory to help them escape Vietnamese troops. From 1979 to 1981, with the support and knowledge of China and the United States, the Thais sheltered, fed, and armed Khmer Rouge troops, allowing them to keep up the resistance against Vietnamese occupiers. UN agencies and other organizations fed, clothed, and housed Khmer Rouge wives and children in refugee camps.[2]

Thailand was also reluctant to accept Cambodian refugees because it was among the several Asian countries already flooded with Vietnamese boat people. Most rural Thais were poor and resented these foreigners who did nothing but receive free food from the government. By June 1979, there were perhaps three hundred thousand Vietnamese in camps in the Philippines, Thailand, Hong Kong, Malaysia, Singapore, and Indonesia waiting for some country, any country, to take them in—and the number was growing.[3] Beginning June 8, 1979, Thailand sent back some forty thousand Cambodians at a mountainous spot called Preah Vihear on the northwestern Cambodia border.

That day fleets of buses began dropping off refugees on a plateau atop a steep bluff overlooking Cambodia. Thai soldiers shoved the terrified and wailing Khmers through holes in the wire border fence. They stumbled and slid hundreds of feet down to the edge of a forest loaded with mines from decades of border conflicts between the Khmer Rouge, Thailand, and Khmer militants. A man named Ly, whom Radha would later meet and befriend, was among the Khmers pushed into the minefield.[4] He saw people stumble and slide down the path. Older, weaker people had a terrible time getting down without injury, and parents dropped their meager supplies to grab their children and keep them from tumbling away. As Ly made his way down the slope, he could hear ahead of him booms and human cries and see the flashes of explosions. The stench of death rose to meet him.

He found a path at the bottom and joined a line of other people picking their way through the jungle. They went in single file, clutching children and the elderly, not daring to put a foot off the path. Nearby craters were littered with bloody human remains. Few people had any water, and it was dangerous to go near the pools, which were polluted with the dead bodies of those who failed to realize they were mined. They dared not leave the trail to relieve themselves, so excrement soon littered the paths underfoot, adding to the smell of the victims already rotting in the heat and covered in insects.

Ly passed many grievously wounded people who had been abandoned by friends or family, and he often heard them call out faintly, "Help me! I need water!" But he had no way to help them—no one on that trail did. At night, the forest seemed to echo with their cries. Every so often, another mine went off, and Ly's ears rang with the explosion and the screams of the dying.

Nobody knows how many thousands died on this trek, whether by mine, thirst, or something else. On the third day, Ly's group finally met some Vietnamese soldiers who directed them down safe paths through the last section of the forest. Many of the refugees were stuck in holding camps on the Cambodian side of Preah Vihear for months, but Ly hiked one hundred miles to the city of Siem Reap. He later married a woman he had met earlier in a Thai refugee camp, became a Christian, and moved to the United States.

Radha, hearing this story years later, realized how easily he and Samen might have died had they decided to try for Thailand that June. Again, God had protected them.

Thai and Chinese aid helped the Khmer Rouge recover and made them very dangerous. Worse, the international community still officially recognized the Khmer Rouge as the "legitimate" government of Cambodia; Khmer Rouge officials, representing Pol Pot and his senior officials hiding in the Thai border region, still held Cambodia's seat at the United Nations. Vietnam and the Soviet Union tried to get the United Nations to recognize the People's Republic of Kampuchea in September 1979, but the United States, China, and other nations voted down the measure by a 2–1 margin.

Some were wringing their hands over the fact that America and the West were indirectly supporting a regime that had slaughtered vast numbers of its own people (estimates from Hanoi put the figure at three million, although respected historians such as Ben Kiernan later settled on about 1.7 million). It was distasteful but more important to Western nations, strategically and politically, to resist anything that might advance the interests of Communism and the Soviet Union than it was to punish a homicidal bunch of rogue Rouge. With outside aid, over the next few years, the Khmer Rouge became strong enough to keep the Vietnamese in a bloody stalemate for another decade. In Washington, some were satisfied that Vietnam itself was bogged down in its own quagmire, just as the Americans had been a decade earlier.[5]

It's difficult to understand today how recognizing and supporting a venomous regime, thereby enabling appalling human rights abuses to continue, in exchange for an opportunity to undermine a Cold War enemy could have looked like a reasonable trade-off. But the dangers of worldwide Communism and nuclear war seemed very ominous a decade before the collapse of the Soviet Union.[6] In the late 1970s, nuclear war between the superpowers was considered not just possible but, in some circles, likely. Moreover, it's not certain that the United States could have pressured Thailand into not supporting the Khmer Rouge, given the Thais' security concerns. Still, in retrospect, it looks stunningly cynical.

By July 1979, the political situation was already changing. International media had thoroughly covered Preah Vihear, generating an international uproar. Vietnam's initial resistance to foreign aid had softened in May, and in July, the new Cambodian government allowed the International Red Cross and UNICEF to send in a joint two-man delegation to survey the needs. They found, unsurprisingly, a traumatized population, appalling malnutrition, and almost no available medical care. The PRK government in Phnom Penh formally requested aid, claiming that the Khmer Rouge devastation was so severe that millions were in danger of starvation in the next several months.[7]

In July, the PRK also held a show trial in which Pol Pot and Ieng Sary were sentenced to death in absentia. Their own lawyer declared his clients "criminally insane monsters" whose actions implicated "the manipulators of world imperialism, the profiteers of neocolonialism, the racist philosophers, the hegemonists." That is, Western countries, along with "fascist China," should be "sharing the sentence."[8]

In July and August 1979, representatives of more aid agencies arrived at the refugee camps and issued more dire reports for Cambodia, and there was growing concern within Thailand that vast numbers of refugees might suddenly storm the border and overrun the country. A Thai report in early September suggested that between 260,000 and 360,000 desperately hungry and ill Cambodians were massed in the border regions. The Thais began pushing for more international aid—both inside Cambodia and in the border camps. The Thai government said it might offer refugees temporary asylum until the situation in Cambodia improved and they could be sent back.[9]

22

Free Trading

Stumbling on reed-thin legs through the high elephant grass that grows along the frontier, they form a grisly cavalcade of specters, wrapped in black rags. Many are in the last stages of malnutrition, or are ravaged by such diseases as dysentery, tuberculosis and malaria. Perhaps the most pathetic images of all are those of tearful, exhausted mothers cradling hollow-eyed children with death's-head faces, their bellies swollen, their limbs as thin and fragile as dried twigs.

— "Deathwatch: Cambodia," *Time*

Despite Radha's restlessness, he and Samen chose to settle into Battambang. As May flowed into June, Amma and Samen started making and selling rice-flour cakes. These are desserts made from ground rice, flavored with pumpkin or banana, and then steamed in banana leaves. Amma and Ravy made the cakes in the morning, and then Samen and the others went house to house bartering them for more rice. The family ate some of the rice they earned and used the rest to make the next batch of cakes the next morning.

219

Samen's personality, they soon discovered, wasn't suited to driving hard bargains. They also discovered she was pregnant. Profit margins were tight and so they lived the definition of a hand-to-mouth existence. Radha, meanwhile, looked for a job or some way to earn some gold or extra food.

Radha's family group was a little better off than most, in part because they got to know some of the Vietnamese soldiers bunking in the rooms of the high school across the street from them. The Manickams weren't ethnic Khmer, so that was a point in their favor with the Vietnamese. Also, Radha and his brother were some of the only Cambodians around who spoke Vietnamese, so sometimes the soldiers' cook would drop by to chat, bringing some extra rice or meat.

One afternoon in June as Radha walked through the city, he saw a man named Kha, one of the cruelest leaders of any from the several youth brigade crews Radha had worked on. He was also the son-in-law of the Khmer Rouge leader of Kok Porn, where Radha's father had died. Radha stared at the man as visions flashed through his mind of how Appa had been abused and starved to death. Radha started to shake with rage. Kha glanced up and saw Radha; he ducked his head, but in the middle of the street, there was nowhere to hide. Radha started toward the man, murder on his mind.

But as he walked, he again heard a voice in his head. "Now remember," it said, "I've forgiven you for everything you've done. You should forgive others." Radha tried to block it out and kept walking, but the voice persisted: "I forgave you. I died for you."

Kha himself was shaking as Radha stopped in front of him. "Kha," he said, "I'm not going to do anything to you, and I'm not going to report you to the authorities." If Radha had identified Kha as a former Khmer Rouge, the Vietnamese would have arrested him. "I forgive you for what you did to me and my family, and I forgive your father-in-law." Tears began to roll down Kha's cheek, but Radha didn't know if the man was sorry or just relieved. All he said was,

"Thank you for not reporting me." They both turned and walked away.

Considerable resentment and anger had built up among the Khmer people over the previous four years. That summer Amma became frantic when she heard that Bich, one of Radha's former crew members, had come to Battambang and was looking for Radha; she assumed he was out for revenge. Bich, however, just wanted to invite Radha and Samen over for dinner.

Conditions had been improving so gradually that Radha didn't notice what a big step it was to offer or receive such an invitation. Under the Khmer Rouge, normal social interactions were impossible. Who could you trust enough to invite over to your house for an evening of conversation? Who had any food to share, especially since Angka controlled the cuisines? Who could have a private chat and not arouse the suspicion of the cadres and *chhlops*? But now, with the aid Vietnam was importing to the cities and towns, people were starting to behave like neighbors again.

At dinner, Bich asked Radha if he had heard of the Freedom Fighters. Radha had not. They were Cambodians, also known as Khmer Serei, who had taken up arms against the Khmer Rouge. People called any of several armed groups that sometimes worked together Freedom Fighters; former Cambodian Prime Minister Sonne Son led the largest. Many Freedom Fighters were just disorganized bandits who weren't above robbing their own countrymen. They skulked in the jungles near the Thai border and probably got their arms from the Thais, who gave them to anybody who might attack the Vietnamese. Freedom Fighters had set up some camps in the mountains north and west of Battambang. Also in the mix were anti-Vietnamese guerrillas, Sihanoukists who considered themselves loyal to the prince.

But Radha was tired of fighting, and he still hated guns, so he was not interested in joining the fighters. However, he did want to hear from Bich about the trading camps along the Thai border. People were managing to get food and other goods into Battambang, and Radha knew they must have been coming from Thailand. The camp nearest the city was called Nong Samet or the "007 Camp."

That night he talked things over with Samen and suggested that it might be worth the risk to make a trip to the camps to do some trading. The Manickams were doing better than most but could always use extra money. The next day, Radha swapped their last water buffalo for a few hundred grams of gold and soon after that stepped onto one of the trailheads leading to the border.

The path was only two or three feet wide, and it was extremely dangerous to stray off it. The forest floors contained many land mines and traps, deep pits with sharpened bamboo sticking up to impale the unwary. The paths wound their way between the mines and traps, the result of many travelers whose caution had led them through on safe ground.

Radha set out through the forest. He passed through several areas littered with corpses in rotting clothes, the remains of those caught by Khmer Rouge patrols, and some with baskets or other belongings scattered around. Halfway to the border he stopped in a province called Banteay Mean Chey and slept on the side of a dike with a bunch of other travelers.

Through the trees, Radha could occasionally see Khmer Rouge soldiers, usually resting at a small camp. At this time, though, they were not harassing the Cambodians passing through the forests. Radha saw several parties of Khmer Rouge over two days of traveling, and many of them carried brand-new M-16 rifles, black as charcoal, and even some grenade launchers. The M-16 was the American military's rifle of choice in Asia. Any left over from the civil war, when the Americans had been pouring aid into the Khmer Republic, would have been faded and scuffed. *Where'd they get all these new guns?* he wondered. He kept his eyes down. He didn't realize the degree to which the Thais, Chinese, and Americans were directly and indirectly supporting the rebuilding of the Khmer Rouge military.

At Nong Samet, Radha found thousands of people and hundreds of stalls and tents spread out over a large area. The people were bartering and buying food and consumer goods of all types—from jewelry to clothes to small appliances. The International Red Cross also had a tent.

Freedom Fighters maintained a sort of loose order over the massive open-air markets. Every morning thousands of Thais set off from nearby towns in brand-new pickups laden with everything imaginable: cutlery, whiskey, makeup, car parts, stereos, cigarettes, batteries, rope, toothpaste—anything one needed to start a new life.[1]

Cambodians who were able to make the trip eagerly bought up the goods that crossed the border. Each day in the other direction flowed hundreds of thousands of dollars in gold that Cambodians had squirreled away during the revolution. A series of middlemen, each taking a cut, passed the goods and gold along. The corrupt Thai military commander who ruled the region made a fortune collecting unofficial tolls and tariffs. Vice flourished.

Radha wandered through the camp for a couple of days. He soon realized that something small and valuable would be a lot easier to carry home than sacks of food. He bought a nice-looking watch for two grams of gold and headed home to Battambang. There he sold the watch for four grams of gold, a tidy profit for a few days' work. Radha made the same trip a month later but didn't make any money; the supply of consumer goods was picking up, apparently, and the market had tightened.

The Manickams stayed in Battambang for the next three months, into November, making and selling the rice-flour cakes. Radha sometimes went out to chop firewood to supplement their income. Amma still longed to go back to Phnom Penh. Other people they knew left

223

for their home villages or headed for the Thai border. Samen and Radha didn't know what to do; they prayed and asked God for a sign.

They knew nothing of the outside world's dire predictions of famine. Food was certainly scarce—most people were malnourished to one degree or another—and few had decent clothing. Overall, however, real freedom made life far better than it had been under the Khmer Rouge.

Meanwhile, the rest of the world was convinced millions of Cambodians were on the verge of death, in part because of a change in Thai policy. In October 1979, the Thai prime minister went to see the awful conditions at the border and declared an "open door"—no Cambodian would be turned away. He may have had some humanitarian reasons, but the move was certainly to get aid to the Khmer Rouge troops and their families and so prevent a Khmer Rouge collapse.

Thailand promptly dumped responsibility for tens of thousands of refugees—both those who were there and those who were coming—on the relief agencies that had been clamoring for access to the Cambodians, primarily the Red Cross and the United Nations High Commissioner for Refugees.

With mere days to prepare, the agencies managed to set up a camp called Sa Kaeo, about forty miles from the border. The camp consisted of tents atop swampy land with grossly inadequate drainage, a particular problem around the latrines because of torrential rains. The refugees, when they started streaming in, initially found a lack of food, medical care, shelter, and clothing.[2]

Journalists, missionaries, relief workers, and many others came to Sa Kaeo. They returned with stories, images, and film of starving, wretched people under appalling conditions. Sa Kaeo smelled terrible and looked worse. Dysentery and other diseases spread among refugees living atop each other in muck. Some desperately ill people, unable to move, reportedly drowned in the puddles that formed around their mats. One Red Cross poster of a badly emaciated child read, "Some children in Kampuchea look like this . . . the rest are dead."[3]

The Cambodian crisis shot to the top of the world's agenda because, for once, humanitarian concern aligned with political imperatives. Western governments wanted to draw attention to the crisis so they could blame the Vietnamese and its client PRK government. US Secretary of State Cyrus Vance called Cambodia a "human tragedy of almost unfathomable proportions. . . . An entire generation of Kampucheans may have been lost." The PRK wanted to attract as much aid as possible from capitalist countries and was secretly shipping significant amounts to Vietnam. Worldwide, fund-raising for Cambodia exploded amid constant comparisons to the Holocaust,[4] while Pol Pot earned comparisons to both Hitler and Stalin.

The camps were grim places, especially Sa Kaeo in its early days. But the campaigns were sadly misleading regarding Cambodia as a whole. In Sa Kaeo, many of the refugees were the ones the Communists had driven ahead of them like hostages when fleeing the Vietnamese, and most of the rest were Khmer Rouge soldiers and cadres. They stumbled out of the jungle in horrible shape, and even in Sa Kaeo they were still under Khmer Rouge control. The Khmer Communists maintained a corrosive presence, controlling food distribution, terrorizing inhabitants, and forcing refugees to return across the border as the Thai soldiers looked on.

But in other camps with lively black markets, where the people coming across the border had been living for months or weeks outside Khmer Rouge control, refugees were much better off. Moreover, the public relations blitzes failed to clarify the distinction between conditions in the camps on the border and conditions in Cambodia's interior countryside. The latter was in much better shape. Despite the PRK government's inability (or refusal) to distribute properly the limited aid that it allowed into Phnom Penh, when relief agency officials were finally given permission to travel around inside the country in the fall of 1979 and into 1980, they saw little evidence of famine. They found instead exactly what Radha had been experiencing: people were dirty, poor, often malnourished, and badly clothed, but managing to survive.[5] Many people were very hungry, but they didn't starve because of Cambodia's natural provision. Rural people returned to harvesting mangoes, pineapples, sweet potatoes, palm sugar, vegetables, bananas, shrimp, fish, and crabs. All this was supplemented by food and goods supplied by enterprising traders.

The aid agencies realized fairly soon that initial fears of a countrywide famine were exaggerated but, having generated so much support and outrage using those camp images of starving refugees, most were unwilling to admit they'd been wrong. The images, stories, and donations continued to flow.

23

Traveling Mercies

It was the LORD our God himself who brought us and our parents up out of Egypt, from that land of slavery, and performed those great signs before our eyes. He protected us on our entire journey and among all the nations through which we traveled.

—Joshua 24:17

In November, Samen's younger sister Samith and her husband, Try, announced that they were leaving Battambang for Thailand. Radha told Samen he didn't want her to lose track of her sister. About then Radha also heard that the Vietnamese were registering people and assigning them to rice farms. Radha had seen enough socialism; they decided to head for the border, although Radha was reluctant to leave Cambodia. He figured at the border he would have a better chance of taking care of his young family, and Samen's due date was coming up.

Amma, Ravy, and the two "adopted brothers" decided to stay in Battambang and someday make their way to Phnom Penh. Ravy wanted to go with Radha but was too sick to travel at the time. On the morning they left, Amma gave Radha all the rice she had—twenty-one ounces—and to Samen she gave a gold ring. "This is all I have," she said.

The four of them (Radha, Samen, Samith, and Try) met at Try's place outside Battambang, gathered up their belongings, and headed west toward the border. Samen and Samith were both about seven months pregnant, so Try hired a porter to haul his and Samith's stuff. Radha and Samen carried their own things—just a couple of bags for food, a pot, a few clothes, and some other items.

That evening, as the sun was going down, the group set off from Battambang northwest through the fields, traveling parallel to Highway 5. They were hiding from the Vietnamese and the Khmer Rouge, picking their way along the tops of dikes and through stands of trees. When the day dawned, they found a place to sleep in some bushes. They looked out and saw that the paths were completely empty. When the sun set again, they emerged from their hiding place and suddenly hundreds of people were there with them in the starlight, stepping carefully along the dikes. They hiked all night, and when the eastern sky began to lighten, the crowds began thinning. By the time the sun appeared, the fields and paths were empty again.

The tops of the dikes quickly started to break down with use, narrowing from two or three feet across to less than twelve inches. The broken ground was wet and slippery, so people slipped off into the muck and had to clamber back up. It became too dangerous for the expectant mothers, so on the first night, the Manickam party set off directly across the paddies. It was a hard slog for both women but slightly easier for Samith because her porter carried much of their load. All through the long hours of the night, Radha and Try pulled their wives through thick mud and sometimes water up to their waists.

On the second night, the rice fields gave way to forest and firm ground. They spread out plastic sheets and collapsed into sleep. It soon began to rain, and they tried to pull some of the plastic over their heads to keep the water out of their ears.

The next day as they were getting up, Radha looked over at Samen, who was just turning over. He flashed his hand over and grabbed her arm. "Don't turn," he said as calmly as he could. "Get up straight." Right behind her on the edge of the plastic sheet was a land mine. One wrong roll, and all five of them would have died.

They resumed their hike, traveling during the day now that they were well into the forests and could travel undercover. Samith, Try, and their porter were much less fatigued and set off briskly through the forest, soon outdistancing Radha and Samen. They heard later that Samith and Try went on to Nong Samet, also known as the "New Camp."

Radha and Samen arrived at the "Old Camp," a large trading settlement called Nong Chan right on the border in the evening of the fourth day of walking. Thailand had at this time both informal trading camps right along the border and internationally run refugee camps located farther into Thailand. Freedom Fighters, with AK-47s hanging from straps, lounged around the huts and markets, playing cards and killing time. Some of them were farm boys with very little exposure to the outside world. Radha saw several of them wearing rouge and lipstick—they didn't realize makeup was for women. He didn't dare laugh in their faces.

They put up a shelter and sold a silver bowl, the last family heirloom Samen owned, for four hundred baht (Thai currency, about sixteen dollars at the time) and the gold ring Amma had given Samen for two hundred baht. Those were the last things they owned of any value, but they had enough to get started making and selling fried noodles. As with the rice-flour cakes, it was a day-to-day existence—and a dangerous one. One day Samen heard shelling over the camp, so she grabbed her noodles and rushed back to their hut. That day they ate all their potential profits; it was discouraging.

After a month, in December 1979, Samen got word from Samith that she had found their brother Saman in the New Camp, Nong Samet, and wanted Radha and Samen to come too. So they slipped through the forests to the camp, where Radha got a job in the

International Red Cross hospital in the children's ward working with a Swedish doctor. Radha was usually on duty during the day, slept at the hospital at night as an informal ward supervisor, and also worked as need arose in the pharmacy tent.

Every day UN buses parked in the middle of the camp near the hospital, waiting for Cambodians who might want to travel farther into Thailand to the refugee camps. Most days only a few took advantage of them. The word was that the Thais were not especially welcoming to Cambodians. Military units patrolled the border and guarded the camp gates, and the camps were known as tough places with little food and much disease. Granted, creature comforts were sparse in Nong Samet, but at least they had some freedom there.

That month a missionary with the Christian and Missionary Alliance, Norman Ens, came to Nong Samet. He had known Samen's family in Phnom Penh before its fall to the Khmer Rouge. He recognized Saman and passed on word that two of their older sisters, Sameth and Samoeun, were already in the United States. After escaping with their six children through Thailand in 1976, Sameth and Savin later settled near Portland, Oregon. Samoeun, Vek Huong, and Wiphousana had survived the entire Khmer Rouge regime as well. They had been among the first to flee to Thailand in early 1979, and then Campus Crusade for Christ sponsored them for American visas. They were living in Long Beach, California.

Ens told Saman that he needed to get into the UN refugee camps in Thailand and then his sisters could sponsor him into the United States. Samen was thrilled when Saman delivered the news. Radha still wasn't quite sure he wanted to leave Cambodia forever. But he had their new baby to consider, and Samen was due in just a few weeks. What kind of life would the child have in Cambodia, and what about medical care?

Near the end of the month, the decision was nearly made for him when a party of Khmer Rouge raided the camp, trapping him, his family, and hundreds of refugees in the crossfire.

It was a midmorning in late December. One of Samen's cousins named Limchheng and his wife and two children had just arrived in Nong Samet. Radha was working at the hospital; one of the regular helpers hadn't shown up, so the Swedish doctor pulled him in to help.

Suddenly they heard gunfire nearby and explosions. Radha glanced out of the tent and saw the black pajamas of the Khmer Rouge soldiers running through the camp, grabbing what they wanted and blasting away at any Freedom Fighters they glimpsed down the streets. Then a pistol-waving Khmer Rouge burst into the hospital tent, trailed by a handful of soldiers, and demanded to know who was running the pharmacy. Nobody said anything while he ranted and threatened and demanded medicines. And then one of the soldiers spoke up. Radha realized with a jolt that it was the surgery assistant who hadn't shown up for work that morning. He was a Khmer Rouge spy.

"This comrade," he said, pointing at Radha. "He works in the pharmacy." Radha forced a teeth-grating grin—he hated being called comrade. They hustled Radha over to the pharmacy tent and forced him to explain which medicines were which and how to use them. Radha did his best, and they swept hundreds of the bottles and boxes into bags. Then they left without shooting him.

He looked out the tent door and saw that the camp was in chaos, with people dashing everywhere. He ran back to his family. They had to get out. They gathered up some stuff and left their hut, rushing west to get deeper into Thailand.

They weren't alone. Hundreds of people had the same idea, running hunched over as bullets ripped through the air around them. They heard yelling and more gunfire. It looked to Radha like the Khmer Rouge were on the left and the Freedom Fighters on the right, and the crowd was dashing through the crossfire. Saman became separated from the others in the confusion (he eventually ended up back at Nong Chan; Samith and her family had left the day before on a bus for the refugee camps). Many people in the crowd just fled into the jungle.

Radha, Samen, and her cousin's family kept their heads down and followed the bulk of the crowd. They were maybe two hundred yards outside the camp boundaries when a huge explosion blasted dirt and rocks high into the air. More screams. A land mine had ripped apart a group of people just yards in front of them, leaving behind a hole in the ground and shattered corpses dimly visible through the dust and smoke.

"Stop!" he yelled at Samen and grabbed her arm. "Back up!" They gathered up their relatives and hurried back the way they had come. They might have been able to make it across—others did, apparently—but it was too dangerous to try. They huddled in a shelter near the hospital and listened to the gunfire cracking through the morning air.

The firefight continued for perhaps another ten minutes, and then the Khmer Rouge retreated. Radha guessed they had gotten what they wanted—some supplies and medicine, and maybe some prisoners. The Manickams stayed undercover until early afternoon. Radha went back to the pharmacy and collected some of the medicine and vitamins for Samen.

After talking it over, the group decided to make another try for the refugee camps in Thailand. They couldn't stay where they were. In the late afternoon, they joined the scattered groups of people setting out along the red dirt road that marked the border to Thailand. They kept to the Cambodian side, not wanting to risk being shot by the Thai military. That night they bedded down near a rice field.

The next day large UN-sponsored trucks, the kind with wooden slats for sides used for hauling livestock, showed up, and officials set up tables to register refugees for the trip into Thailand. The Manickams got into line and registered, and the following day officials began calling names.

The Manickams eventually heard their names and clambered aboard. Dirty and skinny people packed the truck bed. The situation forcefully made Radha recall the last time he'd been stuffed into the back of a cattle truck with his family. He had expected then to be taken across the Thai border but ended up starting a cooperative at Phnom Tippedei.

According to rumors, the Thai people really didn't like the Khmers and would rob or even kill you. He had heard about Preah Vihear by this time. At the checkpoints harsh Thai soldiers searched the refugees and took what they wanted. *We mean nothing to them*, Radha thought. He prayed for protection. So did Samen.

The soldiers, however, had no intention of killing or sending them back to Cambodia. After several hours, the truck arrived at a UN staging area, and the refugees got off and lined up in front of long tables to register yet again. The Manickams got their "tracing card," which was a booklet that would keep track of their movements through the system and the various UN camps should they be moved from one to another. Officials also searched them again, and this time they confiscated the bag of medicines Radha had collected. He protested, saying, "It's for my pregnant wife!" but they took the bag anyway. "You don't need it. We have a hospital here," the official told him.

They had arrived at Khao I Dang, the latest UN-run refugee camp. The date was January 1, 1980.

24

Church of the Lord Jesus Christ

God loves you and has a wonderful plan for your life.

—Bill Bright, *The Four Spiritual Laws*

Khao I Dang was huge, holding at its peak more than 140,000 Cambodian refugees in row after row of long huts with thatch walls. Most of them were New People or had otherwise suffered persecution under the Khmer Rouge. The camp, operated by the United Nations High Commissioner for Refugees, was set up on a plain next to a mountain in the Cardamom range in late 1979. In theory, there was a room for each family, but conditions were very crowded. Radha and Samen and her cousin's family were assigned to a hut in group 11, and after a couple of days managed to find Samith and Try in another group.

On January 9, Samith delivered a daughter, and on January 12, Samen delivered a daughter as well. Radha and Samen named their girl Chandra, an Indian name that means "Moon."

Had they made it? Were they guaranteed passage to a Western country now that they'd made it to the official UN refugee camp? Were they safe? No. Thailand had set up the refugee camps as tem-

234

porary holding pens, way stations from which the Cambodians were shipped out to other nations. But the process was painstakingly slow and bureaucratic. Not everybody who made it across the Thai border qualified for a visa to one of the receiving countries. Other problems arose as well.

No water was available that first day, so Radha and Samen's cousin Limchheng went to a well at a nearby village. Their group leader later reprimanded them sternly, telling them they must not leave the camp boundaries. "The borders are marked by posts," he said. "If you get caught, the Thai soldiers will put you in jail."

No jail really existed, but there was a small, open-air enclosure of barbed wire into which the Thai guards shoved offenders of various kinds—ranging from food smugglers and suspected bandits to people who had sneaked into the camp looking for missing family members. Those in jail were not entitled to shade or water. They just sat in the sun and baked, lacking even hair for protection because the guards shaved the prisoners' heads. Radha occasionally saw Thai soldiers beating the prisoners or kicking them with their heavy military boots.

Security was low on the Thai soldiers' list of priorities. The camp had no fence for the first several weeks, so bandits raided the camp almost nightly. The wire fences, when they were built, hardly slowed down the bandits. The refugees went to bed in fear of knife- or rifle-wielding criminals dragging them out of their beds and beating them until they gave up their tiny stashes of gold or money, and they could do little to protect themselves. The soldiers didn't bother to patrol; they just hung around the front gates. Few Cambodians spoke to the Thai soldiers, as they could expect only a harsh reply.

Many agencies offered various services. In early 1980, thirty-seven foreign agencies assisted in Khao I Dang, ranging from Catholic Relief Services to Doctors without Borders to a group of holistic healers from California. The Cambodia/Thai border area also had ninety-five humanitarian organizations in addition to the UN agencies and the Red Cross, all with money and some tripping over one another in their eagerness to relieve Cambodians' suffering.[1] Authorities estimated that between informal trading camps like Nong Samet, UN camps, Khmer Rouge settlements, and other groups, about six hundred thousand Cambodians were living in the region. The United Nations and other agencies provided food, and while it wasn't great food, it kept body and soul together. The Manickams received fourteen ounces of rice per person per day—an unimaginable amount of food in the cooperatives—and each week a family of three received a quarter of a chicken, a few dried fish, and a bit of salt.

Radha was grateful that he and his family weren't starving, although the food itself was discouraging. The broken rice often had maggots. The fish was old, dry, and yellow, and it smelled of the salt in which it had been preserved. Samen had to soak the fish for an hour before she could cook it. Over time, many camp residents planted small vegetable patches ("swamp cabbage" was popular), and a kind of gray market sprang up. Local Thai villagers often came up to the barbed wire surrounding the camps to sell food and clothes from small stands, hastily covering up their wares if Thai soldiers wandered by. Refugees who could get their hands on a few baht, usually sent in from relatives, could survive fairly comfortably.

Water was dear because the camp contained no streams or springs. Water trucks arrived regularly to replenish the large tanks from which people could draw their daily ration. A bucket for a family of three had to cover drinking, cooking, and washing. The water shortage, plus the lack of latrines, made hygiene difficult—even more so than in the cooperatives, where a canal was usually nearby. Diseases were a problem throughout the camp. Even though medical relief programs sprang up, conflict among the agencies made effective treatment difficult. Camp residents got a shower maybe once a week. Almost as bad as the conditions was the lack of news from the outside world. The refugees felt forgotten (knowing nothing of the massive publicity given to their plight) and cut off from relatives still in Cambodia.

Then in mid-February 1980, the Nget siblings received a letter from Sameth and Samoeun in the United States. They had heard from a missionary friend who was ministering in the refugee camps that some of their siblings were alive. The letter instructed the siblings to gather all the family members because Sameth and Samoeun were going to sponsor them into the United States. From then on, they regularly sent money and updates to those in the camp.

When Radha and Samen got the letter, they immediately sent word to Saman to come from Nong Chan to Khao I Dang as soon as he could. They also investigated ways to get Sidore and Credy, the two youngest Nget brothers, who were still in Phnom Penh, out of Cambodia. The families didn't have much money, but they pooled their gold and hired a guide to smuggle the boys out. The brothers arrived in Khao I Dang in early March. By this time, other relatives were gathering around the Ngets, including Samoeun's father-in-law and her sister-in-law and family, not to mention a couple of other women and their children who had attached themselves to the party. By the time Saman submitted all the names to the US embassy in Thailand, the list had a couple of dozen names on it.

Radha had heard about some Christian house churches in the camp, and soon after he arrived, he overheard a hymn sung in Khmer while wandering through section 5. He found the hut and saw a white guy leading the music inside. It was Don Cormack, an Overseas Missionary Fellowship missionary Radha had met in Phnom Penh in 1974. Then Cormack hadn't spoken a word of Khmer and now he was leading worship in the language. Radha came in, and Cormack and the other believers told him about a large church that had been set up next to a Buddhist temple at the foot of the mountain, over a half mile away from his section. It was known as Church of the Lord Jesus Christ.

Radha walked right over and met the leaders, including Pastor Nhem Sokun, who had been a pastor at a Christian and Missionary

Alliance church before 1975 and had worked with Samen's brother in Phnom Penh. Things were looking up.

Church leaders were cordial enough to Radha as a believer but understandably also a little cool. Radha was eager to step into some sort of ministry, given his experience at Maranatha Church, but the leaders made no offers. Sure, he was married to the daughter of one of their old colleagues, but that meant little given how the Khmer Rouge had arranged forced marriages. The long-standing tension between the decidedly uncharismatic Alliance Christians and Maranatha Church didn't make things any easier. Radha brought his family the following Sunday, and from then on began spending many of his days at the church.

Over time he earned the elders' trust and began working with various ministries. Radha helped one Overseas Missionary Fellowship missionary, Alice Compain, track down people in the camp whose relatives had sent money and letters from overseas. He kept the money that arrived with the letters locked in a drawer in the church. He was on the evangelism committee and assisted a young Dutch couple who brought a tape recorder and a loudspeaker system into the camp every day. They would tape Radha presenting several Bible stories in Khmer, and then the couple, Radha, and other believers would go into the muddy streets and play the message with music. They would hold up large cardboard pictures illustrating the stories and then mingle with the curious people and spread the gospel.

Meanwhile, Church of the Lord Jesus Christ was growing rapidly. It held about one thousand people for Sunday services, and many more would sit on the ground outside and listen through the thatch walls. They held baptisms in a big tin tank. The UN camp director was reputed to be a believer, so despite the shortage, there was usually water in the tank (even though it was pretty thick by the end of the service—those washed in the waters of baptism understood it was a spiritual cleansing only). The church held lengthy prayer services, some going on all night, and people often slept at the church. The elders also organized a system of house churches and home Bible studies in each of Khao I Dang's eleven sections.

Many refugees were responsive to the gospel despite Cambodia's Buddhist history and tradition. Their lives had been shattered. Where was Buddha when they had lost their family, home, and hope? This Jesus was supposedly alive. The cheerful countenances of the Christians attracted some people, perhaps, and they were realizing that their deeds were not going to save them. Others in the camp were angry at this influx of Christianity into Khmer culture and called the Cambodian Christians "lost crocodiles," meaning they had lost their ponds, their identity as Buddhists. "Yes I did," one believer responded stoutly one day. "My pond was dry, so I went looking for a pond with water, and I found one, Jesus, and that pond never dries up."

The church at Khao I Dang continued to grow for the next few years. At its height in the early 1980s, it had perhaps twenty thousand believers, and this was in a camp in which thousands of people came and went monthly. Many of these believers left Cambodia, but many thousands returned to their home country to become the foundation of the Khmer Christian Church.

On another Sunday, Radha saw through the window of an office in the church a man named Hoy, Kha's father-in-law and the one-time village leader of Kok Porn. In the cooperatives, he was a brutal, vicious man—the one who gave the order to set up the communal kitchen and confiscate the food. In Radha's mind, he was the man who killed his father.

Radha eyed Hoy as he walked into the church and sat down. Radha could feel his anger rising. He thought Hoy deserved to die but not by being murdered in the street. Radha wanted somebody, some authority, to arrest, charge, and execute him. But instead of acting on his anger, he asked God to calm him down and stayed in the office.

Radha could hear the sermon over the loudspeaker and eventually heard the pastor deliver the altar call. Radha watched as Hoy went up front to accept Christ. Radha felt happy in a way he couldn't explain. It felt in some ways like the heady days of ministry before the fall of Phnom Penh.

Radha and his family, however, were still stuck in a refugee camp that was periodically invaded by bandits, thieves, and murderers. One day in April, Radha and Samen moved to an empty hut next door; it was in slightly better condition than theirs was. Its former occupants, a group of young adults, had taken possession of another nearby hut.

About midnight, some noises at the foot of their bamboo bed awakened Samen. Chandra, who was only about four months old, was sleeping with her parents. Samen thought that one of her cousins had sneaked into their hut, and she was angry. "Wake up!" she said, elbowing Radha. "Nol is in here taking noodles again!"

Radha was struggling awake and just starting to sit up, when suddenly a hand lifted up their mosquito netting and he felt something cold and hard against his neck. He froze, and then somebody—perhaps several people, one looked like a woman—yanked him from the bed and started to deliver a sound beating. "Give us the money!" a harsh voice demanded between slaps, kicks, and punches. Radha scrambled to find the few hundred baht (about $4 or $5) he had in the hut, Chandra's milk money, and a watch Don Cormack had given him a few weeks earlier. "Where's the rest of it?" they demanded during a pause in the beating. He managed to stammer out that he had just arrived from Cambodia and didn't have any money.

They didn't believe him and continued to demand money. They tied him up with his krama and threatened to drag him outside the camp and kill him immediately. They pulled Samen from the bed and gave her a few slaps as well. Chandra was wailing by this time, Samen was crying, and the robbers were shouting. Radha began to pray.

Lord, he prayed silently, *all those years under the Khmer Rouge You looked after me. You protected me when I was in danger, You fed me when I was starving, You saved my life many times. You told me You had a plan for my life. My life is in Your hands.*

Then the bandits began to drag him outside. "You're coming with us," they told him. Samen was frantic by then.

"It's OK," he told her. "Stay here. Don't scream. Don't cry."

The robbers pulled him along, and the whole group burst into the next hut. Inside were the young adults who had just vacated Radha's new hut, but they, forewarned by the commotion next door, seemed ready. They fought back with their fists. In the melee, one of the robbers jammed a knife into a refugee's shoulder, and the blood sprayed all over Radha's shirt.

Just then, through the thatch walls of the hut, they heard the sound of military boots rushing up. Thai soldiers were coming to investigate. The robbers dashed out of the hut and disappeared into the darkness. Radha hurried back to his hut. Samen stopped crying and stared at him, shocked. He was covered in blood, most not his own. The neighbors came to their hut, and it was a long time before things settled down and they all went back to bed. *Lord*, Radha and Samen prayed, *You have spared our lives once again. We promise that if we get the chance we will spend the rest of our lives serving You in ministry. We will do nothing else.*

The next morning Radha's left eye was completely black, and Samen had a deep red mark on her cheek. The bruises on his side took a month to heal. Radha soon realized that his assailants had been expecting someone else in the hut. The young people who had vacated it the day before had recently moved in from another camp, one whose residents supposedly had more money than most refugees did. The robbers themselves were probably Khmer, he guessed. They threw in a few Thai phrases to make themselves sound like regular border bandits, but he recognized their Khmer accents. The Thais arrested those particular bandits a few months later trying to get on a bus headed to Malaysia. He was glad to hear it, but he never got his baht back.

Through the steamy summer months, life in the camps was slow. Radha kept more or less busy working with the church ministries, while Samen looked after baby Chandra. They knew their applications were working their way through the international bureaucracy, but it was hard to wait. Everyone talked about getting out, and most people wanted to go to the United States. It was the Promised Land, where everyone was free and there was lots of food. And for the growing number of Christian Cambodian refugees, America was a Christian nation, a place where everyone shared their faith. They couldn't wait. It was going to be good—no, it was going to be wonderful.

In October 1980, Radha and Samen learned that the UN authorities were preparing to shuffle people around to different camps. They were assigned to go to Sa Kaeo II the next morning. The original Sa Kaeo had been home to many Khmer Rouge, and according to rumors, they still basically ran Sa Kaeo II. At the very least, many Khmer Rouge still lived in the camp. Nobody wanted to go there. But at least Radha and Samen knew several other families from the church who were also going, including one of the pastors, Chan Ham.

Samen's siblings and their families and several friends and fellow ministers from the church came the next morning to see them off. Most of the people on the bus were fellow believers. Even more encouraging was the bus itself, which was nice. Radha was accustomed to traveling in a filthy railcar or cattle truck, or just walking. Now here they were, each in their own padded seat—with air-conditioning!

After a short ride, they arrived at Sa Kaeo II and were assigned a room—two families to each room, two rooms to a hut. Radha and Samen arranged to switch so they could stay with three other Christian couples from the church. In Sa Kaeo II, the food improved a bit—more vegetables, more of everything, really—so they all decided to cook together, eat together, and pray together. Each night they lit a kerosene lamp and read their Bibles together. Overall, it wasn't too bad.

Radha's immersion into ministry had not relieved all of his bitterness, especially for the loss of his thirteen family members. He doubted he would ever see his mother and brother again. He doubted he would ever return to Cambodia. Still, his anger was slowly passing. He and some of the refugees were even able to joke about the bad old days under the Khmer Rouge.

A church was already operating in Sa Kaeo II, but no one asked Radha to do much officially until one of the Christian and Missionary Alliance missionaries recognized him as the guy who was married to the daughter of Pastor Nget Choy and pointed him out to the leadership. They asked him first to work with the youth and then to plan a Christmas pageant, which was coming up in a couple of months. He recruited some young people and started practicing every afternoon.

Radha also happened to run into Don Cormack again. "Take this Bible," Cormack said, "and keep it with you. I can't come back here very often, so I don't know when I'll see you again." Radha later opened up the Bible and found 400 baht inside. It came at a perfect time; Chandra needed milk, and he didn't have any money.

The next day he was out doing street evangelism with one of the youth, a sharp teen girl named Sopheary. On this day, Radha, walking down the street, looked into a hut and saw Leap, the liver-eating Khmer Rouge cadre, the one who had pulled on Radha's beard. He was sitting in a hut with his wife and a baby. "Older Brother Leap!" he called. The man swiveled his head around, fear in his eyes. Leap was short, and now he also was thin and pale. So were his wife and daughter. Radha stepped into the hut and sat down.

Leap didn't seem quite so frightening anymore. "I'm not going to do anything," Radha said. "I'm not going to take revenge for anything. What's past is past."

Leap was silent as Radha talked about Christ and the forgiveness of sins. He talked for what seemed like a long time. Finally, Leap said, "I'm glad you don't hold a grudge, and I thank you for it." The Khmer word he used for grudge was *kum*, the desire for disproportionate revenge.

Then Radha remembered when Leap had caught him with a magazine. "Yes," he said. "I can read and write."

Leap allowed a small smile. "I knew it, but you still lied to me."

"Could you blame me?" Radha asked.

Then he looked at Leap's little girl. "Doesn't she have enough food?" he asked.

"We have the daily ration," Leap said, "but my wife doesn't have much milk."

Radha went home to find Samen making dinner. He told her that he had seen Leap and his wife and that they didn't have enough milk for their baby.

Samen suggested that they share some of their money. They settled on half of Cormack's gift, 200 baht, and Radha went back to Leap's hut.

"Older Brother," Radha said, "my wife and I would like you to have this to buy milk for the baby." Tears came to Leap's eyes. "Thank you, Dha," he said, and then Radha turned and walked away. He never saw Leap again.

25

Family Ties

A ministering angel shall my sister be.

William Shakespeare, *Hamlet*

In early December 1980, Radha heard a familiar voice exclaim, "I know him!" He turned around, and there was Todd Burke, traveling with another missionary. He had come to Sa Kaeo II looking for believers from Maranatha Church. He embraced Radha, who found it uncomfortable because Burke had always been kind of overbearing, and they both wept.

Radha took Burke to his hut, introduced him to Samen, and described some of what they'd gone through. Burke offered to sponsor him into the United States, but Radha said no because Samen's family was looking after that. "Call me when you arrive," Burke said, and then he left. [1]

The Christmas pageant rolled around a few weeks later. Radha helped the kids dress up to put on a nativity scene with Mary, Jesus, Joseph, shepherds, angels, wise men—the whole works. It was another reminder of happier times in Phnom Penh. The church was packed, and hundreds more people sat on the ground at the edges.

245

Thai Christians brought toys, cookies, and candies to give away to Khmer children who were, of course, very excited. Any child younger than six had never known life apart from either the camps or the Khmer Rouge, who forbade toys. Chandra, who was almost one, received a Barbie doll. She was very happy. So was Radha. They sang "O Holy Night."

Christmas of 1980 was his first since 1974. The refugee camp still felt like no-man's-land, but just being able to celebrate Christmas gave Radha a sense of hope. The Christian families in Radha's group pooled their UN rations and food they had grown to put on a dinner: fish and swamp cabbage and some vegetables. Samen, the couple had recently realized, was expecting their second child.

That month UN officials began to post names for the next stop on their trip, a place in Chonburi province called the Holding Center. Just after Christmas, Radha, Samen, and Chandra's names appeared on the list, but none of their Christian friends were listed. The next day they got on the bus.

The Holding Center, Phanat Nikhom, where refugees were processed and interviewed, looked a lot like Sa Kaeo II, only more forbidding with a double fence around the perimeter. Officials arrested anyone caught between the fences. Refugees whose visas were finally approved were sent through the fences and across the highway to another building, the Transit Center, where they waited for the bus that would take them to the Bangkok airport.

It was quickly clear that the less time they spent in the Holding Center, the better. Refugees were housed in shelters made of corrugated asbestos-cement sheets and erected on concrete slabs, each hall holding perhaps ten families. Radha and Samen stepped into their shelter and looked around in dismay at the dozens of other gaunt, struggling refugees. It was packed and noisy—but not with cheerful hum and chatter. Radha could hear babies crying and the conversation of stressed adults. The scene was so gloomy it reminded Radha of the huts in Tuol Mateh. Radha and his family were assigned a spot a little larger than a mat, perhaps five feet wide and eight feet long.

They spent six months in the Holding Center. The Christians, as they always did, quickly found one another. Samen's brother Saman had just arrived with some relatives, and several evangelical pastors and elders were already in the camp, including some of Radha and Samen's Christian friends from Phnom Penh. Soon they began a church with Sunday services, using musical instruments donated by Thai Christians. Radha led Bible studies, helped out a church of Laotian believers, and worked with a Catholic agency distributing clothes from a small warehouse. He also worked with missionary Alice Compain, who had him typing up tracts on a Khmer language typewriter she had hauled into the camp.

Compain had first arrived in Cambodia in 1974, and a short time later the Khmer Rouge tossed her out. She was a slightly severe-looking woman with a big heart and a strong will. She came to Thailand when the refugee camps opened.

"You should go back to Cambodia," she told Radha regularly. "The church there needs you. Cambodia needs you."

"You don't know what it was like," he would tell her. "You can't imagine. And I think God wants me to leave, to move forward, to go to America."

The slightly tense discussions eventually turned into arguments that, for a Cambodian man and a Western woman, were quite heated. Radha eventually refused to talk to her about it. "You don't understand," he told her.

He simply could not bear the thought of going back to Cambodia, even though he knew his mother and brother were still there. The Vietnamese might be an improvement over the Khmer Rouge, but he'd had enough of Communism. They were already organizing people into collectives when he left. He wanted a future for his wife and children, and America offered freedom, security, and prosperity. You could get the job you wanted—no more wading through rice paddies. No more fearing a cadre would take you into the fields and murder you on a whim. And the food! Radha didn't really know what it would be like, but he was sure there would be lots of it.

When he was growing up, nobody in Cambodia seriously thought they could one day go to America. It was just a pipe dream—too wonderful to take seriously. This romanticized view of the United States was especially true for many Christians. They viewed it as a heaven on earth, a place where righteousness ruled and everybody was a Christian. It was a Christian nation, right? That's what everybody said.

In April, officials called the Manickam name, and after some preliminaries, they stood before an American immigration official seated at a table. A Cambodian interpreter stood beside him. Radha, not wanting to interfere in the process, answered the questions in Khmer. He swore to tell the truth, the whole truth, so help him God, and then the interrogation began. Radha confirmed his birthplace (Phnom Penh) and citizenship (Indian), and Samen did the same. The officer also asked about Radha's religion.

"I'm a Christian," Radha said.

"He's a Buddhist," the interpreter said, apparently because all Cambodians should be Buddhist.

"Pardon me," interjected Radha in English. "I'm a Christian."

The American looked up in surprise. "You speak English?" he asked. "Why didn't you say so before?" They continued in English until he had more questions for Samen, who told him about her sisters in California and Oregon.

Without another word, the immigration official stamped their papers. They watched him anxiously, hearts pounding, because they didn't know what the stamp meant. Then the official looked up and smiled. "You passed," he said. "Congratulations." Broad grins broke out over Radha's and Samen's faces, but they restrained themselves until they got outside—and then they jumped and laughed and celebrated.

They had to wait two more months to leave, however. Officials told them they couldn't travel on the plane while Samen was pregnant. They would have to wait until she had the baby.[2]

Lakshmi was born in April, and on June 22, 1981, they got on the bus for the short trip across the highway to the Transit Center. Three days later, they hopped aboard a bus to yet another transit camp inside Bangkok. The huts in this one had gravel floors and no walls, but they were only there a day. At midnight on June 26, they were roused and herded onto a bus that took them to the airport, about an hour's drive away, so they could have their paperwork processed in time for their 6:00 a.m. flight to Los Angeles.

They had only a few possessions—their clothes, a plastic bag containing their immigration documents, and one small bag. The passengers on the plane were all refugees, as far as Radha could tell, but only a few were Cambodian. The rest were Vietnamese, likely boat people who had managed to land on Thai beaches.

Radha and Samen had never been on an airplane before, but given the stress of leaving their homeland, they didn't quite appreciate the novelty of the experience. They sat in their seats, feeling stunned, each with an infant on their laps. After a brief stop in Japan, the Manickams touched down in Los Angeles. Two women from Cambodian churches in the Los Angeles area met the young couple (they were twenty-eight and twenty-six) when they disembarked and helped them through the immigration process.

When Radha and Samen came through the airport gate, Samen's sister Samoeun and her husband, Vek Huong, greeted them. Samoeun hadn't seen Samen since 1975 and looked at her little sister with shock. She and Huong had expected her to be thin, but they hadn't expected her to be so brutally skeletal, like a bamboo pole. Samoeun took Chandra out of Radha's arms, Samen held on to Lakshmi, and they crowded into one another's arms, sobbing.

26

Settling in Seattle

This is what the LORD Almighty, the God of Israel, says to all
those I carried into exile from Jerusalem to Babylon: "Build
houses and settle down; plant gardens and eat what they produce. Marry and have sons and daughters."

—Jeremiah 29:4–6

It was dark, and Radha was standing on the edge of a canal by
a rice field, surrounded by Khmer Rouge soldiers. He'd been
there many times before, only this time his elbows, not someone
else's, were tied behind his back. He could feel the fear rising, and
he hunched his shoulders against the blow that was coming, the
club about to smash into the back of his neck. It was coming, any
second now, it was coming, and it was about to descend. He started
screaming and screaming, and then he was shaking and then . . .

He was in bed, still screaming. Samen was shaking him and calling,
"Wake up, Bong! Bong! Wake up!" Slowly the bedroom of their Long
Beach apartment came back into focus, and he caught his breath
and felt the sheets and his sweat.

It was November 1981, five months after they had come to California, and both he and Samen had been having nightmares. They would both continue to have them for many years. Radha's varied a bit, but the gist was always the same: Khmer Rouge cadres had arrested and were about to kill him in the same places and the same ways he had seen others executed. Sometimes it was a hoe to the back of the neck; sometimes he was about to be shot or have his throat cut.

He and Samen had landed in America, and he was grateful to be there, but it was not quite heaven on earth. There were lots of churches around, sure, but the United States just wasn't as Christian as Radha had anticipated. He couldn't have explained what he had thought America would be like, but he wasn't feeling the warm fellowship of believers he had remembered from before 1975—or even what he had experienced in the refugee camps.

Everything was different, but everything reminded him of Cambodia. When he and Samen rode in a car, he would remember what it was like to ride in the back of an oxcart. When they ate, they would talk about how they used to eat—or rather, not eat—in the cooperatives. Once Radha was sitting outside Samoeun and Vek Huong's house when the sound of a siren flooded the neighborhood. He jumped up and dashed into the house, visions of air raids flooding through his memory. "No, there's no war here in America," Vek Huong said. "It's just an ambulance."

Radha was studying eight hours a day at California Trade Technical School to become a welder. A state aid program for refugees covered his tuition, and the state also provided a stipend for food and rent. The college had no dining area, so at lunch he would sit on the ground in an alley behind the school and pull out the rice and chicken Samen made for him each day. He would lean against a wall, surrounded mostly by Vietnamese and Laotian classmates, and chew on the chicken thigh cooked in a spicy marinade just as they had made in Cambodia. Eating on the ground, bowl on his knees, was like being back in a cuisine, only the food was better and nobody searched him for contraband snails.

Food on street corners Radha and Samen understood, but Americans had food everywhere—at church and in gas stations. And fast-food joints seemed thick upon the ground. And the amount of food wasted! And the grocery stores! They had never seen such things. It wasn't just the variety and sheer volume of food on display, although that was overwhelming. It was that nobody bartered. How could anyone expect to get the best price without bargaining? It didn't make sense.

He and Samen had a running joke about making "chicken dessert"— mixing rice porridge with sugar and adding chicken. It struck them as funny because back in Cambodia they had spent all their time yearning for food, and now they could put together all the foods they had wanted then but couldn't have—and as much as they wanted. They didn't actually make chicken dessert, but they could have. That was the point. No more cadres loomed over them to order their deaths at this abuse of Angka's generosity. No more prepubescent spies turned them in for disloyalty to Angka's provision. They were free, and sometimes it left them giddy, and sometimes it seemed they just couldn't move on.

The immigrant settlement agencies offered a variety of career training programs. Radha chose welding for the pay—a promised $20 per hour when he was state certified. That was good money back in 1981 in the United States, and wealth beyond imagination if you converted a year's wages back into Cambodian riels.

He sometimes recalled the promise he and Samen had made after the bandits robbed them in Khao I Dang that they would enter the ministry, but at the same time, he had just had enough. He was in the wealthiest country in the world. Many other refugees, including many Cambodians, had landed in Los Angeles, Chicago, or Atlanta and had built very comfortable lives for themselves. They had started small with jobs in restaurants and construction and other fields, and soon they had their own prosperous businesses.

Certainly, he could make a comfortable living for his family as a welder. That was important to Radha because he felt, almost immediately, that a few in Samen's family were skeptical about him. He was Indian, and they were Khmer. When they first met him, he was very scruffy, thin, and dark, and there is a powerful Cambodian cultural stigma against dark-skinned people. He suspected that some relatives regarded him as a "round potato"—in English, an ignorant country bumpkin who couldn't take care of his family. They knew Radha was from a wealthy Phnom Penh family, but what had he ever done himself? They didn't say much to his face, but he believed they had real doubts about whether he was able to look after Samen in America's wide-open society. So he was anxious to prove himself and determined to make serious money. His father had been successful in a new country; he would be too.

So Radha worked from the fall of 1981 to April 1982 completing the welding certification. When he graduated, it felt like he had finally arrived. Their third child, daughter Priscilla, arrived a month later.

But somehow Radha never landed a job as a welder. He applied at several different places, but nobody called him back. He and Samen continued to survive on state assistance. He was too busy to be very disappointed, however, because he became involved with several different Khmer ministries in the region. For example, he assisted with English classes at the Cambodian Christian Center, a ministry affiliated with Campus Crusade for Christ that Vek Huong had started in Long Beach. He worked with Paul Ellison (son of David Ellison, one of the original Christian and Missionary Alliance missionaries to Cambodia) on translating theological education by extension courses into Khmer. He also became a board member of the Cambodian Evangelical Church in Long Beach, which was affiliated with the Christian and Missionary Alliance, and sometimes preached in Khmer Alliance churches in the area.

Once he came across a pile of Campus Crusade's "Four Spiritual Laws" tracts. He opened one up and read for the first time, "Law 1: God loves you and has a wonderful plan for your life." This made him vividly recall singing "This World Is Not My Home" on the termite hill.

Radha's involvement with the Alliance created complications. His father-in-law had left the Alliance back in Phnom Penh before the revolution because of a bitter dispute, and he could tell Samen's family didn't approve of his involvement with the organization.

As well, Radha became part of a group of pastors, including his brother-in-law Saman, who wanted to start a network of Khmer churches of various denominations. Tens of thousands of Cambodians had arrived in the United States in recent years, and several Khmer churches had sprung up in southern California and other nearby states. The pastors ran into conflict with the Alliance's Khmer leaders, who were unwilling to have their people working outside denominational lines. That was a problem, because he was ministering in an Alliance church. He was forced to leave the network even before it got going, which he found both disappointing and hard to understand.

Despite the conflicts and frustrations, Radha soon realized that he did want to enter full-time ministry after all. His experience in California was a sort of capstone for his informal ministry training in Phnom Penh and the camps. It also got his name out among Khmer churches looking for pastors. In November 1982, University Presbyterian Church in Seattle, a four-thousand-member urban congregation, invited him to candidate for and then work with its ministry to Cambodian refugees. The Manickam family packed up and arrived in Seattle on January 10, 1983, with two suitcases and three girls from eight months to three years old.

The church had rented for them a two-bedroom unit in Mt. Baker Apartments, which was in a poor part of town and infested with rats and cockroaches. The church chose it because many of the Cambodian refugees had settled in the neighborhood. The church additionally supplied the Manickams with some household items and furniture, as well as a banana-yellow Honda Civic to drive. The first time he drove the car to his office at University Presbyterian, he got lost coming home in the dark. Samen, for her part, struggled to adjust to the weather, the neighborhood, and the distance from her family in California. She found it difficult to become confident speaking English, in part because she was able to spend much of her time with fellow Khmer refugees. The children grew up speaking English, of course. Overall, the Manickams had somewhat of a tough start in Seattle. But eventually Samen and the children settled in.

Radha's ministry went well from the beginning. About fifty Cambodians were attending the Khmer service at University Presbyterian when Radha first came. He started a series of Bible studies for men, women, and youth, and began training people to lead them. He visited homes, prayed with people, preached, and generally did the work of a pastor.

He also asked the church to stop handing out food or household items to Cambodians who had been in the country long enough to establish themselves. Some families left as a result, but the church grew anyway. By 1985, Khmer Evangelical Church had grown to close to two hundred people. Radha and Samen's son, Jonathan, was born in December 1985, and his fourth daughter, Sarah, arrived in January 1987.

Cambodian Ministries for Christ was incorporated in 1984 out of that initial network of Khmer pastors, with Samen's brother Saman as the president. Radha became involved there as well. He helped organize conferences and over the next several years regularly counseled and advised Khmer churches across the country.

As the years went by, Radha kept as informed as he could about affairs in his home country. The news was dismal. By 1983, with the threat of famine receding, international aid began to draw down. As living conditions improved somewhat, the stream of Cambodian refugees to the United States slowed from a high of 27,100 in 1981 to just a few thousand per year by the end of the decade.[1]

The People's Republic of Kampuchea, still led by ex–Khmer Rouge officer Heng Samrin, solidified its hold on the country, even as many of its most educated and capable citizens continued to flee. When it first came to power, the PRK government allowed considerable local control of affairs but was less forgiving when it came to politics. It implemented an indoctrination program (including "reeducation camps") designed to impress a Vietnamese-flavored Communist ideology on the devastated population. It jailed thousands of political prisoners, and most of them were not Khmer Rouge. Instead, many officials in the new administration were themselves ex–Khmer Rouge soldiers and cadres. The Vietnamese justified this by blaming the past atrocities on the "genocidal Pol Pot–Ieng Sary clique."[2] The problem with the Khmer Rouge, according to the Communist Vietnamese, was not Communist ideology faithfully implemented but maniacal leaders.

The maniacal leaders, including Pol Pot, spent much effort right after 1980 on an international public relations campaign. They claimed that not only were they misunderstood and their "mistakes" exaggerated but also that they weren't even Communists anymore. And whatever had happened was all Vietnam's fault.

A *New York Times* article in March 1980 described the leaders' luxurious jungle accommodations to which they invited reporters: beds with mattresses in tidy bungalows, fresh flowers, French food, and Johnnie Walker Scotch whiskey.[3] "With their Chinese dollars, the formerly Spartan Khmer Rouge began to throw lavish parties at the United Nations and assiduously courted delegates from around the world," writes Shawcross in *The Quality of Mercy*.[4]

The dissolution of the Communist Party of Kampuchea and the Khmer Rouge leaders' repudiation of socialism, which nobody believed, came because the Chinese insisted on a three-way alliance that included the Khmer Rouge, the People's National Liberation Front led by a former Cambodian politician named Son Sann, and Norodom Sihanouk himself. "Papa King" had spent most of 1975–1979 under house arrest in Phnom Penh, "spit out like a cherry pit" when his usefulness was over, as he had predicted. After the Vietnamese rolled through Cambodia, the Chinese took him to Beijing, and now they were calling him back once again to be an impotent figurehead. None of the "allies" were enthusiastic about this alliance, but the Chinese were determined to rebuild a viable military resistance to the People's Republic of Kampuchea so that Cambodia remained a thorn in Vietnam's side. In 1982, this alliance, the supposedly capitalist Coalition Government of Democratic Kampuchea, became the West's preferred government of Cambodia, even though it was in exile.[5] The United Nations recognized the Coalition Government of Democratic Kampuchea as Cambodia's representative in New York.

The Khmer Rouge, with its roughly twenty-five thousand troops compared to a few thousand National Liberation Front fighters, were clearly in charge of the Coalition Government forces. They controlled large areas in the northern and western Cambodian jungles. Various anti-Communist rebel groups totaling several thousand fighters were also in the same area. The result was a confusing and deadly guerrilla war between the Khmer Rouge, the Vietnamese army aligned with forces from its puppet government, the People's Republic of Kampuchea, and armed rebels. With armed black marketers and bandits also roaming the mine-infested forests, the Cambodia/Thailand border region was a dangerous place.

Pol Pot himself retreated during the 1980s into the Cambodian and Thai jungles and controlled the war from there. "He mystified and frightened his opponents because his invisibility echoed that of many magically endowed Cambodian heroes in traditional literature. Like his guerilla armies, he could appear (and disappear) at the times and places he chose," wrote one historian. Pol Pot's wife, Khieu Ponnary, suffered a nervous breakdown and was hospitalized in Beijing. With her permission, in 1985, Pol Pot married a young woman who bore him a daughter and later told reporters, "Since I married him, I never saw him do a bad thing."[6]

For much of the 1980s roughly 230,000 Cambodian refugees were still languishing in refugee camps, and none of the armed groups worried much about civilian casualties. Humanitarian organizations tried to help the victims and civilians in this mess, but it was simply impossible to get food or medicine to mothers and children without supplying troops as well. The aid agencies ended up strengthening both the Vietnamese/PRK and the Khmer Rouge. Consequently, humanitarian aid contributed, at least in part, to prolonging a deadlocked civil war throughout the 1980s in which tens of thousands died. The aid agencies, however, faced a rotten choice: deliver aid that would help both sides in an unjust conflict or stand by while innocent victims starved.

For its part, Vietnam, the major player in Indochina, refused to consider compromises that would have disarmed the Khmer Rouge but included Vietnam's withdrawal from Cambodia. Some charged that Vietnam needed the threat of the Khmer Rouge as an excuse for its continued occupation of Cambodia. The result was, as Robert Johnson, the UN secretary general's representative, put it, "sheer, unending, bloody tragedy."[7]

Ex–Khmer Rouge officer Hun Sen became prime minister of Cambodia in 1985 and gradually but inexorably consolidated his power after that. The Vietnamese and PRK troops had some success pushing the Khmer Rouge into Thailand but failed to crush the organization. In September 1989, the Vietnamese withdrew the last of its troops.[8] The decision was partly because the PRK, which by then had changed the country's name to the State of

Cambodia, had become strong enough to continue on its own. Further, that summer the Soviet Bloc in Eastern Europe had started to crumble; clearly, the days of major Soviet aid to Hanoi were numbered. Freed from Vietnamese control, Cambodia was getting ready to open up.

27

Home Again

"Return home and tell how much God has done for you." So the man went away and told all over town how much Jesus had done for him.

—Luke 8:39

By 1989, Radha had been praying for months about returning to Cambodia. The country at that time was closed—and certainly to individual Christian Khmers. He didn't really want to go back. He was still having nightmares and was frankly afraid to put himself in the hands of a Communist government. But his homeland still called to him and, just as important, he had no idea if his mother and brother were still alive. He was thirty-six and hadn't had any contact with either since he left Battambang in 1979.

Then in January, University Presbyterian invited him to join its nine-member delegation to the Second International Congress on World Evangelization (also known as Lausanne II) in Manila, Philippines, that July. Radha needed an American passport to travel, so he filled out the paperwork, had an interview in February, and received his citizenship and passport in April.

Radha thought he might be able to find a way to visit Cambodia from Manila, so in June he sent a telegram to the State of Cambodia asking for permission to enter the country. He was Cambodian and a Christian, he explained, and he wanted to do whatever he could to help the country recover and rebuild and to help the poor. No reply.

Samen was very unhappy about Radha's decision. She was supportive of his ministry, and attending the Congress was fine, but returning to Cambodia was a step too far. "You don't have to go back," she said. "Cambodia is still Communist. You're going to get caught, and they'll throw you into prison, and I'll never see you again."

"God wants us to minister to the Cambodian people," he insisted.

"Well, there are Khmer people in places other than Cambodia," she retorted. He eventually agreed; he would just go to the Congress.

The team from University Presbyterian arrived in Manila on July 15, joining about 4,300 people from 173 countries. Radha soon met up with other Cambodian Ministries for Christ officers, President Chhong Kong and Vice President Setan Lee. They hadn't been invited to Lausanne but came to Manila hoping to make contact with other Cambodian Christians and visit Cambodian refugee camps in the region. Radha and his colleagues met some Khmer pastors who had come to the Congress from Australia and France, as well as a number of Westerners interested in Cambodia, including Alliance missionary Cliff Westergreen and Dale Golding of the Far East Broadcasting Company. The group formed an unofficial committee and prayed that God would allow one of them to set foot in the country.

Nobody at that time knew how many Christians lived in Cambodia or how much persecution they were suffering under Heng Samrin's Communist regime. Khmer believers had made contact with Christians in Thailand, and the Congress had issued invitations to a few pastors, but the Cambodian government had refused to let them leave.

Many people at the Congress were interested in Cambodia because of worldwide publicity about its many crises. Also, some delegates remembered how at the 1974 Lausanne Congress in Geneva some Khmer leaders had made a passionate and memorable appeal for aid and prayers, only to be lost or killed when the Khmer Rouge came to power a year later.[1]

After the Congress ended on July 25, the University Presbyterian team headed home. Radha, despite his promise to Samen, decided to fly to Bangkok and try to find a way into Cambodia from there. In Bangkok, a missionary named Paul Utley with Campus Crusade for Christ picked him up. Radha explained that he hoped to get into Cambodia from Vietnam, but the last time he had checked all the flights from Bangkok to Ho Chi Minh City were full. He still hadn't heard from the Cambodian government, but he asked Paul to help him find a flight. "Let's pray about it," Paul said as they drove away. "Don't close your eyes," Radha said, eyeing the road as Paul maneuvered the car through the heavy and chaotic Thai traffic. At the Utley residence, Radha phoned Samen to let her know he was safe. He also met a staffer with an aid organization who had recently come back from Cambodia. This man explained how to contact the underground church if they did by some miracle get into the country.

The next morning, July 26, Radha got a call from one of the University Presbyterian secretaries back in Seattle. The People's Republic of Kampuchea had received his request and via telegram had formally invited him to visit. A visa would be waiting for him at the Cambodian consulate desk at the airport in Ho Chi Minh City (the only airport then with flights into Phnom Penh), and a representative of the Ministry of Foreign Affairs would be waiting for him at the Phnom Penh airport.

Radha could hardly believe it. He and Paul prayed and then rushed off to a local travel agent to see about a plane ticket to Vietnam. As they sat in the travel agent's office, she examined her monitor and said, "You're really lucky. One seat just came open."

"Book me," said Radha, and then his stomach began to churn as he realized what he'd done. He sent a telegram to Phnom Penh notifying the government of his arrival. He didn't call Samen.

"I don't know whether I'm coming back or not," he told Paul as they drove back to his house, "but I know for sure God planned this trip."

The next morning they drove back to the airport, and Radha boarded his Air France flight to Vietnam.

"Where are you headed?" he asked the friendly Caucasian man in the seat next to him.

"Cambodia," he said.

"Cambodia?" Radha replied. "I am too." And they fell into conversation. The man turned out to be a senior World Vision officer in Cambodia.

Once the plane landed, Radha exited and found the Cambodian consulate in the Ho Chi Minh City airport and showed the official a copy of the telegram University Presbyterian's secretary had faxed over the day before. After some discussion, the official issued Radha's visa, but Radha still had no ticket with the Vietnamese airline, the only one that flew into Cambodia. It looked like he'd have to spend the night in the airport. He prayed and waited, and then the plane began to board. Just before the doors closed, one of the clerks called him over.

"One seat just became available," she explained.

The churning in Radha's stomach got worse. "I'll take it," he said.

The flight to Phnom Penh was a little rough. The crew of the old Soviet jet declined to turn on the air-conditioning until they were in flight, so it was stiflingly hot. And the plane was so overcrowded people were sitting in the aisles. Radha could see the World Vision officer in a seat ahead, and he looked unconcerned. They took off, but Radha thought that the jet never did fully level out; he suspected it was due to overloading. After a fifty-five-minute flight, Radha found himself standing on the tarmac of the Phnom Penh airport in the early evening, taking his first steps on Cambodian soil since fleeing across the Thai border a decade before.

It was dark and humid. The grass was taller than his head around the edges of the cracked runways. The airport in Ho Chi Minh City had been full of planes and bustle; this one was almost empty. The terminal's floor tiles were so dirty he couldn't tell what color they were. He was sweating heavily and near tears. This wasn't the Phnom Penh of his youth.

After going through customs, Radha stood outside, wondering whether the Foreign Ministry had sent someone to meet him as promised. Then the World Vision official offered Radha a place to stay at the Samaki Hotel, where the organization had set up quarters and offices; he gave Radha a spot in a bungalow.

The next morning, July 28, Radha hired a cyclo-pousse (a three-wheeled pedal-powered rickshaw) for a short, unofficial tour of the city. People looked healthier than when he had left, if not exactly prosperous. Smoke and the smell of burning trash tainted the air because so many people burned their own. Everything looked old and beat-up, out of repair, and gray. Garbage dotted the sidewalks. The streets were quiet, with many bicycles, a few military jeeps, and some Russian cars. Propaganda billboards bore anti–Khmer Rouge messages, while others depicted armed PRK soldiers in fatigues with sayings like, "We are united to protect our country." The soldiers on the street, however, wore Vietnamese uniforms; the official pullout of Vietnamese troops was still two months away.

Radha struggled to explain to the driver where he wanted to go because the new regime had changed all the street names. Even the language had changed. That morning, despite himself, he kept correcting people's word choices and accents. He went into a restaurant to get something to drink and the clerk called him a *soviet*, which was the new term for a foreigner, instead of *barang* (literally "French").

To someone else who complimented his Kampuchean accent, he insisted that he spoke Khmer, not Kampuchean. It all drove him nuts.

He bought lunch at a restaurant for himself and his driver, for whom soda was a luxury. The servers, he noticed, were eavesdropping on the patrons, especially foreigners. As he chatted with the driver, he heard his server, standing just behind him, comment to another in Vietnamese about his foreign looks. He called her over and scolded her mildly for talking about people behind their backs. Provoking local informers was, in a Communist country, a reckless move. But he was already feeling more comfortable in his home country; it definitely wasn't like it had been living under the Khmer Rouge.

After lunch, Radha headed down to the Ministry of Foreign Affairs, and an official apologized that no one met him at the airport.

"As I said in my telegram, I'm a Christian," said Radha, "and I'd like to talk about the believers here. Who should I see?"

"The ministry in charge of religion is the National Front," the official said. "It is also in charge of the military."

It seemed an odd combination to Radha. "So if I do something wrong regarding religion, the military comes in?" he asked.

The official smiled faintly and said, "That's the way the government is set up."

He assigned Radha a big black sedan with a driver (but no air-conditioning) and a tour guide named Kan Man who was surprisingly free with his opinions for a functionary in a Communist state. As they drove, Kan described how the Vietnamese made the farmers work in cooperatives, but at least they kept some of their crops.

Kan went further, complaining that the Vietnamese didn't treat Khmer people as equals and Cambodia should be under Khmer leadership. He even asked Radha to sponsor his two children into the United States. Saying such things to a stranger was a major risk. Radha was noncommittal; he wasn't willing to jeopardize his new relationship with the Cambodian government by entertaining such ideas. Kan seemed sneaky to Radha, like a snake with two heads, but in the end, he played an important role in Radha's relationship with the Cambodian regime.

First, they visited Tuol Sleng. The Vietnamese were still emphasizing the horrors of the prison and blaming the Pol Pot–Ieng Sary clique for the country's bloody revolution. Radha looked over the school-turned-torture chamber, with its barbed wire and bloodstains on the classroom floors and ceilings. As the memories flooded back, he started to tremble.

"Comrade Man, why did you take me here?" asked Radha after the third cell. "I've seen such things with my own eyes during the Khmer Rouge."

"Well, this is what the government wants foreigners to see," Kan said and shrugged.

Then they went to Choeung Ek, the Killing Fields. Radha saw the mass graves, which were sunken with scraps of clothes still visible on the edges. He took a picture of the large map of Cambodia filled in with human skulls that the PRK had created for its anti–Khmer Rouge campaign. He saw the bloodstained killing trees against which soldiers had smashed children and babies, and then he had to close his eyes. It was just too much.

As they walked, Kan had been explaining Khmer Rouge methods. "Enough," Radha said. "I know how it was. Your job is to show me around. Get it over with." So they went back to the Samaki Hotel for dinner with the World Vision staff and then to a villa reserved for guests of the government. Radha later realized that his nightmares ended after he toured Tuol Sleng; he figured it finally helped him realize that the Khmer Rouge were, if not completely gone, at least no longer in power.

The next morning, July 29, Kan took Radha out to the countryside south of Phnom Penh. The roads, running between rain-soaked rice fields and forests, became steadily rougher until finally they had to get out and walk. A short distance on they came to a small canal next to a dike. Atop it, a soldier in black pajamas, carrying a rifle and wearing what looked like a Khmer Rouge cap and krama, walked toward them. Radha's heart seized, and then he hurriedly stepped back, ready to flee. "It's a Khmer Rouge," Radha gasped to Kan.

"Don't worry," said his guide. "He's one of ours—just village security." The soldier walked up, introduced himself, and shook Radha's hand.

Kan and Radha spent most of the day viewing fields and canals, which all needed costly repairs. Radha slowly realized that the Cambodian officials didn't know what he was, exactly, and thought he was there to offer aid. He guessed that they believed he represented a large charity with lots of money that was based in the American capital, a mistake possibly encouraged by the fact that his initial telegram came from "Washington" and offered to help poor people. He decided not to clear that up for the time being. Instead, he nodded and looked over the fields with the skeptical eye of an experienced plowman. When Kan suggested he provide money to fix this or that, Radha was careful not to offer any specific aid. "I'll think about it, but no promises," he kept saying. On the way back to the city, he asked Kan to set up a meeting with the National Front.

Radha insisted on returning to World Vision's bungalow to spend the night. The next morning, July 30, Kan agreed to take Radha to look at the Manickam family's former home, east of the Central Market. When they got there, Radha stepped out of the car and then stood looking at the house for a moment. The street was mostly empty. He recalled sitting with his father on the second-floor balcony every evening listening to his radio and watching people pass below. He also noticed the warehouses across the street where Appa had kept his electronics and other goods. He didn't know what to do next.

"What do you want to do?" Kan asked.

"Can you ask the people who live here now if I can see inside?" Radha said.

So Kan walked over and spoke with a middle-aged woman who had come out. She refused because she knew the house had been Radha's.

"When she moved in, all your photos and furniture and decorations were intact, so she knows it belonged to an Indian family, and you're Indian," Kan said.

But Radha asked him to try again, with no luck. Finally Radha came over to talk with her. "Has anyone else besides me come to look at this house?" he asked.

"No," she answered shortly (he found out later that that wasn't true).

"What happened to the furniture and things?" he persisted. "How about the photos?"

"No, we threw it all out," she said.

An empty feeling came over Radha as he and Kan returned to the car. He wanted Amma and Ravy to still be alive. He prayed that they were, but it was getting harder and harder to believe.

He and Kan then drove to an orphanage in Phnom Penh called "Rose 1." Most residents were teenagers. Radha sat at a table with a row of children on wooden chairs in front of him, and some of them performed a traditional Khmer dance. Radha felt uncomfortable; he wasn't used to being the guest of honor. Then the director explained that they needed more beds, more clothes, and more money. "I'll see what I can do," Radha said.

Kan then took Radha to a facility in Kampong Speu, west of Phnom Penh, for older youths under twenty. The girls learned to sew in a big hall, and the boys learned carpentry. They all stood when Radha walked in. There the director described the need for more sewing machines and other resources.

On the way back to the city, Kan explained that some of the orphanage staff had a little sideline business prostituting the youths. They would take their charges to visitors, mostly European, staying in Phnom Penh hotels. Come see the foreigners, they would tell a girl, and then lock her in a room until the client came to rape her. Radha had unknowingly brushed up against the beginnings of one of the world's worst child prostitution problems, one that began in part because the Khmer Rouge era left so many orphans. Cambodia is still considered a destination spot for pedophiles and sex tourists.

Radha was outraged. It felt like a personal attack on not just children but Khmer children—his people.

"Well, is the government doing anything about it?" Radha asked.

"Not that I'm aware of," Kan said.

"You should report it."

"I can't do that," Kan said. "The staff needs that money to survive."

Kan then took Radha to an orphanage for babies near Phnom Penh's downtown. He saw packed into halls dozens of infants, many of them handicapped and abandoned by their parents. They looked hungry. Radha could feel the anger and frustration in his stomach but, once again, declined to promise much help.

The Ministry of Information was next door, so Kan brought him inside and arranged for a brief tour. He saw an elderly Soviet printing press. Radha also learned that electricity was sporadic, usually working a few hours per day, and that there was a curfew in place. It all reminded him of Phnom Penh in the last days of the civil war.

28

Such a Time as This

And who knows but that you have come to your royal position
for such a time as this?

—Esther 4:14

Radha and Kan stopped for lunch and then went to the
National Front offices in downtown Phnom Penh. After
some preliminaries, they found themselves in the reception
room of Chairman Min Kihn. Radha sat on a wooden bench, Min
sat facing him on a wooden chair, and his assistant, Tea Bunlong,
stood nearby.

Radha introduced himself as being from Washington State, not
Washington, DC, but he wasn't sure if they grasped the distinction.
He also declared that he was a Cambodian Christian who had come
to do whatever he could to help the Khmer people.

"I'd like to discuss whether the government would consider recognizing the Christian church in Cambodia," Radha explained.

Tea, the assistant, had handled the conversation up this point,
but now the chairman spoke for the first time. "Christians?" he said.
"We have no Christians in Cambodia. We are a Buddhist country."

Radha looked at Tea, who nodded. Freedom of religion had been a part of the constitution since 1979 under the PRK. Most Cambodians had reverted to their traditional Theravada Buddhism. World Vision president Stan Mooneyham that same year had a similar conversation with Hun Sen, then Minister of Foreign Affairs. When he asked Hun Sen for official recognition of Christianity, he said it wasn't necessary because Cambodia had no Christians.

Mooneyham later brought it up again in a second meeting with Hun Sen, but Radha was neither that diplomatic nor that patient. "Oh, but there are Christians here!" he replied to Min Kihn. "They probably just don't want to show themselves because they're afraid of persecution."

That was, charitably speaking, an imprudent remark. The chairman's brown, lined face turned a deep red. "Are you accusing the government of persecution?" he demanded. "We liberated this country to give people freedom to live, not to punish them!"

"I'm sorry, sir, but the country is Buddhist, and I don't think the government understands Christians just yet," Radha said. "That's why they are afraid to show themselves—"

"Please excuse us for a minute, sir!" Kan said, grabbing Radha's hand and pulling him from the room. "Look," he whispered to Radha, "do you know that nobody talks to that guy like that? Do you know what could happen to you? He could arrange for you to 'lose' your passport. You could even be killed!"

Kan was right. Under Heng Samrin and then Hun Sen the government regularly made political opponents disappear.

"I know Jesus, and I follow Jesus," Radha told Kan. "I became a Christian back in the 1970s, and I didn't change my beliefs just to get into the United States. I believed even before the Khmer Rouge took over. I survived the four years. I nearly died many times, and I lost many members of my family. God took me out of Cambodia, but now He has sent me here, and if this government is going to kill me, so be it!"

271

Kan was looking at him strangely, as if he had just realized something. Then he pulled Radha back into the chairman's reception area. "Pardon us, sir," Kan said. "You should know that this man survived the Khmer Rouge."

The chairman examined Radha with new interest, and the hostility in his eyes started to fade. He asked about Radha's life in the cooperatives. So Radha began with the evacuation from Phnom Penh and explained that his family had spent time in camps south of the city before being sent up to Battambang to help start the cooperative at Phnom Tippedei.

And when he pronounced "Tippedei" with an authentic Khmer accent, the mood in the room lightened even more. Radha kept talking, but from their expressions, he could see they now considered him a local. He told them he had worked twenty-one hours per day on two spoonfuls of rice and a little bit of salt and had lost thirteen members of his family, including six brothers and sisters.

"So you're one of us?" the chairman asked.

"I survived the Khmer Rouge just like you," said Radha, adding that he didn't skip the country when things got tough. He didn't leave Cambodia until November 1979, after the Khmer Rouge had left.

"So," the chairman continued, "why don't you contact your people, your Khmer Christians, and have them write me a letter asking for official recognition? Better yet, I'll have Comrade Man go with you to meet with them." The chairman smiled.

So much sudden friendliness was alarming. The last thing Radha wanted was to expose the underground church to the Cambodian regime without their knowledge or consent. "No, that's OK," Radha said quickly. "I can go by myself. I wouldn't want to trouble your staff."

The chairman shrugged. "Up to you," he said.

"Before you go," the chairman added, "tell me about this Jesus."

So Radha launched into how Christ is the Creator of all things and how He died for everyone's sins on the cross and rose from the dead.

"You know why people put a cross on their doors after some-one in the household dies?" he asked. "It's because the cross has power."

The chairman seemed somewhat interested but clearly wasn't convinced. He smiled faintly sometimes as he listened for another half hour and then ended the interview.

"You don't need to pick me up tomorrow," Radha told Kan as they left the office.

The next morning Radha caught a cyclo-pousse up to the Central Market, a large yellow-and-white dome with four long wings extending out onto the grounds. When it was built in 1937, it was reportedly the largest indoor market in Asia, covering several city blocks and housing hundreds of stalls. Vegetables, kramas, watches, paintings, rice, dresses, jewelry, knives, fish—everything imaginable—were piled in display cases, dangled from rods, and protruded into narrow aisles. The shopkeepers stood beside their wares or sat on stools as customers meandered past, sometimes stopping to finger the fabric or the fruit while deciding whether to bargain.

At the east entrance, Radha found a flower stall watched over by its owner, a middle-aged woman. He bent over to sniff the blossoms while looking sideways at the passersby, checking for spies and eavesdroppers. The owner immediately brightened up when she saw him; here was another foreigner ready to be plucked.

He gestured to a bunch. "How much for these?" he asked, and she looked more closely at him.

"You can speak Khmer?" she asked, coming over to talk.

And then he addressed her directly. "Eang," he said in a low voice, and then explained that a worker with an aid agency had told him she could put him in touch with the Christian leadership in Tomnop Teuk. "Can you arrange it?"

"I don't think I can do that," she said carefully.

"Tell them I am Pastor Choy's son-in-law," said Radha. "I married his daughter Samen."

Eang considered him for a moment. "Come back later today," she said.

Radha wandered around for a bit and returned to the market after lunch. Eang introduced him to a man named Soth, who took him a mile or so south of Phnom Penh to the Tomnop Teuk area. They came up to a house with several people, including some of Soth's relatives, on its balcony. They joined the group, and the believers started to examine Radha casually. They wanted to know if Radha knew Pastor Ens, a longtime missionary.

"Oh yes, I saw him in 1985 in California," Radha said.

"How about Paul Ellison?"

"Yes, I know him well and have often worked with him in California."

They began to mention Samen's siblings by name. Radha informed them that the Ngets lost only two siblings. Using the word for "older brother," he said that Bong Sichan died in a cooperative under the Khmer Rouge, and Bong SaKhun and his wife went missing. Gradually, they relaxed.

Finally, Radha delivered the chairman's message. They talked it over and decided to open discussions with believers in other underground churches. Meanwhile, a few of the believers took Radha to see Sieng Ang, one of the only pastors from before the revolution to have survived. He had known Nget Choy quite well.

Sieng was wearing a T-shirt with a cross on it. In early 1979, after the fall of the Khmer Rouge, he too fled Cambodia. He had drawn the ire of the PRK regime for speaking openly about Christ and opening his home for church meetings, so he sneaked into Khao I Dang in Thailand some months after Radha and Samen left. But he decided that the Lord wanted him back in Cambodia and returned to Phnom Penh. In 1986, he was caught and jailed for six months.

It was a sobering conversation. Radha wondered whether he too should have gone back to Phnom Penh in 1979, as Alice Compain had wanted. He decided he was grateful for what happened.

Radha also worried that the chairman had fooled him, that the offer of official recognition was just a ruse to smoke out the underground church. However, some openly Christian organizations, including World Vision, had worked in Cambodia for years. The regime, despite its Communist roots, seemed unlikely to be that hostile to Christianity, despite the occasional persecution of pastors like Sieng. Radha decided it was all in the Lord's hands.

———————————— ✦ ————————————

On the morning of August 1, Radha hired a cyclo-pousse and went first to the building where Maranatha Church had met in western Phnom Penh. He stood in front of the chained front double doors, peered through the windows, and then took a picture of the empty building. It once had been a busy place. The church held services and sometimes Bible studies upstairs during the day, and on the ground floor was a library where he used to help teach the children's Bible club. He recalled walking out the doors with his friends and fellow church members, laughing even in the midst of a terrible civil war, to go out street witnessing or head down to the river.

Ever since he had arrived back in Phnom Penh, he had watched people on the streets and sidewalks, hoping to see somebody from the old days. He had especially hoped to see Huoth, probably his best friend, the one who first took him to Burke's English class. He doubted whether any of them were even alive anymore: Pastor Thay, Van, the other Van, Hach, and others. His vision blurred with tears.

But then he thought that perhaps they were just in other provinces. Maybe some of them had survived. Maybe he wasn't the only one left from Maranatha Church. He wiped his eyes and took a deep breath. He believed God had saved him for a plan, and maybe he would meet them later.

After ten minutes or so, he got back into the cyclo-pousse. He and the driver visited a few landmarks and other places significant to Radha: the site of Nget Choy's former pastorate, Bethany Church; Wat Phnom ("Temple Mountain," which was a Phnom Penh landmark), where Amma had taken the family for long walks when he was a child; and Independence Monument. He eventually found himself on the bank of the Mekong River, not far from the Royal Palace. He could almost see himself on the boat chugging past on his way up to Battambang and feel the breeze and sunshine of that day when he thought he would never see Phnom Penh again. God had brought him back; he had been wrong. *Thank you, Lord*, he prayed.

Then he remembered that Appa, Amma, and all his siblings had been on the boat with him. Now they were all dead or missing. He had been labeled an "alien" when he came to the United States, and the border officials called him an alien when he landed in Phnom Penh. He was back in the city, but he still felt like an exile.

Radha flew to Ho Chi Minh City and from there caught a flight to Bangkok, where he met with the other Cambodian Ministries for Christ staffers, Chhong and Setan. He reported what he'd seen and done and told them a ministry in Cambodia looked possible. They promised to discuss it further.

He also called Samen, who was happy to hear from him after a week without contact. "I just got back from Cambodia," he said.

There was a long pause, and then Samen asked, "What do you mean you just got back from Cambodia?"

After he explained, Samen was glad he was fine and seemed to understand why he had gone. She asked about Amma and Ravy. He reported that he went to the house but his family wasn't there and that he visited the old churches and saw some people who knew her family. He didn't raise the prospect of returning again.

That first trip helped Radha realize that Cambodia was opening up to the idea of Christianity. He brought his ideas for working in Cambodia to the church board of West Seattle's Khmer Evangelical Church; about half supported the idea, while the other half wanted him to focus on ministry within the church.

Radha was certainly busy. On Sundays, he got up early to preach and train leaders at a Khmer Episcopal congregation down in Tacoma and then came back in time to speak at his home church in the afternoons.

Still, Radha found himself pulled ever more deeply toward ministries aimed at his homeland, and he went back to Cambodia several times over the next few years. In January 1990, he had breakfast with Min Khin and met with other officials about the government recognizing the Christian church. On that trip he also attended a conference in Singapore for Khmer church leaders from the United States, as well as France and Australia. In Singapore the delegates founded Cambodia Christian Services, which later became the Evangelical Fellowship of Cambodia.

They also heard that the Cambodian government would officially recognize Christianity, in addition to Buddhism and Islam. Several factors besides Radha's visit likely played into the decision, such as Hun Sen's meeting with World Vision's Mooneyham and the letter from Khmer Christians. And perhaps the government wanted to appear to be liberalizing in advance of the UN vote on whether to admit Cambodia's new government into membership.

Church leaders suspected that the real purpose of official recognition was to let the government keep an eye on them. They faced some surveillance, certainly in the early years; often they saw people who looked like spies visiting their services. But the recognition allowed the Christian community in Cambodia to worship openly—no small change.

Most churches had very few Bibles or Christian materials. In 1990 and 1991, at the request of a missionary, Radha made two trips by car from Vietnam into Cambodia with trunks full of Christian literature. He told border guards (both Vietnamese and Cambodian sides searched travelers for banned political materials) that he had educational books, slipped them a few dollars each not to look in the trunk, and made it in. Radha was also involved in starting the Phnom Penh Bible School in 1992. It is still the only inter-denominational evangelical pastoral training school in the country, and later he taught there regularly and sat on its international board of directors for several years.

All this steadily led Radha away from his Khmer congregation in West Seattle. He was beginning the ministry that the last twenty years had prepared him for, but first there was his family.

29

. . . And of the Holy Ghost

Then he threw his arms around his brother Benjamin and wept,
and Benjamin embraced him, weeping.

—Genesis 45:14

In the late summer of 1990, Radha was jolted awake by a ringing
telephone. He looked blearily at the clock beside his bed, which
read 2:00 a.m. He picked up the receiver and heard some gibberish.
He hung up and tried to go back to sleep. A few minutes later it rang
again, and he heard a Cambodian operator: "Sir, you have a phone
call from Cambodia, please don't hang up."

"Radha!" said an elderly female voice. "This is your mom!"

Radha doubted that. It didn't sound like her, and he knew that
scams were common in the refugee community. Con men would
phone over to the United States asking "relatives" to send money.

"Do you know where Ravy is?" he asked suspiciously.

"Oh, he's here in Phnom Penh," the voice said.

"Well, how about the rest of my siblings?"

"They're all gone, you know that."

The woman seemed anxious that Radha believe her. It still didn't sound like his mom—and it wasn't. It was Pa Dylay, his father's informally adopted sister. Amma had eventually made it back to Phnom Penh after separating from Radha in 1979, and some years later she reunited with Pa Dylay. Amma was standing right next to her but was too nervous to speak to Radha herself, so Aunt Dylay kept up the pretext for the entire call.

A few months before this call, Radha had been in Phnom Penh with his brother-in-law Saman. They were working with the Cambodian Red Cross to help a Khmer family immigrate to the United States. The Red Cross office was just a block from Ravy's apartment, where Amma was living. Ravy's wife, Roeun Sokha, happened to be looking out the window when Radha and Saman drove by slowly, and she called Amma over to see the Arab guy in the beard. Amma glanced out the window. "He's not Arabic," she said. "He's Indian." She looked more closely as the car continued down the street. "And he looks just like my husband, Manickam."

On that same trip, Radha asked a friend in Battambang to ask around about his mother. This friend found someone who knew she had moved to Phnom Penh, and that, eventually, led to the late-night phone call. Soon after that call, while Saman was again in Cambodia, he stopped in to see Amma and Ravy and led them both to Christ.

In early January 1991, Radha arrived at Ravy's tiny Phnom Penh apartment. The reunion with Amma was joyful, but she also seemed nervous and distracted. The one-room flat, divided up with curtains, was on the second floor of a crowded, run-down three-story complex. The kitchen was on the covered balcony. The apartment felt even smaller because inside Radha encountered several people, including Aunt Dylay, another young woman Amma had informally adopted (she was still taking in lost young people), and a strange man and a young boy who weren't introduced.

Ravy came home an hour later. He ran up the steps and into the apartment. When he saw Radha, he dashed across the room and put his hand around the back of his brother's neck. Radha had maintained his composure when seeing Amma, but now his tears flowed. After everything the brothers had been through, they had both made it back to Phnom Penh with their mother.

Ravy had been a teen and somewhat small for his age when Radha left him behind in Battambang. Radha hardly recognized him as a grown man with a beard and was shocked at how skinny he was. He had joined the PRK military in the 1980s and had become an officer in the civil war against the Khmer Rouge. He'd been wounded twice and led troops into many battles but now was barely eking out a living as a military driver. He and Roeun Sokha had four kids.

The family spent much of the next few days together and soon caught up on news. Ravy and Amma had gone back to the Manickam family home in Phnom Penh in the early 1980s and spoken with the new residents, including the same woman Radha had encountered. The new owner had offered to let them stay in the ground level, but Amma had refused. Radha realized that he had often come within a couple of blocks of Ravy's apartment during his initial trips to Phnom Penh.

Throughout the visit Radha had noticed a child running in and out of his mother's sleeping area, a very private place. "Who is this boy?" he finally asked, and Amma, who had been edgy for days already, began crying quietly.

She told him he was her son, Radha's half brother. His name was San Rany and the other man in the apartment was Heng San, her new husband and Radha's stepfather. She hadn't told him earlier because she was afraid of how he might react. Before Appa died, Radha recalled Amma saying that after he was gone she would never share her bed with anyone else. He felt betrayed but tried not to show it.

Through her tears, Amma related how she'd been all alone after the Vietnamese invaded, like so many women across the country, and it was incredibly difficult for a middle-aged woman to survive on her own. The Khmer Rouge had left thousands of women bereft of husbands and unable to find a new spouse. Radha and Samen had left for Thailand, Ravy was in the military and always gone, and she had nobody to look after her. So she married Heng and had one more child in her middle age.

Radha assured her that he didn't blame her for her decision to remarry. That evening he took everybody out for a nice dinner at the fanciest hotel they could find, the Cambodiana. Radha went back to Seattle and started sending Amma money—enough so that she no longer had to cook for a living.

Radha stood waist-deep in the river water and listened to yet another believer's testimony of faith in Christ. The sun was hot on his white dress shirt. "I baptize you in the name of the Father, and of the Son, and of the Holy Ghost," he said. He supported the man as he dropped backward into the Mekong River, then pulled him up and out again. Todd Burke had done it that way. The other pastors were allowing people just to bend their knees and sink under the surface, but Radha felt that falling on your back better symbolized the Christian's death to self, followed by rising up to everlasting life.

It was January 1992. He was one of eight pastors spread out along the banks of the Mekong, about fifteen miles east of Phnom Penh just off the No. 1 highway. About one thousand people lined the riverbank. In Phnom Penh, all those people had been loaded into a long line of grain trucks and driven out earlier that day. Radha was glad a fellow missionary had offered him a ride in someone's air-conditioned Mercedes.

As they rode, images of his last two rides in grain trucks flashed through his memory: when the Khmer Rouge hauled the Manickams up to the railway at Pursat, headed to Phnom Tippedei, and again when the United Nations took him and Samen across the Thai border to the refugee camps. Those weren't exactly happy memories. He tried to chat with the other passengers so he didn't have to look at the convoy—at the people packed into the trucks with their hair blowing in the wind.

"Do you believe that Jesus saved you from your sins and that He is your Lord and Savior?" Radha asked a woman. She said yes, she believed. "I baptize you . . ." The evangelical churches had enjoyed official recognition from the Cambodian regime for almost two years by that point. The church leaders decided it was time for a public display, both for individual Christians and for the evangelical churches. This was the first mass baptism since 1975. The pastors and elders had invited everyone in their congregations. About three hundred candidates for baptism had divided themselves among the eight pastors. They lined up on the shore, waited for their turn, and then eased out into the slow current. ". . . and of the Holy Ghost." The woman wiped water out of her shining eyes and waded back to shore.

Radha was vaguely aware that yet another person was coming out toward him. How many were there? He'd lost track of how many people he'd baptized that day. And then Radha looked up, and there before him stood Ravy, wearing a big smile. He had no idea Ravy had come to the baptism. His brother hadn't told him he wanted to be baptized, hadn't even decided to come out until the last minute when he and his wife and a couple of the young people Amma had taken under her wing just figured they would go. And here they were—standing in line for Radha to baptize them. Ravy was first.

Radha choked back his tears. "I baptize you in the name of the Father, and of the Son, and of the Holy Ghost." He gave Ravy a big hug and watched him step back toward the shore.

Epilogue

But Joseph said to them, "Don't be afraid. Am I in the place of God? You intended to harm me, but God intended it for good to accomplish what is now being done, the saving of many lives."

—Genesis 50:19–20

In 1993, Radha and Samen decided he would leave the pastorate of their West Seattle Khmer congregation to be a full-time missionary, working with Khmer churches in America and ministering in Cambodia. Samen had warmed to the idea since his first unscheduled visit to Cambodia in 1989. After the robbery in Khao I Dang, they promised the Lord that they would go into ministry full time. And when Radha admitted to Samen that the prospect of raising support scared him, she told him to have faith. "When we were enslaved to the Khmer Rouge, God provided," she said. "Now that we are enslaved to the gospel, God will not forget us."

Radha joined the Conservative Baptist Home Missions Society (now called Missions Door) as his sending organization and became the third and current president of Cambodian Ministries for Christ. Support was slow coming in, and money was very tight, but somehow at the last minute just enough would come in to cover their expenses and keep them going. Samen also later took a job with an auto parts maker in Seattle.

By 1995, he was raising enough support to take two or three trips to Cambodia per year. He has started or been involved in dozens of ministries and projects in the years since then. He taught for several years at the Phnom Penh Bible School. Under his leadership, Cambodian Ministries for Christ has done orphan ministries and educational programs and worked with eleven different denominations to help evangelical Khmer churches connect. The ministry now has a two-story training center on the outskirts of Siem Reap, featuring classrooms, office space, a kitchen and dining area, and a large, cool chapel with a beautiful marble floor. Radha still runs pastoral seminars and job skills programs and consults and ministers at different American Khmer congregations. He has brought teams of American volunteers over to help build church buildings for small, rural congregations and helped American mission agencies make contacts in the Khmer evangelical community.

No one knows exactly how many Khmer Christians were in Cambodia at the start of the Khmer Rouge regime or how many survived. A fair guess might be several hundred believers in the whole country in 1979. The Church in Cambodia has grown steadily since then. Christians now make up 1–2 percent of a population of more than fifteen million, certainly over 150,000 believers and perhaps many more in about two thousand registered churches.[1] An unknown number of unregistered churches also exist. For more than twenty years Radha has been a major contributor to the growth of today's evangelical community in Cambodia, a community that is, despite many challenges, thriving.

———————

The Vietnamese withdrawal in 1989 set the stage for the reintroduction of Cambodia into the international community. In July 1990, the United States quit pretending that a genocidal regime was a legitimate government and stopped supporting the Coalition Government of Democratic Kampuchea as Cambodia's representative to the United Nations. China also cut its aid to the Khmer Rouge and warmed up to Vietnam.

At an international conference on Cambodia in Paris in October 1991, all the parties—the State of Cambodia, Khmer Rouge leaders, Sihanouk, and militia leader Son Sann—formed a Supreme National Council presided over by Sihanouk. National elections were planned for 1993. It looked like Khmers would finally be able to settle their own affairs. The prospect of stability prompted the United Nations to embark on its costliest and most ambitious project to date—to rebuild an entire nation. It poured three billion dollars as well as thousands of military and civilian aid staffers into the country via the United Nations Transitional Authority in Cambodia, known as UNTAC.

Hundreds of thousands of Cambodians who had been stuck in refugee camps on the Thai border returned. Human rights and aid organizations—educational, agricultural, and health—of all sizes poured into the country. However, the Khmer Rouge declined to disarm, refused to allow UN monitoring, and expanded the territory under its control. This was more about building its rapacious logging, mining, and smuggling operations than Khmer Rouge ideology.

The State of Cambodia also refused to give up its weapons and stymied UN inspections. Moreover, the sudden infusion of UNTAC cash and goods into the country contributed to massive inflation, brothels, AIDS, crime, homelessness, and corruption in the cities without doing much to alleviate the pervasive poverty and disease in the countryside.

UN observers deemed legitimate the 1993 elections, which eventually resulted in a coalition government between Hun Sen's Cambodian People's Party and a party called Funcinpec, led by Sihanouk's son, Prince Ranariddh. The coalition government declared the Khmer Rouge illegal, and without Chinese support, the Khmer Rouge started to crumble. Pol Pot reassumed direct control of the group in an attempt to hold it together, but many supporters, able to read the writing on the wall, defected to the Cambodian government. Khmer farmers, vividly recalling life under the Khmer Rouge, had no interest in supporting its return.[2] Angka degenerated into bunches of smugglers and bandits controlling large sections of Cambodia's jungles.

Hun Sen and the new Cambodia People's Party (CPP) gradually overpowered the other emerging political factions in Cambodia, including Funcinpec, usually with violence and sometimes with guile. He finally took control in a July 1997 coup that showed that, while UNTAC had accomplished some good things, its attempt to bring meaningful democracy to Cambodia had failed. Radha happened to be in the country at the time and barely escaped on a plane with some World Vision staffers.

Sihanouk, no longer any threat to Hun Sen, became king again after the 1993 elections. To the annoyance of Hun Sen, Sihanouk frequently inserted himself into political controversies and occasionally offered to abdicate the throne if he didn't get his way. He died in Beijing in 2012.

Only three of the top Khmer Rouge officials were convicted of any crimes. "Brother Number Two," Nuon Chea, and Khieu Samphan, president of Democratic Kampuchea from 1976 to 1979, were convicted of human rights crimes in an international tribunal in 2014 and sentenced to life in prison. In the spring of 2016, Nuon and Khieu were again on trial on charges of genocide.

Kaing Guek Eav, alias Comrade Duch, hid out in the Cambodian jungles for many years under the name Hang Pin. On January 6, 1996, exactly seventeen years after Tuol Sleng was shut down, he became a Christian and was baptized. A Western journalist later recognized him, and in 2007 he turned himself in. Before his arrest, he planted a church in his village, where he taught the Bible and baptized other believers. In 2012, he was sentenced to life in prison for war crimes and crimes against humanity.

Pol Pot is dead. In June 1997, he ordered the assassination of a top aide he suspected of collaborating with the government in Phnom Penh. Pol Pot's troops killed the aide and fourteen family members, some of them young children. It was the last straw, even for the Khmer Rouge. Previously faithful military units deserted, and Pol Pot fled into the jungle. But he was unable to walk due to a stroke and had to be carried in an army hammock slung on a bamboo pole. His long-serving general, Ta Mok, arrested him the next month and held a show trial at Anlong Veng to which he invited Nate Thayer and other journalists.

According to Thayer's account in the *Phnom Penh Post*, "'Crush! Crush! Crush! Pol Pot and his clique!' shouted the crowd on cue, a chorus of clenched fists striking down in unison toward the ground. There, in a simple wooden chair, grasping a long bamboo cane and a rattan fan, sat Pol Pot—the architect of Cambodia's 'Killing Fields'—an anguished old man, frail eyes struggling to focus on no-one, watching his life's vision crumble in utter, final defeat." Witnesses, some missing limbs or eyes, came forward to denounce Pol Pot, and he "seemed often close to tears as the vitriol was unleashed."[3]

Pol Pot was sentenced to house arrest. Two months later Nate Thayer conducted a two-hour interview with him, in which he declared, "I would like to tell you that I came to carry out the struggle, not to kill people. Even now, and you can look at me, do I look like a savage person? My conscience is clear."

On April 15, 1998, Pol Pot heard on a Voice of America broadcast that his captors had decided to turn him over to a tribunal to face charges of crimes against humanity. That night he lay down on his bed, gasped, and died. Ta Mok told reporters Pol Pot died of heart failure, but later reports speculated he committed suicide by overdosing on his medication to avoid arrest. Ta Mok paraded his body in front of journalists for two days, and on April 18, he was taken five hundred yards inside the Cambodian border and cremated under a pile of rubbish and personal possessions.[4] The "era of the contemptible Pot,"[5] as some call it, was over.

———————————

In December 2014, Radha took me to see what Cambodia has become under Hun Sen—in many ways an aid-dependent society struggling under a kind of crony capitalism—and how Khmer churches and other Christians are trying to deal with that reality.

On the first day, we left Phnom Penh in a borrowed Rav 4, heading north on Highway 5 to Battambang. Open-air vendors crowded the roadside, and tiny taverns of uncertain hygiene bore signs for Angkor Beer and Metfone cell phones. On Highway 5's two semi-smooth lanes, when we passed oxcarts and farm tractors, oncoming scooters swerved to the shoulder; we dodged when trucks, Mercedes sedans, and Lexus SUVs approached in our lane. Right of way belongs to the bigger vehicle carrying wealthier people.

That's about how Cambodia's economy works. The Hun government has in recent years approved projects that "resettled" tens of thousands of poor Phnom Penh residents into tarp towns to clear downtown land for condos and high-end shopping centers. Diamond Island City, for example, features the Elite Golf driving range, a water park, and million-dollar villas.

A common billboard along Highway 5 showed Hun smiling benevolently as he does the *sampeah* to passing motorists in the palms-together gesture of respect. He has become the poster boy of corrupt dictators in Southeast Asia. Watchdogs charge the CPP has sold off billions of dollars of timber, oil, and other natural resources with the benefits going to Hun's patronage network of military and business insiders. Since 2008, the garment industry has exploded into a $5.5 billion per year export business; the well-connected families who own the factories pay below-subsistence wages to the young women who migrate to Phnom Penh for work.

To its credit, the Hun government has liberalized the economy somewhat. Late that afternoon in Battambang, we pulled into the driveway of a bakery, a large house with a high cinder-block fence. The ovens were in a big metal outbuilding where several women sat around a low table wrapping meat-filled snacks. Delivery scooters came empty and left with large cardboard boxes on the saddle stacked higher than the driver's head. The son of the Christian owners explained that they distribute all over the region and just set up a new bakery in a rented house in Phnom Penh.

Cambodians with business experience and some capital, like the bakery owners, can thrive. Per capita income, according to the World Bank, has quadrupled to $1,000 per year since 2003.[6] Poor folks used to rely on bicycles, but now throngs of scooters, often carrying three riders, pack city streets. People check phones, swig water, and clutch babies while weaving through heavy traffic. Helmets are optional.

Cambodia's poor rural areas are also a bit better off. One day we visited Tuol Mateh, the cooperative where Radha and Samen spent much of their time. Radha pointed out canals, still in use, that he had helped dig with a hoe. Amid acres of table-flat rice fields, thatched huts without power huddled next to groves of banana trees and farmers dipped water for washing and drinking from nearby ponds.

A World Bank study released in 2014 said 20 percent of Cambodians lived in poverty with another 20 percent on the verge. But it called the country "one of the best performers in poverty reduction worldwide" because the poverty rate had dropped from 53 percent in 2004.[7]

After hunting through stands of trees and scattered huts, we found the concrete foundation of the dining hall where Radha and Samen wed. It was their first time back to Tuol Mateh—what was left of it—since 1979. Radha, then sixty-one, stood looking thoughtfully at the piles of nuts and grain spread out to dry on the cement and pointed out where they had said their vows as young adults in their

291

twenties. Samen posed for a picture but then, looking a bit shaky, sat down in the shade. Neither of them said much.

The next day we drove to Siem Reap to visit Cambodia's biggest tourist draw and the symbol of Khmer identity: Angkor Wat. The massive temple complex is now a World Heritage Site. Stunning carvings of Hindu and Buddhist imagery cover the five-towered ruins.

Here Buddhism meets politics. Opposition politicians allege that the corporation collecting the twenty-dollar (US) entrance fees from the 4.2 million annual visitors skims millions of dollars off the top. Sebastian Strangio reports in *Hun Sen's Cambodia* how top monks swap blessings and legitimacy for large donations: "The Cambodian path to Nirvana, it seems, now runs directly through the CPP."[8]

The Buddhist hierarchy sometimes uses its political clout to harass Christians, but seldom fatally. In 2007, the Ministry of Cults and Religions forbade evangelizing and distributing religious literature outside church grounds. Officials said churches had been buying converts with food and clothing; a more charitable explanation is that Christians had been ministering to the needs they saw around them. Enforcement of the ban depends on local authorities. After the 2007 edict, Cambodian Ministries for Christ set up a well-drilling program and now sinks more than thirty wells annually on rural church properties in villages that lack water in the dry season. According to Radha, villagers come for the water, "Then we share the gospel, and it's legal."

CMC still faces official harassment. Local authorities expect to collect "licensing fees" from Christian charities. "At CMC we don't do that," Radha said. "But when they don't get the money, they keep giving us problems. It's like a Communist country."

Near the end of the week, we drove south back to Phnom Penh. The "Play Penh" is a comfortable posting for tens of thousands of foreign aid workers. The city is exotic, cheap, and fairly safe by third-world standards. My fudge MooLatte from a spotless Dairy Queen near the banks of the Mekong River was quite tasty. It helped me forget seeing the Stung Meanchey dump west of town where workers, including many children, pick recyclables from a breathtakingly large and putrid "trash mountain."

The presence of non-governmental organizations (NGOs) is pervasive. Expensive SUVs with aid agency logos are common, and development jargon pops up everywhere. One store sign read, "Sonatra Microloans" in a misspelled reference to the crooner. "It's a pawnshop," Radha explained.

Cambodia's aid culture began when Vietnam permitted World Vision into Cambodia to help avert a famine after the Khmer Rouge fell, and the aid culture mushroomed in the UNTAC era. Since then, crisis after crisis—from AIDS orphans to landmine amputees to child trafficking—has attracted worldwide attention and donations. The 2,600 government-registered NGOs range from the twenty-four UN agencies to faith-based humanitarian giants like Samaritan's Purse and World Vision to dozens of Christian missions and projects of varying sizes.

Strangio writes that any apparent progress in Cambodia is a "mirage." Year after year governments and NGOs send billions of dollars of well-intentioned aid in exchange for Hun Sen's human rights abuses and empty promises of reform. The CPP government has off-loaded its costly responsibilities for health, education, and other areas onto the NGOs while failing to tax the wealthy. The result is a "dependence spiral," he writes, enabled by a massive development complex that entrenches a predatory elite.[9]

The Khmer Christian leaders I spoke with were not quite that negative, but the aid culture troubled them. Training and resources can help people emerge from poverty, said one pastor, but churches that depend on foreign aid struggle to develop strong leadership or support their own pastors and ministries. Many of the graduates of the Phnom Penh Bible School don't end up leading churches but, instead, aspire to work for aid agencies.

Some Khmer Christian leaders chase titles or exaggerate the impact of their ministries because the credibility helps raise money from Western donors. One told Radha, "All you have to do is cough, and [Americans] will give you money."

"When they start a church, it is the same thing," says Timothy Ith, a Khmer Rouge survivor and board chairman of the Evangelical Fellowship of Cambodia. "They wait for the [mission agency] to give them something. Some of the church members are waiting for a gift from the church too."

Some churches are struggling to break free from dependency. Ith, who oversees twenty-eight tiny rural churches in ten provinces, developed a program that helps people earn a living and reinforces biblical teaching on work and giving. At a sixty-member congregation in Takeo province, for example, new members receive rice seed or a cow; they tithe seed at the next harvest or the first two calves back to the church. Those go, in turn, to the church's newest members.

At week's end, Radha took me to Tuol Sleng, the prison where the Khmer Rouge tortured at least fifteen thousand "traitors." Glass cases hold the racks, manacles, and knives the guards used to extract the confessions. Large displays show photos of thousands of victims taken by Comrade Duch's staff, and tourists gawk at the barbed wire and bloodstained cells.

We then visited the "Killing Fields" memorial at Choeung Ek. Underneath stands of chankiri trees, the path meanders beside grassy depressions and sandy hollows where thousands of corpses were dumped. Signs say, "Please don't walk through the mass grave!" A little farther along are the "killing trees," and a bit beyond that is a tall Buddhist stupa, or tower. Inside are hundreds of human skulls sitting on shelves in glass cases. Visitors can look through the cases to the sunlit grounds outside the door or up to see the shelves of skulls, one after the other, rising to the ceiling.

Many explanations exist for why the Khmer Rouge murdered more than 20 percent of Cambodia's population between 1975 and 1979. Some Western socialists, trying to distance Communism from the Cambodian bloodbath, have conceded that Pol Pot's methods were excessive but insist he was heading in the right direction. This reduces the Khmer Rouge to well-intentioned homicidal maniacs, thereby illustrating the observation of French philosopher Raymond Aron that Marxism is the opium of intellectuals.[10]

Others try to identify some flaw in the Cambodian national character, while others look for parallels in similar mass murders—from Stalin's Soviet Union to the Nazi extermination camps to Rwanda's bloody frenzies. Were the Khmer Rouge simply monsters? Ideological fanatics? Opportunistic ladder-climbers prepared to cross any boundaries? True believers in a Communist utopia? Or were they just following orders from the genocidal Pol Pot–Ieng Sary clique to try to save their own lives?

Scholars have suggested many social, political, and economic factors that are tied to issues of class, race, revenge, power, modernity, and honor to help explain why people commit genocide. Anthropologist Alexander Hinton, for example, describes how socioeconomic upheaval leads to a breakdown in morality and the rise of ideologies that, first, make sense in the culture and, second, offer scapegoats, dehumanized to permit their elimination.[11]

In Cambodia, the process no doubt varied from person to person, but surely Khmer Rouge ideology played a key role. In trying to create the "new socialist man," Pol Pot believed he could shape human nature in any way he chose—that there is no such thing as a fixed human nature.

But Christianity teaches that people are not blank slates; rather, they are sinners made in the image of God. Because human nature is real and people are fallen, human institutions are not perfectible, nor are people "infinitely malleable," in Big Brother's memorable phrase. One of the things that weakened the Khmer Rouge was the peasants' refusal to deny family ties or their faith.[12] The Communists tried to exert more and more control over their victims, leading to more and more violence, but it was futile.

Before his arrest, Brother Number Two spoke several years ago with the makers of a Cambodian documentary called *Enemies of the People*. Why, he was asked, did all those people have to die? After some stonewalling, he finally blurted out, "If we had let them live, the party line would have been hijacked!"[13]

Exactly. If you think you're building utopia, you can justify mass murder.

Some, mystified by the violence of the Khmer Rouge, end up terrified to realize that within their own hearts lies the capacity for deeds vile beyond comprehension. François Bizot writes in *The Gate*[14] of being the prisoner of Comrade Duch, who would later run Tuol Sleng, in the Cambodian jungles for several months in 1971. Bizot testified at Duch's trial for human rights violations, telling the court that while a prisoner he was shocked to discover that Duch, with whom he had developed a strange sort of intimacy, personally beat prisoners:

> Your Honor, I should say that until then, I had felt reassured. I believed that we were—that I was—on the right side of humanity; that some men were monsters and, thank heaven, I could never be one of them. I believed that this was a state of nature, that some of us were born evil while the rest of us could never be. But that evening, Duch's response, combined with my perception of him throughout the course of various interrogation episodes, opened my eyes. . . . I realized that this was far more tragic and infinitely more terrifying, because in front of me stood a man who looked like many friends of mine: a Marxist who was prepared to die for his country and for the Revolution. . . . I saw that this monster was, in fact, human, which was just as disturbing and terrifying. I was no longer sheltered from this knowledge—we are no longer sheltered—and the worst mistake

296

we could make would be to separate such monsters into a different category of being.[15]

Those surprised by the evil found in human hearts don't yet know themselves, and those terrified by the discovery have not grasped the grace of God. The desire for disproportionate revenge isn't limited to Cambodian society. Genesis 2 records how Lamech boasted that if Cain was avenged seven times, he would be avenged seventy-seven times. In a fallen world, sin is crouching at the door of every heart. The question is not "How could the Khmer Rouge be so evil?" but "Why are we all not more like the Khmer Rouge?"

Yet by God's grace, the institutions common to all reasonably free societies—family, church, voluntary associations, democratic government—keep evil in check to the degree that they reflect a biblical view of human nature. When those pursuing some vision of a perfect society sweep away these institutions, the human capacity for evil is unrestrained. It grows and distorts and corrupts all it touches, until violence explodes out of one heart and escalates from person to person until, as the prophet Hosea lamented, "They break all bounds, and bloodshed follows bloodshed."[16]

It's something to keep in mind when a society's leaders, claiming to have a better way forward, insist that institutions like the traditional family—or, in the West, Christianity—are outdated, irrelevant, or oppressive and need to change with the times.

When we visited Tuol Sleng, Radha showed little emotion; he's seen it before. Once I asked Radha what he thought it meant, everything he went through under the Khmer Rouge. He said that while living under Angka, he was deeply angry with the Communists and with God, who he thought was punishing the whole country for its unbelief. Now he believes God preserved Cambodian Christians and his own life through those horrific years to bring good out of great evil. And who knows what good those many thousands of Khmer Christians will accomplish in the future?

Radha could have fled his homeland years before the Khmer Rouge took over, but he didn't. He believes God protected his life because God has a plan for his fellow Cambodians and the church in Cambodia—and that plan includes Radha. It was a hard plan, with much suffering. "But if I hadn't stayed in Cambodia," he says, "I wouldn't know the pain of the people."

Acknowledgments

Portions of this book previously appeared in articles I wrote for the *Weekly Standard* ("A Walk Past the Mass Graves," May 18, 2015), *WORLD Magazine* ("Waiting to Break Free," May 2, 2015), and *Touchstone* ("Cambodian's Anti-Exodus," September/October 2015).

I'd like to thank my wife, Jennifer, for her patience during the many evenings and weekends I spent gazing at a computer screen or a book. Her presence, support, and love make my life very, very sweet.

Thank you to Radha's friends and family who agreed to speak with me about his life and theirs. I owe a great debt to David Aikman for introducing me to Radha and putting me in touch with the fine folks at Baker. Thanks also to Lynn Vincent for helping me believe this book could happen.

And thank you to the excellent staff and editors at Baker whose encouragement and support made this process such a blessing.

Finally, I dedicate this book to Radha and Samen, whom I greatly admire. Their example of faith has changed how I think about—well, many things. I can only pray I would have such courage in the face of so many harsh trials.

Notes

Prologue

1. *Democratic Kampuchea Is Moving Forward*, Phnom Penh, August 1977, 10.

2. Taylor Owen and Ben Kiernan, "Bombs Over Cambodia," *Walrus* magazine (October 2006), 68.

3. Ben Kiernan, *The Pol Pot Regime: Race, Power, and Genocide in Cambodia under the Khmer Rouge, 1975–79* (New Haven: Yale University Press, 1996), 464. He wrote, "Despite its underdeveloped economy, the regime exerted more power over its citizens than any state in world history."

4. François Ponchaud, "Social Change in the Vortex of Revolution," in *Cambodia 1975–1978: Rendezvous with Death*, ed. Karl D. Jackson (Princeton: Princeton University Press, 1989), 161.

Chapter 1 Civil War

1. "US Planes Bomb Cambodia Town in Error," *New York Times*, August 7, 1973; William Shawcross, *Sideshow: Kissinger, Nixon, and the Destruction of Cambodia* (New York: Touchstone, 1987), 294–95.

2. David Chandler, *A History of Cambodia*, 4th ed. (Boulder, CO: Westview Press, 2008), 224–27.

3. Philip Short, *Pol Pot: Anatomy of a Nightmare* (New York: Henry Holt and Company, 2005), 207.

4. Elizabeth Becker, *When the War Was Over: Cambodia and the Khmer Rouge Revolution* (New York: PublicAffairs, 1986), 125.

5. Timothy Carney, "Unexpected Victory," in Jackson, *Cambodia 1975–1978*, 25.

6. Owen and Kiernan, "Bombs Over Cambodia," 67.

7. David Chandler, *Brother Number One: A Political Biography of Pol Pot* (Boulder, CO: Westerview Press, 1999), 96.

8. Kiernan, *The Pol Pot Regime*, 16–23.

9. Owen and Kiernan, "Bombs Over Cambodia," 67–68.

10. Kiernan, *The Pol Pot Regime*, 16. The bombing was "probably the most important single factor in Pol Pot's rise."

11. Kevin Ponniah, "US Bombing Defended," *Phnom Penh Post*, September 9, 2014, http://www.phnompenhpost.com/national/us-bombing-defended. The article is a summary of Henry Kissinger's interview with NPR in which he defended the decisions to bomb Cambodia with responses from noted historians.

Chapter 2 Talking Theology

1. Todd and DeAnn Burke tell their story in *Anointed for Burial* (Plainfield, NJ: Logos International, 1977). Personal recollections from DeAnn are from telephone and email interviews conducted on July 15 and September 23, 2015.

2. Don Cormack, *Killing Fields, Living Fields* (London: Monarch Books, 1997), 59.

3. Ibid., 78.

4. Ibid., 117.

5. Ibid., 142.

Chapter 3 Two Worlds

1. Cormack, *Killing Fields*, 157–58.

Chapter 4 Streets of Fear

1. Kiernan, *The Pol Pot Regime*, 36–37.

2. François Ponchaud, trans. Nancy Amphoux, *Cambodia: Year Zero* (New York: Holt, Rinehart, and Winston, 1977), 6.

3. John Barron and Anthony Paul, *Murder of a Gentle Land: The Untold Story of Communist Genocide in Cambodia* (New York: Reader's Digest Press, 1977), 17.

4. Haing Ngor and Roger Warner, *Survival in the Killing Fields* (New York: Basic Books, 1987), 86.

5. Ibid., 89.

6. Ponchaud, *Cambodia: Year Zero*, 6–7.

Chapter 5 The Khmer Rouge

1. For a description of Khmer Rouge policy in the aftermath of the invasion, see Karl D. Jackson, "Khmer Rouge in Context" in Jackson, *Cambodia 1975–1978*, 8–9. For a detailed account of the Khmer Rouge actions, see Kiernan, *The Pol Pot Regime*, "Introduction: The Making of the 1975 Khmer Rouge Victory" and "Chapter Two: Cleansing the Cities." Also providing inside information on the Khmer Rouge plans is David P. Chandler, Ben Kiernan, and Chanthou Boua, eds., *Pol Pot Plans the Future:*

Confidential Leadership Documents from Democratic Kampuchea, 1976–1977 (New Haven: Yale Center for International and Area Studies, 1988).

2. See Becker, *When the War Was Over*, 140–44, for a good summary of Ith's book and its effect.

3. Becker, *When the War Was Over*, 140–42. See also Carney, "Unexpected Victory," in Jackson, *Cambodia 1975–1978*, 28–30.

4. "Deathwatch: Cambodia," *Time*, November 12, 1979.

5. Ponchaud, "Social Change," in Jackson, *Cambodia 1975–1978*, 153.

6. Short, *Pol Pot*, 25.

7. Chandler, *Brother Number One*, 111.

8. Cited in Ben Kiernan, *How Pol Pot Came to Power: Colonialism, Nationalism, and Communism in Cambodia, 1950–1975* (New Haven: Yale University Press, 2004), 27.

9. Chandler, *Brother Number One*, 25.

10. Kiernan, *How Pol Pot Came to Power*, 119.

11. Chandler, *Brother Number One*, 33.

12. Ibid., 53.

13. Pol Pot used the phrase in a 1978 documentary by Yugoslav journalists, some of the few outsiders granted access during the regime; see David Chandler, *The Tragedy of Cambodian History: Politics, War, and Revolution Since 1945* (New Haven: Yale University Press, 1999), 304.

14. For a very good description of Khmer Rouge ideology, see Karl D. Jackson, "Ideology of Total Revolution," in Jackson, *Cambodia 1975–1978*, 37–78.

15. Chandler, *Brother Number One*, 6–7.

16. Short, *Pol Pot*, 73.

17. Locard, *Pol Pot's Little Red Book*, 96.

18. Short, *Pol Pot*, 59.

19. Ponchaud, "Social Change," in Jackson, *Cambodia 1975–1978*, 161.

20. Kenneth M. Quinn, "The Pattern and Scope of Violence," in Jackson, *Cambodia 1975–1978*, 190.

21. Alexander Laban Hinton, *Why Did They Kill? Cambodia in the Shadow of Genocide* (Berkeley: University of California Press, 2005), 48.

22. Short, *Pol Pot*, 316.

23. For an authoritative summary, see Chandler, *A History of Cambodia*, 35–90.

24. Jackson, "Total Revolution," in Jackson, *Cambodia 1975–1978*, 59. He describes the Khmer Rouge not as turning back to an earlier time but as "rushing forward at a dizzying pace regardless of the consequences."

25. *The Constitution of Democratic Kampuchea*, Article 20, The Documentation Center of Cambodia, last accessed March 15, 2016, http://www.ddccam.org/Archives /Documents/DK_Policy/DK_Policy_DK_Constitution.htm.

26. Jackson, "Ideology of Total Revolution," in Jackson, *Cambodia 1975–1978*, 71.

27. Ponchaud, *Cambodia: Year Zero*, 127.

28. Ponchaud, "Social Change," in Jackson, *Cambodia 1975–1978*, 173. For a slightly more detailed discussion of the Khmer Rouge mix of Marxism and Buddhism, see Hinton, *Why Did They Kill?*, 144–46.

29. Chandler, *A History of Cambodia*, 247.

Chapter 6 Into the Countryside

1. Teeda Butt Mam, "Worms from Our Skin," in *Children of Cambodia's Killing Fields: Memoirs by Survivors*, ed. Dith Pran (New Haven: Yale University Press, 1997), 13–14.

2. Hinton, *Why Did They Kill?*, 214.

3. Locard, *Pol Pot's Little Red Book*, 185.

4. Pin Yathay, *Stay Alive, My Son* (Ithaca, NY: Cornell University Press, 1987), xiv.

Chapter 7 Water Buffalo Island

1. Chandler, *Brother Number One*, 102.

2. Ponchaud, *Cambodia: Year Zero*, 41–43.

3. Kiernan, *The Pol Pot Regime*, 97.

Chapter 8 Angka the Idol

1. Rithy Panh, *The Elimination: A Survivor of the Khmer Rouge Confronts His Past and the Commandant of the Killing Fields* (New York: Other Press, 2014), 103.

2. Locard, *Pol Pot's Little Red Book*, 171.

Chapter 9 Don't Let Them Count One

1. *Democratic Kampuchea Is Moving Forward*, 8.

2. Locard, *Pol Pot's Little Red Book*, 306.

3. Yathay, *Stay Alive, My Son*, 63.

Chapter 10 A Strange Dance

1. *The Constitution of Democratic Kampuchea*.

2. Short, *Pol Pot*, 332.

3. Locard, *Pol Pot's Little Red Book*, 42.

4. Hinton, *Why Did They Kill?*, 289–94.

Chapter 11 Something Rotten

1. Hinton, *Why Did They Kill?*, 130.

2. Locard, *Pol Pot's Little Red Book*, 107.

3. Mam, "Worms from Our Skin," 13.

4. Locard, *Pol Pot's Little Red Book*, 228. See also Ponchaud, *Cambodia: Year Zero*, 108–12.

5. Job 13:28.

Chapter 12 A God of Disorder

1. Quoted by prosecutors in the trial transcript of "Comrade Duch," or Kaing Guek Eav: Extraordinary Chambers in the Courts of Cambodia Trial Chamber, November 26, 2009, Trial Day 76, Case No. 001/18-07-2007-ECCC/TC, KAING GUEK EAV, 46.

2. Chandler, *Brother Number One*, 129.

3. Chandler, Kiernan, and Boua, *Pol Pot Plans the Future*.

4. See the introduction to *Pol Pot Plans the Future*; Jackson, "Ideology of Total Revolution," in Jackson, *Cambodia 1975–1978*; and Chandler, *Brother Number One*, 114–22, for more detailed discussions of the Khmer Rouge approach to revolutionary consciousness and its relationship to the Four Year Plan.

5. Chandler, *Brother Number One*, 118.

6. Ibid., 120.

7. Pol Pot, "Preliminary Explanation before Reading the Plan, by The Party Secretary," in Chandler, Kiernan, and Boua, *Pol Pot Plans the Future*, 156.

Chapter 13 Super Great Leap Forward

1. "Deathwatch: Cambodia," *Time*.

2. Locard, *Pol Pot's Little Red Book*, 190.

Chapter 14 Rebels Within

1. These examples are taken from Locard, *Pol Pot's Little Red Book*, 81, 113, 119, 292; for a discussion of the subversive nature of these revisions, see Kiernan, *The Pol Pot Regime*, 246–50.

2. Isaiah 59:15 NIV.

Chapter 15 The Plan

1. Locard, *Pol Pot's Little Red Book*, 204.

Chapter 18 Inevitably, Angka

1. Kiernan, *The Pol Pot Regime*, 387.

2. Ibid., 394.

3. E. San Juan Jr., "Book Review: The Challenge of the Kampuchean Revolution," *Alive*, 127, March 17, 1979, published by Encyclopedia of Anti-Revisionism On-Line https://www.marxists.org/history/erol/ca.secondwave/alive-k.htm.

4. George Orwell, *1984* (London: Penguin Books, 2008), 261.

5. Kiernan, *The Pol Pot Regime*, chapters 8 and 9.

6. Chandler, *Brother Number One*, 147.

7. Ibid., 123–30. For a survivor's account of Tuol Sleng, see Mey Chum, Sorya Sim, and Kimsroy Sokvisal, *Survivor: The Triumph of an Ordinary Man in the Khmer Rouge Genocide* (Phnom Penh: Documentation Center of Cambodia, 2012).

8. Chandler, *Brother Number One*, 168, see also 143–44.

Chapter 19 Risking Angka's Wrath

1. See Kiernan, *The Pol Pot Regime*, chapter 11, on the disintegration of the regime.

Chapter 20 A Killing Field

1. Chandler, *Brother Number One*, 162–63.

2. "Deathwatch: Cambodia," *Time*.

3. For a good summary of the political and humanitarian crisis this chapter describes, see "Deathwatch: Cambodia," *Time*.

4. Chandler, *A History of Cambodia*, 278–79.

5. Ibid., 278.

6. "Deathwatch: Cambodia," *Time*.

7. This description is a summary of William Shawcross, *The Quality of Mercy: Cambodia, Holocaust, and Modern Conscience* (New York: Simon and Schuster, 1984), chapters 3–8.

Chapter 21 Hard Waiting

1. For fuller accounts of Thai-Cambodian relations in the aftermath of the Khmer Rouge, see Shawcross, *The Quality of Mercy*, 58–59, 83–94.

2. Chandler, *A History of Cambodia*, 281.

3. Shawcross, *The Quality of Mercy*, 93.

4. Not his real name. Ly recounted his story in an interview with the author on December 14, 2014. The story of the "repatriation" of Cambodians at Preah Vihear has been reported in numerous other sources and was reported in news media at the time; see Shawcross, *The Quality of Mercy*, 83–89; Cormack, *Killing Fields*, 273–76.

5. "Vietnam bogged down in Cambodian quagmire," *Washington Post*, March 3, 1979.

6. The Office of the Historian, US Department of State, notes, "Although the decade [1969–1979] began with vast improvements in bilateral relations, by the end of the decade events had brought the two superpowers back to the brink of confrontation" as shown by the breakdown of discussions on nuclear arms control. "Milestones: 1969–1976, Dentente and Arms Control," US Department of States Office of the Historian, accessed October 31, 2015, https://history.state.gov/milestones/1969-1976/detente/.

7. Shawcross, *The Quality of Mercy*, 109.

8. Ibid., 121.

9. Ibid., 131–33.

Chapter 22 Free Trading

1. Shawcross, *The Quality of Mercy*, 236–37.

2. Ibid., 172–78.

3. Ibid., 190.

4. Ibid.

5. Ibid., 212.

Chapter 24 Church of the Lord Jesus Christ

1. Shawcross, *The Quality of Mercy*, 302.

Chapter 25 Family Ties

1. Author interviews with DeAnn Harris, July 15 and September 23, 2015. Radha occasionally crossed paths with Burke over the next several years. In 1980, Todd and DeAnn were working with a group called the New Covenant Commission. But they lost a child, Jeremi, in 1989, and Todd drifted away from his Christian faith and left his family. DeAnn remarried in 1990. Todd died in 2006.

2. Some months later, Radha and Samen discovered that Compain had asked World Relief officials to hold up the couple's paperwork, apparently hoping that with a bit more time she could convince Radha to return to Cambodia after all. After living for a decade in the United States, he met her again in Bangkok. When she saw his black, leather-bound Bible she said, "You're an American now! You don't even read the Cambodian Bible anymore!" Irritated, he opened it for her. "Older Sister, why do you say that? Do you want to see?" he said and showed her the Khmer text. She apologized, and they got along well enough after that. Sometimes they even worked together, but Radha felt the incident reflected a condescending and controlling attitude he encountered among some Western missionaries toward Cambodian Christians. Compain passed away in September 2008.

Chapter 26 Settling in Seattle

1. "Cambodian Refugee Admissions to the United States," Cambodia, accessed March 30, 2016, http://www.mekong.net/cambodia/refugees.htm.

2. "Judgement of the Tribunal, August 19, 1979," in Paul R. Bartrop and Steven Leonard Jacobs, eds., *Modern Genocide: The Definitive Resource and Document Collection* (ABC-CLIO, 2014), 611–27. The People's Revolutionary Tribunal of the People's Revolutionary Council of Kampuchea was a creation of Vietnam, and its report blamed Pol Pot and "Peking reactionaries" for implementing Maoist ideology in an attempt to extend Chinese rule over all of Indochina.

3. "Pol Pot Living in Luxury in Midst of Deprived Cambodia," *New York Times*, March 4, 1980.

4. Shawcross, *The Quality of Mercy*, 335. See also Chandler, *A History of Cambodia*, 282.

5. Chandler, *A History of Cambodia*, 282–84.

6. Chandler, *Brother Number One*, 164–65.

7. Shawcross, *The Quality of Mercy*, 406–13.

8. Chandler, *A History of Cambodia*, 285.

Chapter 27 Home Again

1. Cormack, *Killing Fields*, 140.

Epilogue

1. According to various Christian leaders in Cambodia, a 2014 US State Department report lumps Christians, Jews, Bahais, and a handful of other religions into a group comprising about 1.5 percent of the population or about 230,000 people, http://www.state.gov/j/drl/rls/irf/religiousfreedom/index.htm?year=2014&dlid=238286#wrapper (accessed October 30, 2015). The same report from 2010 says Christians make up 2 percent of the population of 13.4 million, or almost 270,000 people, in 1,300 churches with about 1,000 of those registered, Department of Democracy, Human Rights, and Labor, *International Religious Freedom Report 2010*, US Department of State, November 17, 2010, http://www.state.gov/j/drl/rls/irf/2010/148861.htm.

2. Chandler, *Brother Number One*, 180.

3. Nate Thayer, "Brother Enemy No. 1," *Phnom Penh Post*, August 15, 1997, http://www.phnompenhpost.com/national/brother-enemy-no-1.

4. Chandler, *Brother Number One*, 183–86.

5. Arthur Cotterell, *A History of Southeast Asia* (Singapore: Marshall Cavendish International, 2014), 336.

6. "World Development Indicators," The World Bank, last accessed March 30, 2016, http://data.worldbank.org/country/cambodia.

7. The World Bank, "Where have all the poor gone? Poverty Assessment Cambodia 2013," news release, February 20, 2014, http://www.worldbank.org/en/news/press-release/2014/02/20/poverty-has-fallen-yet-many-cambodians-are-still-at-risk-of-slipping-back-into-poverty.

8. Sebastian Strangio, *Hun Sen's Cambodia* (New Haven: Yale University Press, 2014), 203.

9. Ibid., 226.

10. Raymond Aron, *The Opium of the Intellectuals*, trans. Terrance Kilmartin, (New York: W. W. Norton and Company, 1962).

11. See "Conclusion," in Hinton, *Why Did They Kill?*

12. Kiernan notes that "along with the massacres that threatened peasant life itself, it was the CPK's attack on the family that alienated peasant supporters." Kiernan, *The Pol Pot Regime*, 215.

13. *Enemies of the People*, DVD, directed by Thet Sambath and Rob Lemkin (London: Old Street Films, 2009).

14. François Bizot, *The Gate* (London: Vintage, 2004); translated from French by Euan Cameron.

15. Therry Cruvellier, *The Master of Confessions: The Making of a Khmer Rouge Torturer* (New York: HarperCollins, 2014), 163–64.

16. Hosea 4:2.

Les Sillars grew up in Red Deer, Alberta, and went to Dallas Theological Seminary intending to become a basketball coach (it's a long story). After graduating from DTS in 1993, he fell into a job as a reporter in Calgary and later earned a doctorate in journalism from the University of Texas at Austin. He has taught journalism at Patrick Henry College since 2002 and is on staff at *WORLD Magazine*. He and his wife, Jennifer, have two grown children. This is his first book.